Chaucer and Menippean Satire

Chaucer
and
Menippean
Satire

F. ANNE PAYNE

THE UNIVERSITY OF WISCONSIN PRESS

Published 1981

The University of Wisconsin Press
114 North Murray Street
Madison, Wisconsin 53715

The University of Wisconsin Press, Ltd.
1 Gower Street
London WC1E 6HA, England

First printing

Printed in the United States of America

For LC CIP information see the cólophon

ISBN 0-299-08170-2

Chapter 6, "Foreknowledge and Free Will: Three Theories in *The Nun's Priest's Tale*," first appeared in *Chaucer Review* 10 (1976): 201–19 and is reprinted here with a few changes by permission of The Pennsylvania State University Press, copyright © 1976.

Publication of this book was made possible in part by a grant from the Julian Park Publications Fund of the State University of New York at Buffalo.

For
Mary L. Greenhoe

Contents

Preface

To discover a new literary genre like Menippean satire is a great joy. To discover that its conventions do much to explain the relation between Boethius' *Consolation of Philosophy* and Chaucer's poetry, as well as the techniques of both writers, has proved to be an even greater joy. My work on the subject of the relation between Chaucer and Boethius began as I was completing my book on King Alfred's adaptation of the *Consolation*.[1] I seemed to myself primed with information about the Latin work which would lead immediately to a satisfactory analysis of its influence on Chaucer. I soon discovered that with the light of Chaucer's eyes upon it, the *Consolation* turned into a text I had never seen before. I had read the Latin work many times, but had certainly not come upon the thought that Boethius was adapting models from an important genre which could be studied in other works. The *Consolation* is usually treated as a minor philosophical text, written by a writer not up to the standards of the classical writers to whom he alludes. It is instead his intentional adaptation of those models in a Menippean format. It is also commonly supposed to be a personal utterance of a man trying to come to terms with unjust punishment, an utterance which is, however, too passionless to be engaging. The work is instead an intellectual's supremely powerful, even amused, assertion about how the mind can stay free of its own and others' formulations.

I had, however, had a couple of hints that what seemed an inadequate apple was actually a pear. One was the odd recognition, which kept surfacing, that although I was not much taken with the Latin work, repeated intensive readings did not lower my opinion of it. There are very few texts I enjoy that would not have sagged under such persistent attention. The second hint came from one of the moments of greatest intellec-

1. *King Alfred and Boethius* (Madison, 1968).

tual freedom that I have experienced in my life, which at the time I did not connect with the *Consolation* as I sat working at it, much less with the joy of Menippean satire. Struggling to find some way of getting beyond the depression that graduate study sets off, I felt the injunction flash through my mind: "'The words in which you formulate your despair are your own. They describe no fixed reality. Choose others and go free." But the understanding of what was implied by these hints came later.

I was prepared to argue as soon as I began to look closely at the two authors that Chaucer's attitude toward the Latin work was satirical rather than serious. I would thus have been arguing along very different lines from such major Boethian scholars as Patch and Jefferson.[2] But I was unable to find a method of describing the complexities, much less the point of the satiric employment of the Latin text. I could see that Chaucer manages to combine not only freewheeling parody of Boethius' work but also absolute respect. I found this paradoxical attitude difficult to endure as a feeling and seemingly impossible to describe as an activity of an intelligent poet. After several—for this purpose useless—years of forays into medieval theology and philosophy, at the nadir of exasperation over my inability to handle a problem whose outlines I could sense so clearly, I was sitting one day in Duke Humphrey at the Bodleian, reading H. F. Stewart's *Boethius* (Edinburgh, 1891) for the twenty-first time, and the words, which I had seen many times before, "Satura Menippaea" registered suddenly, along with the realization that I hadn't the remotest idea what a Menippean satire was. That moment led me to the classical Menippean satires by Seneca, Petronius, Apuleius, and especially to those by Lucian, whose brilliant delights tantalize the mind and satisfy the soul. I soon found Northrop Frye's brief description of Menippean satire in the *Anatomy of Criticism* (Princeton, 1957); it gave me the catalyst I needed. Mikhail Bakhtin's book, *The Problems of Dostoevsky's Poetics* (Ann Arbor, 1973; revised Russian edition, 1963), came to hand rather late in the writing, but again at a

2. H. R. Patch, *The Tradition of Boethius* (Oxford, 1935); B. L. Jefferson, *Chaucer and* The Consolation of Philosophy (Princeton, 1917).

moment when my feelings were badly in need of corroboration. His book, being the only full-scale analysis I know of the Menippean qualities in the works of a great author, is indispensable.

The study which follows is an exploration of this genre through the readings of selected works by three great Menippean satirists. The underlying problem that I formulated, once I had become aware of the existence of Menippean satire, was essentially one of analogy: How is Lucian like Boethius like Chaucer, and vice versa. I focus on Lucian and Boethius as Chaucer's two predecessors because Lucian is the first Menippean satirist from whom we have complete works—he acts, therefore, as a kind of touchstone for the genre—and because Boethius' *Consolation* is the Menippean satire that Chaucer cites most frequently. I do not offer an evaluation of Boethius' works other than the *Consolation*, nor of its commentaries. I have kept footnoting to a minimum, particularly in the chapters on Chaucer, partly because the recent volume of critical work renders total citations impractical, mainly because I have found few writers dealing directly with Menippean satire and its relation to Chaucer. I have also not attempted to deal with all the major Menippean satires, much less the minor satires which Chaucer read or might have read. To do so would have been to write a second book. The dialogue literature, the cento literature, and the prosimetrum literature all offer potential Menippean satires. Many works not mentioned in this study will suddenly reveal themselves to the reader as Menippean satires.[3]

---

3. Those with whom I have discussed Menippean satire and readers of my manuscript have made numerous suggestions. One mentions Cicero's *Dialogues* as a possibility, another Bernardus Silvestris' *Cosmographia* and Alain de Lille's *De Planctu Naturae*. Martianus Capella's *Marriage of Philology and Mercury* and Jean de Meun's part of the *Romance of the Rose* are obvious candidates; the *Divine Comedy* and the *Book of Good Love* are also, I believe, Menippean satires. One friend commented after reading the list of traits of Menippean satire which I compile in the first chapter from Frye, Bakhtin, and my own reading: "That's what *Tristram Shandy* is, a Menippean satire." Another penciled in the margin of my Lucian chapter: "Ahab on the whale, Pierre on the Black Knight." A recent discussion with Robert Durling convinced me that Boccaccio's *Decameron* very likely belongs to the tradition. Hamlet springs to everyone's mind. I comment briefly on some, but not all, of the works that have been suggested.

The ubiquity of works which employ, or at first blush seem to employ, the genre is nearly as astonishing as the absence of attention it has received.

The Chaucer text used in this study is F. N. Robinson's *Works of Geoffrey Chaucer* (Boston, 1957). The Middle English translation of Boethius' *Consolation of Philosophy* quoted in the Chaucer chapters is the one which appears in this edition; references will be given by book and prose or meter. For the convenience of the parallel texts, the translations of the *Consolation* in the early chapters and of the works of Lucian I have cited are those of the Loeb editions: H. F. Stewart and E. K. Rand, with a new translation by S. J. Tester, *Boethius* (London, 1973); A. M. Harmon, K. Kilburn, and M. D. Macleod, *Lucian*, 8 vols. (London, 1913–67).

My debts are many. I would like to thank the New York State Research Foundation for three years' of summer support, the Julian Park Foundation for a subvention to aid in the publication of this book, and the Bodleian and English Faculty Libraries at Oxford for sanctuary. I thank friends at Buffalo and elsewhere for the time they took to read and comment on parts of my final manuscript: Fred See, Larry Michel, Mili Clark (Buffalo); Kirstie Morrison (Oxford) and Jack Ogilvy (Colorado). I thank the Wisconsin readers who were identified to me: Jerome Taylor and the classicists Fanny LeMoine and Barbara Fowler for their reading and comments. I would also like to thank Bryan P. Reardon (Irvine) for reading and commenting on the first two chapters. Last, I am grateful to those who helped with the technical side of the preparations for this book: my parents, Frank and Bill Payne, Mary Greenhoe, and Annie Carter for proofreading the manuscript submitted to the press; Jerrie Page for reading galley proofs; Robert Edwards for reading page proof. I thank you one and all.

F. Anne Payne

SUNY Buffalo
June 12, 1980

Chaucer and Menippean Satire

1

Menippean Satire and Menippean Satirists

The failure to recognize that a work belongs to a particular literary genre causes universal difficulties to critics; at its worst, it causes us to attack pear trees for not producing apples. Menippean satire, a genre common in antiquity and the Middle Ages, still written today, but ignored by literary history and criticism,[1] is frequently involved in such a failure. This satire—one of Western Civilization's great literary forms, in a league with epic and tragedy, and to judge by the number of those now writing it, for modern writers, preferable to others,[2]—is a literary form we never encounter as such in our study of literature. This is not to say that we have not all been familiar with major works in the genre. We have all read *Candide*, *Gulliver's Travels*, and *Brave New World*. We may even have read the *Satyricon*, *Gargantua and Pantagruel*, and *Portnoy's Complaint*. But if my own experience and that of the friends and colleagues I have asked is any guide, we have not read Lucian, the first writer whose complete Menippean satires survive and perhaps the most brilliantly funny of all of them.

Our ignorance about the genre remains deep-seated, in part because even when we have read the satires, we are quite unlikely to have seen them associated with their genre. Both Northrop Frye in the *Anatomy of Criticism* and Mikhail Bakhtin in the *Problems of Dostoevsky's Poetics*, who deals with the Menippean qualities in the works of Dostoevsky, point out that in approaching this heavily intellectual form, with its parody of ideas and parodies of parody of ideas, the critic is apt to deal with something like style or content (I add that source study is also a prevalent mode of investigation for works in this genre) rather than with the form, its traits and intents.[3] If these approaches yield lean pickings, then the work fades from literary interest; or in the case of a work like the *Consolation*, its fame is regarded as a peculiarity of tastes we no longer share. In part, our ignorance remains because, uninstructed and unsuspecting, we do not attempt to master the necessary art of reading this satire. For instance, it requires that we accept as necessary the presentation of simultaneous unresolved points of view. Those used to looking for the significance in the resolution to the conficts presented in the narrative are disappointed; they remain blind to the realization that no resolutions are provided at the usual level, that the author's single meaning inheres in his form and is consequently difficult to approach. Bakhtin complains that critics treat Raskolnikov and Ivan Karamazov as if they were philosopher-spokesmen for Dostoevsky rather than single unsupported voices among other voices clashing over the insoluble problem of the universe and the moment which Menippean satire calls up. Bakhtin speaks of Dostoevsky's novels as "dialogical" and "polyphonic" and opposes them for illustration to those of Tolstoy, whose works he calls "monological."[4]

Menippean satire is frequently called a medley and so it is, a medley of prose and verse, of tones, of attitudes, points of view, philosophies, of places high and low, fantastic and realistic, of characters divine and human, living and dead. Often dismissed because of its disregard for the decorum of consistency or the demands of any kind of hierarchical order, it is in fact a profoundly thoughtful genre. Its serio-comical utterances, its parodies of all that the human mind has ever succeeded in formulating, call into play and juxtapose the extreme perceptions of total intelligence. There are resolvers but no resolutions here, a profound concern with ultimate questions but no trust in any one's "ultimate" answer. There is no possibility in this satire for the sublime innocence of epic and tragedy, for it suspects that fate and God are only human names, formulations which probably have nothing to do with what is "out there," and death a boring eventuality which is, in the long run, too commonplace to be of significance. Its time is now, its province all that the mind has created, its problem what is truth, its reward intellectual freedom, its pet hate the tyranny of any Establishment.

4

Menippean Satire and Menippean Satirists

The term "Menippean satire" is at least as old as Varro's "Menippea Satura," where the first word celebrated the inventor of the form and the second meant "medley." It has sometimes been called "encyclopedic satire"; the first term picks up the connotations of "satura" and "satire" is used in the modern sense. Bakhtin and Frye see "satire" as a troublesome and misleading part of the ancient name; Bakhtin abbreviates to "menippea" and Frye substitutes "anatomy." I keep the original term in the recognition that it names a high and elaborate satiric form which bears to its category the same relation that tragedy bears to melodrama, epic to heroic tale. The pattern that underlies its satiric vision cannot be confined to the pattern so often in evidence in lesser grades of satire, which is to posit an ideal position, show something in default of that position, and then attack the defaulter (the energetic worker, lazy John, attack on lazy men or lazy John; ancient Roman virtue, modern Roman vice, attack on modern vice or human vice). Though parody is one of the Menippean satire's consistent features, it does not necessarily reductively mock its target. When it does, it does so without the confining "papa-knows-best" attitude of the lower-level satiric author. If it exposes fools and knaves, it also democratically exposes the presumptions of those who piously expose them. Questioning and complaining about the universe is a pervasive activity of both characters and author, but those who complain are treated comically and those with the "answers" ironically. The purpose of the satire seems to be to make us capable of existing independently in the midst of old answers, not to send us off to where no answer can be found. Even though relentless, it is a companionable sort of satire. Its ultimate purpose is not to expose but to set free, to keep the magic of the mind and the world alive.

What Menippean satire questions is thus not deviations from an ideal standard, but the possibility of ideal standards. This questioning, however it is expressed, is the distinguishing mark of works in this genre. Any one of its conventions (or a number of them perhaps: I shall go on to list the most important ones in a moment) can appear in a work without producing a Menippean satire. For instance, the often cited convention of alter-

5

nating verse and prose passages, as my friend J. D. A. Ogilvy points out, also belongs to the saga. The profound belief that no idea is capable of being validated, if accepted, allows a consequent intellectual freedom of the highest order. The will is treated as free, and choice is the dominant factor, not only in human thought, but also in human action. The conventions to be found in the satires are merely aids to the dramatization of this fundamental assumption. The specific treatment of the idea that the world is largely what we make it varies, of course, according to author, and in Chaucer even according to narrator. The state of affairs frightens the *Troilus* narrator into frantic coverups, wearies the Knight and sends him on a search for some momentary beauty, and maniacally delights the Nun's Priest, who proposes that men's free will has always left them incapable of rising above the desires of roosters.

Northrop Frye, in his brief analysis of Menippean satire, remarks on the lack of attention the satire has received and goes on to deal with its intellectual and analytical focus. "The Menippean satire deals less with people as such than with mental attitudes. Pedants, bigots, cranks, parvenus, virtuosi, enthusiasts, rapacious and incompetent professional men of all kinds, are handled in terms of their occupational approach to life as distinct from their social behavior. . . . A constant theme in the tradition is the ridicule of the *philosophus gloriosus*. . . . The novelist sees evil and folly as social diseases, but the Menippean satirist sees them as diseases of the intellect, as a kind of maddened pedantry which the *philosophus gloriosus* at once symbolizes and defines." Frye points out further that the satire is not interested in the exploits of heroes or the structure of society. "At its most concentrated the Menippean satire presents us with a vision of the world in terms of a single intellectual pattern. The intellectual structure built up from the story makes for violent dislocations in the customary logic of narrative, though the appearance of carelessness that results reflects only the carelessness of the reader or his tendency to judge by a novel-centered conception of fiction." Menippean satire, Frye continues, can be pure fantasy or contain a serious moral vision of society; its short form is a dialogue, as in Landor's *Imaginary*

Conversations or the ubiquitous "dialogues of the dead"; the symposium and the country house weekend provide settings for the clash of ideas and the piling up of enormous masses of erudition. Finally preferring the term "anatomy" (dissection, analysis) to "Menippean satire," Frye concludes: "A clearer understanding of the form and traditions of the anatomy would make a good many elements in the history of literature come into focus. Boethius' *Consolation of Philosophy*, with its dialogue form, its verse interludes and its pervading tone of contemplative irony, is a pure anatomy, a fact of considerable importance for the understanding of its vast influence."[5]

Bakhtin's analysis and definition are more extended. As do others,[6] he relates Menippean satire to a group of writings in antiquity called "spoudo-geloion" (serio-comical) and names as the three dominant traits of this group (which includes the Socratic dialogue) an insistence on examining everything in terms of the present, a deeply critical attitude toward myth, and a love of multifariousness and discordance.[7] He lists fourteen points that describe the salient traits of the specific member of this group Menippean satire (his term is "menippea"). I summarize:

1. The weight of the comic element is greater in the menippea than in the Socratic dialogue, but there is considerable variance. It is heavy in Varro, reduced in Boethius.
2. The menippea is fully liberated from the limitations of the historical and memoir forms characteristic of the Socratic dialogue; it is free of legend and not bound by any requirements of external verisimilitude. It is characterized by extraordinary freedom of invention in philosophy and plot. "Indeed in all of world literature we would not be able to find a genre with greater freedom of invention or fantasy than the menippea."
3. The purpose of the fantastic is "to create extraordinary situations in which to provoke and test a philosophical idea," not to act as an embodiment of the truth. "The wildest fantastical adventures are brought into organic and indissoluble artistic unity with the philosophical idea. . . . it can be

7

said that the content of the menippea consists of the adventures of an idea or the truth in the world: either on earth, in the nether regions or on Olympus."

4. Menippean satire is frequently an organic combination of free fantasy, symbolism, and mystical-religious elements with (from our point of view) extreme, crude underworld naturalism. "The organic combination of philosophical dialogue, lofty symbolism, fantastic adventure and underworld naturalism is a remarkable characteristic of the menippea which was preserved at all subsequent stages in the development of the dialogical line of novelistic prose right up until Dostoevsky."

5. Bold invention and fantasy combine with extraordinary philosophical universalism and extreme ideologism. The menippea is a genre of "ultimate questions," in which ultimate philosophical positions are put to the test. The nature of philosophical problems in the menippea is much different from the nature of those in the Socratic dialogue. In Menippean satire, all problems in the least academic fall by the wayside, as does complex and extensive argumentation, leaving only bare ultimate questions with an ethico-practical inclination. The juxtaposition of stripped-bare positions is represented in Lucian's *Sale of Philosophies* (*Vitiarum Auctio*). In all of them, the *pro et contra* of the ultimate questions of life are laid bare.

6. The menippea is often characterized by a trilevel construction used in connection with philosophical universalism: heaven, earth, and hell.

7. A special feature of the experimental fantasticality of the genre is the observation of something from an unusual point of view, e. g., a city viewed from the heights. Bakhtin mentions Lucian's *Icaromenippus*.

8. There is often an investigation of unusual psychic states: insanity, split personalities, unrestrained daydreaming, strange dreams, suicidal thoughts. These phenomena destroy the epic-tragic integrity of man and his fate; in him the possibilities of another man and another life are revealed; he loses his "finalizedness" and singleness of mean-

ing. He ceases to coincide with himself. Although these traits are rudimentary in the early menippea, they are already apparent, and they afford a new vision of man. The dialogical attitude of man to himself also destroys his "finalizedness."

9. Scandalous scenes, actions, words, events are characteristic of the menippea.
10. There are many sharp contrasts and oxymoronic combinations.
11. The menippea contains elements of a social Utopia; a journey into another land is frequently involved.
12. It characteristically makes use of other genres, of prose and verse. The inserted genres are presented at various distances from the author's position, i.e., with various degrees of parody and objectivization. The verse portions are always to a certain degree parodic.
13. The presence of inserted genres intensifies the variety of styles and tones.
14. There is a topicality and publicistic quality in the menippea. Lucian's collected work could be considered a "writer's diary."

Bakhtin concludes: "These are the basic characteristics of the genre of the menippea. We must again emphasize the organic unity of all of these seemingly very heterogeneous traits and the profound internal integrity of this genre."[8]

To Bakhtin's list, I would add other important traits of the satire, as follows:

15. Menippean satire frequently employs a dialogue between a pair of stereotyped characters speaking from two differing, clear-cut levels of perception. One is a know-it-all who is free of the restrictions and responsibilities faced by ordinary human beings. The other, his interlocutor, has a view of man's struggle with his human burdens different from the one the know-it-all proposes but is persuaded to listen, like it or not. In Lucian and Boethius, the know-it-all is the protagonist, Menippus or a similar figure in Lucian, and Philosophy in Boethius. But in Chaucer's narrator poems

(the dream visions, *Troilus and Criseyde*, and the frame dialogue of the *Canterbury Tales*) and Roth's *The Breast*, the puzzled human sufferer has the main role. Chaucer's narrator in the dream visions, for instance, is lectured unmercifully by the Eagle, the God of Love, and Affrican, but is nevertheless the dominant character in the poem. The psychiatrist Klinger, who is full of unimpeachable advice about how Kepesh is to live as a breast, is also a minor character. We observe primarily Kepesh's problems of living with the imposed restrictions. (Roth's presentation of the trials this troubled character endures reaches a kind of absolute pinnacle of horror and absurdity.)[9]

16. One character of the satire is frequently involved in an endless quest; the other character of the central dialogue comments on his activities, in a sense "helps" him. The quest is endless; there is a satirization of any norm which tries to provide an end.

17. The satire embodies the knowledge that man's unsuspendable freedom to think is his most elating gift and his most terrifying burden. This idea is represented, for instance, by the satirist's treating action as if it too were free. (Menippus can go to heaven or hell; an abstraction, "the love of wisdom," can appear in a prison cell; a man can turn into a breast.) The main purpose, as I take it, of the fantastic element is to metaphorize this freedom. The physical structure of the world is seen as incapable of imposing what are generally thought to be its usual limitations.

18. The characters exhibit a courteous intention to continue conversing no matter what happens and no matter what must be given up (that is, so long as the work remains in the realm of the comic).

19. The satire radiates an unquenchable hope and a titanic energy for whatever the problem is (represented particularly in the know-it-all figure and his/her activities).

20. No "God" or unquestionable authority is represented. The satire is based on the feeling that there is probably no abstract certainty outside of us that we can know, merely the infinitely elating possibility that there might be, if only we could get by the claptrap of our own concoctions.

21. Obscenity appears without pornography. The proposed mating of the woman and the ass in Apuleius reads like an account of an adolescent's fears over his first date; the Breast's struggle to restrain his scream to Claire to squat on his nipple-penis reads like an account of a man being tortured to death by the ultimate powers of evil who heroically restrains himself from screaming "Kill me!"[10]

All these various traits are related to the dominant concern of the satire, the satirization of the possibility of an acceptable norm. For instance, the changing tone, the nonpornographic obscenity, the heterogeneous catalogues which ignore hierarchical subordination, are all ways of violating decorum, consistency, traditional expectation, and are thus antiestablishment. They deny the possibility of an unquestionable standard, answer, method, attitude which some people mean to force down other people's throats. The fantastic element—the journey into Hades (Lucian), the metamorphosis into a breast (Roth), the unscathed survival of endless catastrophes (Voltaire's *Candide*) —provides the opportunity for situations where other conditions obtain, where two sets of norms (or a half dozen) are present if not necessarily in meaningful conflict. The juxtaposition reminds us continually of the presence of alternatives, and of the uncertainty of any final answers.

The air of hope, the courtesy, and the sense of intellectual freedom we find in these satires are the happy by-products of the satirist's projecting a world without dead ends, without the destructive (if somewhat comforting) dictum, the one or the other. They set up in this disjointed world of Menippean satire an enormous elation. Bickering and unpleasantness are quickly superseded by good-humored tolerance, a desire to keep the dialogue going, no matter what the seeming obstacles. New levels of thought suddenly open up at the moment when it seems that everything is closed off. If these satirists propagate a belief in the unknowableness of truth, they are not agnostics. They are too restless for settled schools. They radiate a profound conviction that the search itself is always worthwhile, that to move uninhibitedly in the truth of uncertainty is better than to be bound in the comfort of false certainty. If the inevitable result of this unhuman choice seems, eventually, to be an uneasy teetering on that boundary which separates sanity from madness, the satirist usually chooses to lurch forward into comedy. There are, however, two great Menippean tragedies in English, *Troilus and Criseyde* and *Hamlet*; in these works the human inability to find any kind of validated method of handling the facets of the problem posed is felt as a destructive incapacity that looms larger than the joy promised by the freedom to investigate alternate possibilities.

The two traits of the satire which prove in the end to have the most profound ramifications are the dialogue structure and the parody of certain selected texts. The dialogue, which is composed of the interactions of a series of stereotyped characters, is probably the most frequent device in Menippean satire for portraying the multiplicity of the universe and the impossibility of finding the ultimate answer to any mortal question. Of the central pair of disputants, one—whom I have already referred to as the know-it-all—speaks for the timeless moment of things, for the state of affairs in which men have seen themselves free, eternal, immortal, and above all certain. Bakhtin calls this figure the "wise man."[11] I would rather, if I had to pick one word, call him or her the "scientist," for this figure has a kind of marvelous sanity but knows nothing about art and beauty, whose power, in the opinion of most of us, the scientist ought to acknowledge. In fact, as we investigate the various representations of this figure, we are often reminded of the parody of Kipling's words: "If you can keep your head when all about you are losing theirs, then perhaps you don't understand the situation" (e.g., Klinger with Kepesh). The other character of the main dialogue, only too well aware of the problem, bears the weight of unseeing and unreasoning time upon his shoulders, and attempts in the course of the dialogue to come to terms, in the face of his interlocutor's objections, with the awareness of the perpetual sequences of unavoidable experience. Both characters are submitted to comic and ironic attack; in other words, neither is allowed to have the final view of matters.

In addition to the two characters of the main dialogue, two other stock characters are common in the satires. One is the "friend," a figure also found in the Socratic dialogue. The other is a *deus* figure, who if present gives the appearance of controlling the dialogue. He is characterized by the intent to give the figures in the central confrontation exactly what they think they want. As might be expected in a satire that makes nothing of the sacrosanctities of the usual categories like "living and dead," "divine and human," the *deus* figure is not necessarily the god of any particular mythical system, only of that system being established in this present, on this stage, in this work. The Host holds this position in the *Canterbury Tales*, Nature in the *Parlement of Foules*. Nor are the gods of the usual mythical system necessarily *deus* figures, though they may be. (Zeus in Lucian's *Zeus Catechized* is not; here the Cynic Cyniscus takes the befuddled Zeus to task over his unexamined opinions about fate. Zeus and Hermes in Lucian's *Philosophies for Sale* are *deus* figures; here they have rounded up the major philosophers of antiquity in a slave market, where the philosophers engage in the dialogue with the potential buyers.) Nor is there any power in this satire like the fate of *Oedipus*, the *wyrd* of *Beowulf*, or the God of the Bible. What happens would happen without the presence of these "gods"; at best, they fluff out an already existent situation, are in a sense merely another facet of a satire which proposes that most of the "reality" we dramatize as life is based on our own unvalidatable projections.

The basic dialogue structure varies in one important respect: sometimes the know-it-all is the protagonist, sometimes the human struggler. The authorial preference for the opinions of one or the other of the figures is a possible clue to his actual beliefs. In Lucian, the know-it-all dominates; on occasion, as in *The Fisherman* and *Hermotimus*, he has the author's name or pseudonym, and even when he does not, he plays the author's clear and chosen role. In Boethius, the know-it-all dominates also, except that we are aware of the harder choice because the human sufferer has the author's name. Philosophy is the free spirit wandering through the universe. In Chaucer, however, the "scientist" figure is much reduced in stature; the human struggler, Chaucer's surrogate, is inept perhaps, but nevertheless in the spotlight on center stage. The insights of the Eagle, the God of Love, and Affrican (the know-it-alls of the dream visions) parody by diminution the power of penetrating to the reality of things which Lucian and Boethius assign to Menippus and Philosophy. In the same way, Theseus, Pandarus, and first Pertelote, then the fox—the know-it-all figures of the three works I shall be dealing with at length—are viewed from angles unpleasant enough to make us in each case, if not prefer, at least give considerable thought to the views of their opposites (the young knights, Troilus, and Chauntecleer). In *The Breast* also, Kepesh, the human sufferer, has our attention, not Klinger, objective though he may be. The preference which each author forces upon us indicates ways of handling whole clusters of ideas that hover around these figures. In a genre whose métier is many-leveled irony, this preference is an important key to meaning.

The textual parody, a common device in the satires, is as important as the dialogue structure. This parody causes us to sense continually the presence of another genre, another story, another mind. In Lucian, the works of Homer and the Greek tragedians are constantly with us; in *The Breast*, those of Gogol, Swift, and Kafka, not to mention those of modern psychiatry. In the *Knight's Tale* and *Troilus*, adaptations of Boccaccio, the "other text" is also a technical device, the "old story" of the Knight, "Lollius" of the *Troilus* narrator. In both works, Chaucer's allusions to the *Consolation* establish the presence of another kind of text, a Menippean satire whose dramatic dialogue centers on philosophical problems. In the *Nun's Priest's Tale*, a take-off on fable and mock-epic, we encounter the presence of the "texts" of Western civilization, the *Consolation* among them. The attitude of the narrators toward the inserted text varies. It can be serious as in *Troilus*, objectively dismissive as in the *Knight's Tale*, or wildly derisive as in the *Nun's Priest's Tale*, where the narrator is overjoyed to point out the idiocies and inadequacies of his cited authors, especially Boethius. The textual parody in all these works is one way of keeping before us multiple views of the universe.

The textual parody has another important function. Like the two-leveled dialogue, it is a way of blocking or at least delaying our defining a norm or point of view from which the satirist proceeds in his attacks. The Menippean dialogue causes the foreground to be occupied with characters whose problems do not coincide and situations that remain unsolved and hence call each other into question. The textual parody provides us with another set of conflicting levels. The inserted text (or texts) provides answers matching, contradicting, or deliberately irrelevant to the perceptions of the main text. Both sources of information hit us simultaneously; they are continually interrupting and undermining our conclusions about the whole work and often about any given passage. But because of our struggle to make all our information cohere, we cannot rush to some simple-minded, pat answer. We experience aesthetically both the complexity and chaotic uncertainty of things.

The process is easily felt in a reading and analysis of a simple form of the dialogue like Lucian's *Zeus Catechized*. Cyniscus tries to get the troubled Zeus to see the philosophical absurdity of his opinions about fate—opinions, it soon turns out, derived from Homer and later Greek poets. The dialogue is a systematic and, it seems at first glance, totally destructive attack on the logical absurdities of the myths. In the beginning, the dialogue is comic. It is very difficult to imagine anyone's reading it for the first time in any state other than high glee. We are only too well amused to see these fallacies, which lurked somewhere in the back of our minds as we read Homer and Sophocles, brought into the light. But as we continue to think about the dialogue, we begin imperceptibly to drift toward a profound uneasiness. This movement is a secondary impulse, but it is a reaction to the demand to investigate the negative as well as the positive, to recognize the *sic et non* which this highly intellectualized form sets up.

As we drift, our uneasiness mounts because a being who is styled a god is so incompetent in his perception of what a god does. It becomes intolerable that Zeus will not make the effort to shift the dialogue into a reality that he can handle or at least into one on neutral ground. He does not. We fear that he cannot. The world slips into chaos. We become aware of another dimension of our terror. The brilliance of Cyniscus' attack has obscured the realization that he proposes no alternative, no solution, no world view which contains the right answers to the questions he raises. The satire laughs at what others say, but is silent about its own resolution to the implications of its questions. In this silence, the great Menippean silence, there is a sense in which the satire maintains by its profusion of points of view that we are saved from primeval despair only by our propensity for exercising our mental talents behind the tentatively secure masks of other, perhaps stupider, men's unknowing plays. For one thing is true: though intellectual freedom is the highest good, we can neither look at nor endure the great Nothing. Nor for that matter, if we think about it, can we endure the humiliation of our inability to formulate some reality that stands independent of our minds and language.

It is generally said that the *Consolation*, which I shall examine in greater detail in the third chapter, is a purified Menippean satire,[12] a statement that need hardly be questioned. There is no obscenity, no underworld naturalism. There are no violent shifts in tone, neither the lighthearted questions of Menippus ("Why are you crying, Tantalus?") nor the irreverent humor of the *Dialogues of the Dead* (though we might catalogue in that fashion Philosophy's amusement over the fate of her pseudodisciples who tore pieces off her dress and were later killed by the multitude who mistook them for her friends). For the portrayal of his ideas, Boethius chooses to use the simplest classical model of the Menippean dialogue. Only the two members of the central confrontation are present; other stock figures are excluded. The views of Boethius are attacked with sophisticated amusement, those of Philosophy with superior irony. Boethius has dedicated himself to philosophy all his life, but instantly falls into hopeless weeping and passionate emotion at his imprisonment. Sympathetic though *we* may be, Philosophy attacks him with righteous indignation: "So I am moved more by the sight of you than of this place. I seek not so much a library with its walls ornamented with ivory and glass, as the storeroom of your mind, in which I have laid up not books, but what makes them of any value, the opinions set down in my books in times past" (bk. 1, pr. 5).[13] Behind the text, we hear the laughter—"reduced laughter," Bakhtin calls it.[14] We can, of course, also hear the despair, but it is slighter than Philosophy's optimistic joy.

Philosophy herself is the supreme know-it-all, explainer, and manipulator, who regards herself and her views as sacrosanct. As new ideas occur to her because of the prisoner's questions, she changes her text accordingly. The result is that she takes Boethius on a sophisticated journey through four great philosophical systems: the Cynic (bk. 2–bk. 3, pr. 9), the Platonic (bk. 3, m. 9–bk. 4, m. 5), the Aristotelian (bk. 4, pr. 6–bk. 5, m. 2), and the Augustinian (bk. 5, pr. 4–pr. 6).[15] Nevertheless, her cheerful and lighthearted movement through schools calls even her position into question. As Philosophy shifts from one norm of thought to another, Boethius' downfall, which is mentioned directly only at the beginning, must simply be remembered and imagined as we read. Her discussion leaves unanswered the obvious questions pertinent to the physical situation of the prisoner. What about my life? What should I have done? How do I get out of here? The Menippean silence intrudes without insistence in the *Consolation*, for its satiric technique is not travesty but sustained irony. In her shifting, Philosophy cheerfully discards all worlds and world views but those of the system she is engaged with at the moment (e. g., she does not deal with the demands of empire, or the human need for a space larger than a prison cell and company other than the most abstract of ideas, her august self; nor does she deign to provide a consistent intellectual confrontation with the issue of despair). However much we may rejoice in the ease of her shifts and her brilliant abstractions from the philosophical systems that delight her, the fact remains that she frequently speaks to issues remote from the prisoner's deepest problems. This discarding, no matter what claims these other problems may have on her interlocutor, is the prime condition of belief as she and her fellow mentor-figures, in both classical and modern satires, represent it. Boethius, with the courtesy of the innocent, out of the state of grace of Philosophy's world even more emphatically than out of his own, goes along willingly with all this, largely because he wants to believe again.

17

The dialogue between these two characters, speaking from their two different levels of being, creates in our minds a continual seesawing back and forth between perspectives. The counters with which the dialogue plays are terrible and awe-inspiring: the great systems of Western thought; a prison cell; a man involved in the bitterest human experience; a towering female figure with flaming eyes whose head on occasion disappears in the clouds, yet who when he asks about evil, offers to improve his digestion. In spite of the colossal differences among these counters and the centripetal force of the satire's power, we feel the two characters there together, nevertheless, providing fitful illumination for us. Bakhtin remarks—probably his most interesting point—that the vision of Menippean satire destroys the epic integrity of man. In the laughter that hovers over this dialogue of the *Consolation*, we feel man's epic innocence break apart. Technically, of course, the writer is split in two; the work dramatizes his dialogization. A man's acceptance of an alien within him and of a point of view his immediate experience does not allow him to take is evident in Boethius' presenting Philosophy in triumph over him. The *Consolation* is a particularly good example of this split, of the fragmented perspectives in us which we cannot reconcile, yet must accept. But it is also apparent that as long as these counters—consciousness, tradition, finitude, and the objective, optimistic energy for the uninhibited search—are there in the universe, we will be able to think within a space which finds freedom meaningful.

Finitude is by no means the least important of the four. Whether we experience it as a prison cell or as form in art, it is an important dimension of free thought because we lack the capacity to endure naked infinity. Sketched-out limitations protect us. Heroes, iconoclasts, and the proposers of an unseen God, for instance, try to push this need in us to the background and persuade us to do without it. This is perhaps the main reason that Menippean satire does not value heroism, the attempt to step beyond the on-going system to create a "new" world. It wants establishments, not to transcend, but as peacefully ignorant opponents to attack; it wants traditions to mimic and texts to parody. It wants these obstacles because it recognizes them as a distractive necessity, as the stable force that has so far managed to keep what there is of the house from falling in. The need of the satire for concrete, limited entities whose existence is not in question also explains its interest in the historical milieu of not only the past, but also the present. Bakhtin calls Lucian's works the "diary of a writer" (point 14). The historical events of the moment intrude themselves strongly into the work of Dostoevsky and the *Divine Comedy*. A whole branch of Chaucer scholarship has dedicated itself to identifying living persons who may be referred to in his works. And while not all critics approve the results of such study, there is something about the concrete quality of the detail in some of Chaucer's poetry which calls up the single, immediate person. The underlying concrete entity which defies universalization is most evident in the dream visions and in the *General Prologue* to the *Canterbury Tales*. There is a sense in which the satire desires that finitude which most balks at an instant drift into a concrete universal, which would imply a "system." It wants the single uncomplicated personage or event of the moment.

As far as textual parody is concerned, what Boethius did was not so much purify a device as drive its implications to their uttermost limits. What we have in the *Consolation* is serious textual parody; that is, it does not attack or view in comic light those texts and philosophers it cites. When Lucian's Menippus asks Tantalus why he is crying, since he obviously has no body and therefore no real need of the things he begs for, Homer is being subjected to comic scrutiny. But when Boethius refers to the *Gorgias*, we sense no intention to mock Plato. Boethius simplifies, moves to the heart of the system. Only the ultimate questions, the core in its bareness, remains, attracts.

Bakhtin, defining this particular kind of parody, remarks:

> A single trait is common to all of these phenomena [stylization, parody, dialogue], despite their essential differences: in all of them the word has a double-directedness—it is directed both toward the object of speech, like an ordinary word, and toward another word, toward another person's speech. If we are not aware of the existence of this second context of the other person's speech and begin to perceive stylization or parody in the

same way that ordinary speech—which is directed only toward
its object— is perceived, then we will not understand the
essence of these phenomena: we will mistake stylization for
the style itself, and will perceive parody merely as a poor work
of art.[16]

Very little reading in the criticism on the *Consolation* is required before it becomes obvious that the work has indeed suffered from most readers' failure to apprehend the intent of the
second level.

Our best support for accepting the *Consolation* as a complex
Menippean satire is the knowledge that Dante, Chaucer, Jean
de Meun, and many thousands of lesser minds saw in it a work
of monumental importance. It is not that they any more than
we, if confronted with two anonymous pieces of writing, one
the *Timaeus*, the other Boethius' abstraction from it (bk. 3, m.
9), would hesitate to say that Plato is the greater writer. It is
rather that as they looked at the *Consolation*, they found an ex-
citing resonance in the parody, while we, brought up in the
cult of originality, if not careful, will regard it with much the
same tolerance as we regard a freshman's jejune summary of
Hamlet. The *Consolation* is a Menippean *summa*. It is not that
all knowledge is there, but all is there that makes knowledge
desirable and tolerable. To go Philosophy one better, it contains the books, the memory of the books, and the mind that
can stay free to make new books even in the face of old books'
authoritative tradition. More positively than any other Menippean satire, the *Consolation* dramatizes the belief not only that
we can remain free to search but also that we come from a noble
intellectual tradition that guarantees us support. With full optimism and faith, Boethius accepts the notion uttered later by
Bernard of Chartres: "We stand on the shoulders of giants."[17]
The power of Boethius' assertion, as well as the technical skill
with which he conveys it, gave hope to many and an imitatable
form and technique to a few, most notably, of course, those
cited above—Dante, Jean de Meun, and Chaucer.[18]

By the evidence of his citations, the Menippean satire most
important to Chaucer was the *Consolation*. B. L. Jefferson
counts 562 instances of specific verbal influence and 479 in-

stances of general influence in some thirty works.[19] The Middle English translation of the *Consolation* printed by Robinson is probably Chaucer's.[20] In the *Retraction* at the end of the *Canterbury Tales*, Chaucer lists the translation of the *Consolation* as the only named work which escapes the Narrator's censure. In his works Chaucer mentions Boethius by name (Boece), quotes the *Consolation*, writes passages in imitation of Boethius, and, as I shall show in later chapters, makes use of certain key structural devices which depend heavily on Menippean patterns also employed in the Latin text. But there is no doubt that Chaucer knew numerous other Menippean satires, both major and minor.[21] As far as the early tradition is concerned, there is no evidence that he had read Lucian.[22] There is also no evidence, but more likelihood, that he knew the works in the early Latin tradition, Seneca's *Apocolocyntosis*, Petronius' *Satyricon*, and Apuleius' *Golden Ass*.[23]

Seneca's *Apocolocyntosis* (first century A.D.) is a parody of the encomium, which deals with the "pumpkinification" instead of the "deification" of Claudius. In this work, a mocking Narrator recounts to us the vicissitudes of the emperor after his death. Having been proclaimed divine by the Senate, the dead Claudius attempts to gain admission to Olympus. The gods, at first unable to make anything out of the mumbling, limping, head-jerking object who messed his clothes at death, finally hold a council to determine Claudius' fitness for membership and reject him. Mercury hauls Claudius past a view of his funeral procession on earth and then down to Hades, where he is tried for his crimes and murders, threatened with the tortures of Tantalus, Sisyphus, and Iacus; and finally sentenced forever to rolling dice in a box with holes in the bottom. But even this minor punishment is commuted when Caligula claims Claudius as a slave he beat frequently. Claudius ends up as a law clerk.

The important structural and thematic traits of this bit of irreverent fluff are the journey in search of a Utopian life and the trilevel construction for the action (heaven, earth, and hell). We have gods whose minor squabbles bear all the earmarks of mortals' inadequacies; the unrequited quest; frequent historical allusions to the doings of the Caesars in the midst of the fantasy; the combination of prose and verse, Homeric poetry and colloquial idiom. Above all, we have the courteous interest of everyone concerned in the nonproblem, especially the god Hercules, who attempts to give Claudius what he asks for but is finally overruled by the council. (A part of Claudius' discussion with Hercules is missing.) The Narrator, for all his strictures against Claudius, is not vengeful. The punishment, such as it is, leaves Claudius spending his death engaged in a profession he is known to have enjoyed in life.

Petronius' *Satyricon*, a long Latin fragment also from the reign of Nero, evidently contained an account of the narrator Encolpius' wanderings through the historical world of the time as he attempts to escape the anger of the god Priapus (as Sullivan points out, a probable parody of Odysseus' flight from Poseidon).[24] The fragments that remain contain a discussion of rhetoric with the teacher Agamemnon and a few scenes between Encolpius and Ascyltus, his rival in love for the boy Giton (first in a brothel, then in a street altercation over a cloak, and finally in a meeting with the priestess of Priapus, Quartilla). The longest and most famous fragment is the dinner at Trimalchio's, to which Agamemnon has wrangled the trio of friends an invitation. Thereafter follow a scene in an art gallery where Encolpius, deserted by Giton and Ascyltus, meets Eumolpus, a poet and poetaster; a ship voyage where the three friends and sundry former lovers and enemies meet once more; and a shipwreck, followed by a moving elegy on the dead Lichas, the unfriendly ship captain. On shore Encolpius meets the lovely Circe, with whom he is impotent. His adventures are counterpointed by the plot of Eumolpus to pass himself off as a wealthy man in need of an heir; for in the city of Croton, where they are headed, as a farmer tells them, there are only two classes of people: "Either they have fortunes worth hunting or they are fortune hunters. In this city no one raises children because anyone who has heirs of his own is not invited out to dinner or allowed into the games; he is deprived of all amenities and lives in ignominious obscurity. But those who have never married and have no close ties, attain the highest honours."[25]

Menippean Satire and Menippean Satirists

What is now extant of the *Satyricon* is characterized by the lack of focus in its satiric thrust, by its random account of events, and by the juxtaposition of matters high and low: learning, art, elegy, on the one hand; brothels, obscenity, the lowest human motives (greed, treachery, lust, cannibalism), on the other. People of all classes—slaves, freedmen, academics, poets, professionals, the high-born—intermingle. Inversions of expectation are frequent. Encolpius wonders that Circe, a lady, has the taste of a whore in men, her maid those of a lady. At the fantastic dinner of the nouveau riche Trimalchio, the nauseated wonder of Encolpius and his two friends is set against the energy and life force of their host. Trimalchio's ostentation, murky mythology, vulgarity, obsessions with his catamites and his death, his bowel movement and the arrangement for his guests' similar needs, and above all his culinary extravagances appall us. Yet he emerges from this debased spectacle as a figure of high comedy. Born a slave, he began his rise to success by making love to both master and mistress, attentions which caused them to bequeath him a fortune. His first venture met with disaster, as all five of his ships sank, but he managed to build others bigger and better, so as not to be thought a "man without courage." His wife, a former slave and whore whom he stigmatizes as a viper, sold her jewelry to help him. If he thinks of nothing better to do with his money than give these ridiculous dinners, he has nevertheless succeeded in transforming the chaotic meaninglessness of life into a world of his own choosing, just as his cooks transform the food for his banquets. Beside his egregious audacity, the objective narrator looks pale.

Another example of the comic triumph of the mocked appears in the longest of the inserted tales, the Widow of Ephesus, which runs as follows. A lady famed for her devotion to her husband refuses all solace at his death and sits day and night in the tomb with his corpse awaiting her own death. A young soldier, set to watch that crucified bodies not be taken down from the crosses nearby, is attracted by the light, courteously offers food, then his love, and at last wins her acquiescence. One night as they make love, however, a body is stolen from one of the crosses by the dead man's relatives. The soldier, knowing the death penalty awaits him, prepares to commit suicide. The widow, to stop him, offers her husband's corpse for the empty place on the cross. Next morning, the people of the town are surprised. This story, which is told by Eumolpus as proof that the modesty of all women is vulnerable, draws laughter from the sailors, blushes from the ship captain's wife, and from the captain, an unamused assertion that the husband's body should have been put back in the tomb and his wife nailed to the cross. But for the reader only the laughter holds as a response. What is done with the husband's corpse is unusual, but exactly what should have been done in the circumstances. The great perversion would have been to let two corpses destroy the life of the living. Like the dinner at Trimalchio's and the *Satyricon* at large, the story is an immoral moral tale in which imagination and the love of life win out in the laughter bought with the knowledge that the clichés of a particular morality are inadequate to the demands of human experience.

Apuleius' *Golden Ass*, a Menippean satire in prose of the second century,[26] is a story told by the narrator Lucius, a young intellectual, about his experience as an ass. It is an extraordinarily warm-hearted book because of its affirmation of the potentialities and beauties of man and his world and because of the good-humored irony with which the narrator recounts the troubles his energetic dedication to knowledge leads him into. By the comic twist of the tale, the quest for knowledge is shortly turned into the quest for rose petals. Hungering to explore the magic lore possessed by his hostess, Lucius is enabled by the help of her maid to witness his hostess' transformation by use of an unguent into a bird. Wanting to experience the same metamorphosis himself, he rubs the unguent on his body, only to discover that the maid has mistaken the boxes. He turns into an ass. Before he and the maid can find the rose petals he must eat to become a man again, robbers break into the house, and he is driven off carrying the booty. The bulk of the book recounts his painful adventures as a beast of burden. The climax of his woes is to find after a successful, if unwilling, secret rendezvous with a woman that his keeper is overjoyed with his prowess and plans to mate him at a public spectacle with a woman who had previously been sentenced to be thrown to wild beasts. His moral nature totally outraged and shocked, and, it must be admitted, also disturbed by the fear that if the wild beasts are loosed on the woman, they may be unable to make a distinction and eat some of the donkey, he escapes to a spot sacred to Isis. She appears in a dream and tells him to eat the rose petals on the sacred wreath in her procession the next day. This he does, is transformed into a man again, and learns that he is to become a votary of her religion. The gods prove demanding, however, for not only Isis, but also Osiris, and then a third god demand his initiation into their cults. His funds running low, Lucius is finally promised that three gods are all who will honor him, and that as a result of their favor, he will rapidly come to the forefront of the legal profession in Rome.

The *Golden Ass* is characterized by a trilevel construction: Lucius' time of purgatorial and insatiable curiosity about forbidden magic, the time of hell spent wandering through the land experiencing all but helplessly the terrors and pains of his unaccustomed state, and the time of heavenly mystical dreams and somewhat ironic final success. The work combines realistic scenes from the everyday life of the period and symbolism, fantasy, and religious revelations. The style is varied, being described by Lindsay as "a mixture of ornate invention and rhetorical ingenuity with archaic and colloquial forms."[27] The prototype of the story (represented in the much shorter Greek work *Lucius or the Ass*) has been greatly lengthened by the insertion of many tales only loosely related, if at all, to the main body of the narrative. There are tales of witches and demons, of criminals, and of tragic love; the long fairy story of Cupid and Psyche, which Apuleius calls a Milesian tale or Old Woman's tale; and various bawdy stories, two of which find their way into Boccaccio's *Decameron*.[28] The function of the tales is vastly to extend Apuleius' portrayal of what Perry calls, in Balzac's terms, "la comédie humaine."[29]

This work provides a particularly striking analogue to Chaucer's *Canterbury Tales*, which exhibits the same diverse collocations of styles and stories. Apuleius' narrator also provides an analogue to Chaucer's portrayal of his own narrator, whose role is in impression sometimes as painful and constricting as that of Lucius as an ass. If the Menippean satires of the first century, the *Apocolocyntosis* and the *Satyricon*, seem more distant from the concerns of Chaucer than the *Golden Ass* because Seneca's narrator is flippant and secure and Petronius' narrator is bawdy and harum-scarum, these two early works nevertheless exhibit common models belonging to the tradition of Menippean satire that Chaucer inherited, namely the journey and the *cena*, or symposium. Both situations easily establish the dialogical milieu that Menippean satire needs for its observations. In dialogues modeled on the journey, the characters confront each other in isolated and sequential encounters; in those modeled on the symposium, all characters are present and participating at the same time. When the fantastic journey is used as a model, the clashes of the dialogue are created by outsiders; when the cena is used, they are created, as a rule, by the members of the group. In the second century, Lucian uses the fantastic journey in the *Menippus* and *Icaromenippus* dialogues and the cena in the *Carousel*, a work thought to be modeled on the *Symposium* of Menippus. Both models lend themselves admirably to the establishing of the dialogical milieu in which the juxtaposition of wildly disharmonius ideas and attitudes seems natural.

The two models also adapt to particular situations with ease. The cena is a slave market in Lucian's *Sale of Philosophies*. The journey can become allegorical, as in the *Consolation*. The "wings of the mind" which Philosophy seeks to give Boethius that he may return to his city create the potential for freedom analogous to that set up by the fantastic element of literal Menippean journeys, with their accounts of journeys to Olympus or Hades. Elaborate Menippean satires are likely to employ both models in combination, though one will dominate. The *Satyricon* combines a literal journey around Italy, in which the characters encounter diverse people and places, with the dinner at Trimalchio's which acts as a long pause during this journey. Martianus Capella's *Marriage of Philology and Mercury* contains the journey of Mercury to Apollo to ask about a potential bride (bk. 1) and the journey of Philology into heaven to Jupiter's palace (bk. 2). The rest of the book is dedicated to the symposium of seven of Varro's nine liberal arts (Architecture and Medicine, though present, are not allowed to speak, as they deal only with mortal matters). In Chaucer's dream visions, we have the journey to the wood in the *Book of the Duchess*, to the House of Fame, to the Garden of Love in the "Prologue" of the *Legend of Good Women*, and to the symposium of the bird parliament in the *Parlement of Foules*.

The *Canterbury Tales* combines a literal journey and a metaphoric cena, the latter being the dominant model of the two. This journey is fantastic only when we see it (as we sometimes do) as mankind's journey to the heavenly Jerusalem. But as far as the literal journey is concerned, we are scarcely conscious of movement from place to place, and no resonances are set up by what is encountered, either by events on the road or strange people at inns.[30] Only the encounter which members of the group have with each other matters. The one intruder, the Canon's Yeoman, is quickly drawn into the concerns of the group; the Canon, who will not be drawn in, leaves. Intruders at Trimalchio's dinner are treated in a similar fashion. Individual *Canterbury Tales* often record journeys which have some element of the fantastic in them. For instance, in the Wife of Bath's segment, we have the rapist knight's encounter, on his journey of a year and a day, with the women who give him conflicting solutions to his question and finally the hag who has the answer. We have the summoner's encounter with the devil, the carter, the old lady. We have the friar's with the wife, the husband, the lord, and the squire. The *Summoner's Tale*, of course, ends with a cena where diverse people speak diversely about methods of handling the gift.

Two later Menippean satires in the Latin tradition, both mentioned by Chaucer, are Martianus Capella's *Marriage of Philology and Mercury* (fifth century) and Nigel Longchamps' *Mirror of Fools*, or the *Book of Daun Burnel the Ass* (twelfth century).[31] The *Mirror*, the less important of the two works, contains the story of an ass who wants a longer tail, then a university education and then wants to found a religious order. The account of the ass's travels is interspersed with stories—

27

Chaucer cites the one of the vengeful cock in the *Nun's Priest's Tale*—and disquisitions on a great variety of subjects. "Nigel reflects on the relative merits of wine and water, the caprice of fortune, the decay of nature, the foibles of old age, the omnipotence of money, the reliability of omens and dreams, and the qualities of nobility. Proverbs and animal lore abound in the poem; so, too, do mythological allusions and classical quotations. The spirit of the satire varies as widely as its subject matter. Nigel's method is frequently to intermingle raillery and derision, judgement and sympathy, earnestness and playfulness."[32] So write Mozley and Raymo, the editors of the work. They go on to point out an important technique of the Menippean satirist: Nigel is "a master of parody and often employs it in whimsical imitations of medical recipes, ecclesiastical anathemas, religious blessings, hymns, *Dies Irae* themes, the language of ecclesiastical pronouncements, and the jargon of logicians."[33]

The earliest extant satire with encyclopedic compendiums is Martianus Capella's *Marriage*.[34] Like the *Consolation*, a prosimetrum and an important school text for hundreds of years,[35] it is loosely based on the Cupid and Psyche story of Apuleius. Martianus calls his tale an Old Man's Tale, echoing Apuleius' Old Woman's Tale; both stories center on the marriage of a god and a mortal which culminates in a heavenly wedding ceremony.[36] Chaucer cites Martianus in the *House of Fame* as a describer of a journey into the heavens (985) and in the *Merchant's Tale*, saying that Martianus's little tongue and pen are too small to sing of January's splendid marriage (1732–37). The catalogue of sins in the *Parson's Tale* and the proverbs in the *Tale of Melibee* have the *Marriage* as an obvious analogue.

The *Marriage* has always baffled and frequently annoyed its critics.[37] C. S. Lewis, kinder to Martianus than most, writes: "It is to the same class of mythological allegory that I would assign the work of another writer, if I felt sure that any classification could hold him; for this universe, which has produced the bee-orchid and the giraffe, has produced nothing stranger than Martianus Capella."[38] The diversity of materials here assembled is, to say the least, astonishing. Lemoine writes: "If *satura* were judged by variety alone, the *De Nuptiis* would surely be at the top of the list. The work contains poetry in fifteen different metres and prose in every style and rhetorical color imaginable. It mixes adventurous travels, humorous divertissements, dry lectures, exotic marvels, and serious philosophical speculations all into one potpourri which seems to be even beyond the bounds of *satura*."[39]

The theme of the work, as Lemoine points out,[40] is the Utopian harmony of all things, which is established by the hymn to Hymen at the beginning. But the perfection of this harmony is opposed and undermined all the way through the book with those chaotic events, happenings, and observations that belong to the Menippean reality. Martianus no sooner finishes his hymn than his son demands to know why an old man should utter such silly trifles. Defending himself, he replies that he is about to tell of a marriage, a choice which instantly reduces the "harmony of all things" to simplistic specificity. Its being a *divine* marriage hardly helps, given the portrayal of these gods with their problems and idiosyncrisies.

Martianus then begins to relate his story. Mercury, feeling the good-humored joy all around him, decides to marry, and has some potential brides in mind, though he is not in love. His first three choices are otherwise engaged (5–8); Apollo tells him to marry Philology (22–23). In the allegory, thus, Eloquence (Mercury) is seen as a suitable adjunct to Learning (Philology), but not to Wisdom, a perpetual virgin; or Prophecy, who loves Apollo; or Psyche (soul), who is the captive of Cupid. Maia favors a marriage because Mercury is too big to run around without pants on (5); Juno thinks that if he does not marry soon, he may be overcome with Venus's charms again and beget a brother for Hermaphroditus (34). Jupiter worries about the marriage because he fears that Mercury may be too enamoured to continue as his messenger (35). When Athena is asked advice about all this, she, the nonbegetting and unbegotten, is embarrassed to be troubled with questions over something so mundane as a marriage. Jupiter insists, and she tells him to call a council (39–40). Philology, as she prepares for the marriage, has doubts of her own (99–113); then she proves too heavy for the celestial journey and must vomit up the learning with which she is burdened. The Arts, Disciplines, and Muses run around gathering up the books into which the spew transforms itself (135–38). The heavenly handmaidens of Mercury's house will, of course, supply anew what she here gives up.

The handmaidens' speeches (bks. 3–9) are counterpointed by various kinds of inattention and levity. Bacchus jokes (331), Silenus snores (804–5), Venus gets impatient (704), and Pleasure tempts Mercury to the awaited consummation (726–28). Athena (326) and Mercury (423) fight to keep the utterances of the handmaidens to some suitable length lest the heavenly company be intolerably bored. Martianus, meanwhile, gets into several exchanges. Between books 2 and 3, he tries to keep his forms straight, with the fable in the first two and the intellectual matter in the last seven, but the Muse tells him that the fable must continue for the entertainment of his audience (219–22). Satura pedantically identifies some figures he is unable to recognize (576–79). Later she reproves him for talking about the snoring Silenus and then falls into a poetic description of the next speaker, Astronomy. Martianus (less polite than Boethius) mocks her for using poetry, since she is usually bent on attacking the poets for their imagery and bombast.

Martianus ends his book with what is probably the earliest surviving description of Menippean satire: "Our garrulous Satire has heaped learned doctrines upon unlearned, and crammed sacred matters into secular; she has commingled gods and the Muses, and has had uncouth figures prating in a rustic fiction about the encyclopedic arts. Herself distressed by awareness of the triviality of her composition, and swollen with gall and bile, she said: 'I could have come forth in a grand robe, to be admired for my learning and refinement, decorous in appearance, as if just coming from the court of Mars. Instead I have been inspired by Felix Capella—whom ignorant generations have observed ranting as he passed judgment on barking dogs'" (998–99).[41] A decided failure, he seems to think, yet the gods are married, the possessors of knowledge have managed to speak some of what they know, an unwilling audience has been sufficiently entertained to remain. And after all, Martianus has managed to finish his book.

Lemoine, the first scholar to turn her attention to the artistic merits of the work, writes in conclusion, after confessing that she does not think Martianus a great writer: "However I do feel that the text as it stands is a grand attempt and deserves to stand in the long tradition of works which are consciously designed to present a synthesis of the total pattern of the cosmos." Martianus is "searching for an orderly pattern in a world which so frequently seems to be total chaos and meaningless confusion."[42]

Whatever Chaucer's reading, the affinities of his poetry with the traditions of Menippean satire listed above are clear.[43] That it shares the heavy intellectual bias of the satire is often noted. Eliason, for instance, writes: "Chaucer's poetry is a product of his mind rather than his feelings. Its appeal is more mental than emotional."[44] One of the most persistent traits of the satire—the reliance on the fantastic—is everywhere in evidence in Chaucer's work, not only in the fantastic journeys of the dream visions, but in the fantastic quality of the tales. Bronson writes: "The devil and man meet face to face; in Homeric fashion Pluto and Proserpina intervene in human affairs, and Phoebus keeps house with a human wife; a 'lusty bachelor' marries an otherworld being; a poor widow, of great sobriety of life, harbours the King of the Cocks. Flemish tavern-haunters set out to slay the person of Death. It is evident that this poet has few compunctions about transgressing the laws of natural probability."[45]

Chaucer's unexpected shifts of tone have probably caused more amazement, not to say exasperation, than any other Menippean feature of his poetry. For instance, Bronson asks whether we can ever understand Chaucer if we do not understand this variableness: "We are not merely disturbed, we are sometimes disoriented and amazed by the rapid shifts of stylistic level, the apparent sacrifice of achieved effects, the reversals of moods and tone, the abrupt stoppage of narrative momentum, the commingling of colloquial and artificial diction, the breathtaking incorporation of the whole range of language into the working texture of the verse."[46] He cites as the most outstanding example the ending of the *Knight's Tale*. Chaucer's structural relationships, furthermore, are characterized by those seemingly random and disconcerting juxtapositions characteristic of the satire. Eliason, for example, analyzes the inadequacies of the five ordinary types of relationship (chronological, dramatic, thematic, positional, parallel) for establishing the key to Chaucer's structure.[47] Jordan adopts the term "inorganic" to describe a structure characterized by "sharp edges" and "unsewn seams," or seams sewn up "with red thread," as Eliason remarks.[48] Again, the *Knight's Tale* affords a particularly good example of the technique.

The Menippean dialogue may be said to be the dominant structural feature of Chaucer's work; know-it-alls (sometimes directly modeled on Philosophy) and their interlocutors abound. I have mentioned this dialogical relationship in the dream visions and the works I shall be dealing with here, but this central dialogue is a consistent feature of nearly all the tales. For instance, we have the Hag and the knight in the *Wife of Bath's Tale*, Nicholas and John in the *Miller's Tale*, the clerks and the miller in the *Reeve's Tale*, the crow and Apollo in the *Manciple's Tale*, Prudence and Melibee in the *Tale of Melibee*. The first member of each of these pairs is intent upon establishing an antithetical point of view for the second member; but the honorableness of their intent varies considerably from tale to tale. The Hag seriously wishes to give the knight a more accurate view of women; Nicholas, on the contrary, befuddles poor John with his scientific knowledge only to get Alisoun in bed with him. *Deus* figures, characterized by their desire to give the other characters what they need, want, or ask for, appear as Roman gods in the *Knight's Tale* (Venus gives Palamon Emily; Mars gives Arcite victory) and the *Merchant's Tale* (Pluto gives January sight; Proserpina gives May the ability to answer). They appear in a form peculiar to the tale, as the Old Man in the *Pardoner's Tale*, who at the rioters' request tells them where Death is, as the magician in the *Franklin's Tale*, who at the squire's request (and promise of payment) removes the black rocks, and as the provost in the *Prioress's Tale*, who at the Christians' request punishes the Jews. Again, the precise function of these figures varies considerably from tale to tale. The friend figure is implicitly present as the undramatized reader (listener) in all Chaucer's poems; in the *Canterbury*

Tales, of course, the pilgrims act as "friends" for each other.

The textual parody—the ubiquitous insertion of other texts and material into a conventional monological form—has engendered a whole realm of nearly self-sufficient Chaucer scholarship: the study of his sources. It has not so far provoked an equivalent body of writing which sets itself to analyzing the result of this study. There are instead hints that Chaucer had not actually read or understood the works he cites. Highet, for example, remarks: "Chaucer was not a very deep or intelligent student of the classics. What he takes from them is always simplified to the point of bareness."[49] I have known at least one contemporary critic greatly disturbed, not to say annoyed, that a student should intend to make a serious comparison between the *House of Fame* and the *Divine Comedy*, a work that provides one of the peripheral dimensions of Chaucer's poem. The difficulty in such comparisons, of course, lies in finding the appropriate fulcrum from which the inserted text exerts its influence. But for all his difficulties, Chaucer fares better with critics than do Lucian and Boethius, who are frequently treated as writers of the second rank.[50] Chaucer, as a rule, is allowed a place in the first. The main reason for the difference would seem to be that the authors whose forms Lucian and Boethius draw upon exceed them in stature. Homer, Sophocles, and Euripides have long been acknowledged as greater writers than Lucian; Aristotle and Plato, greater than Boethius. But in the romance, Breton lai, dream vision, fabliau, and saint's life, Chaucer has few English or Continental peers.

Yet knowing that, as we deal with Chaucer's use of the various genres, we encounter great difficulty in saying calmly that Chaucer stands above other practitioners because he is the greatest writer. We are forced to concede that the work, though seemingly a Breton lai, for instance, is somehow different from a Breton lai. We must make some such qualification even after discounting the fact that we have trouble in saying what a Breton lai is. We must also say that the *Knight's Tale* is not quite a romance—there is too much philosophy; the tone is wrong. The *Miller's Tale* hits high style and raises issues that a simple fabliau somehow ought not to. (We would have had much more success in defining medieval genres if we were not constantly trying to take Chaucer, who elaborates upon them, into account.) Chaucer's habit of employing other texts and genres in that highly selective way of Menippean satire, which invokes their problems without solving them, creates the impression that Salter describes after her analysis of the *Knight's Tale* and the *Clerk's Tale* : "The older literary forms he uses may seem, sometimes, to be under considerable strain because of an inner destructive force: they can barely accommodate the amount of new material Chaucer wishes to introduce. On the other hand, we have seen that he seldom wishes to so re-order this material as to change entirely, to do away with the traditional shapes and attitudes his age provides for him."[51] The extra folds and dimensions occasioned by this inserting of other texts, genres, and styles, which we find so often in Chaucer's poetry, mark him as a prime exponent of Menippean satire.

The perception of the dialogical dimensions in the text, which is inevitable in an accurate reading of his works, causes uneasiness even among the best critics. For instance, Crampton, after very interesting remarks on the peculiarities of the *Knight's Tale* (peculiarities, I might add, that mark it as a Menippean satire), feels obliged to write this disclaimer to her observation that Chaucer's portrayal of the gods suggests "that the universe may be irrational": "This does sound like an unmedieval reading; I can only point to the text. I do not suggest that Chaucer believed the world was irrational or that he was agnostic in a modern sense. I would guess that he believed the world was ordered but noticed that it nonetheless harbored irrationality, and the Knight's Tale reflects that observation."[52] The uneasiness evidently persists because we still do not sufficiently accept that the imagination of the great medieval thinkers were quite as capable as ours of going to the extreme limits and possibilities of the mind. They were just as capable of understanding in a responsible way that if orthodoxy has its uses and its place even for the brilliant, so too do many profound conceptions that cannot be covered by the selection and reduction that enables an orthodoxy to exist.

The unresolved, varying views in Chaucer's work have led at least one Chaucerian, Roger S. Loomis, to feel the need to defend him against the charge of being a Laodicean.[53] His defense, in effect, points out a fundamental aesthetic difficulty that monologically oriented minds confront in the presence of dialogically oriented literature. Because the author does not take sides, does not announce himself for the right, or a right, he seems to be indifferent about major issues. In times of historical crisis, however, such as those Lucian, Boethius, Chaucer, and Dostoevsky lived in—times of clashing philosophical, political, economic, or religious systems—Menippean satire affords a constructive method of containing ideological disagreements, a method of broadening the base upon which we must stand in order to investigate the conflicting evidence that creates the spiritual dilemma of man.[54] Arnold's famous remark that Chaucer's poetry lacks high seriousness is after all correct. (His error was that he made the term the only synonym for *profundity*.) High seriousness belongs to the concerns of epic and tragedy, Arnold's preferred literary forms, with their single-minded commitment to revealing the exalted if momentary significance in human effort, to negating what is for them the dominant fact of human life: death.[55] High seriousness has only a minor place in the dialogical confrontations of Menippean satire. Anyone within its boundaries disposed to be highly serious awakes "the dog who grins when he bites."

The great evil Menippean satire perceives is the propensity human beings have for creating faulty systems and institutions that drag them into the abuse and limited understanding of even such ideals as they have managed to build into those systems and institutions. The divine justice it perceives is that the minds of men and women are created free to transcend their self-made stereotypes, their philosophical systems, their conventional utterances about their gods, their loves, their deaths, only, it is true, to construct new ones which in their turn prove confining and capable of abuse. But the cycle can begin again; human beings can remain free to dissect, to laugh, to reorder. If truth always remains beyond our grasp, nevertheless, in the infinite space allowed for investigation, our divine freedom means that our thinking need never be restrictive, no matter what its conventional tendency in that direction.

While the term *nominalism* inevitably springs to mind as we observe these satirists' treatment of human creations as arbitrary, as representing no divinely authorized reality, their insistence on the freedom of the mind is a way of asserting the existence of God, of the universal beyond men and women, and undermines the applicability of the term.[56] They do not ever accuse their targets of holding the position represented by Humpty Dumpty in another Menippean satire (A. D. Woozley's example of the extreme nominalist[57]): "When I use a word, it means just what I choose it to mean—neither more nor less." "The question is," said Alice, "whether you *can* make words mean different things." "The question is," said Humpty Dumpty, "which is to be master—that's all." Nor do they hold this position themselves. These satirists write with an innate conviction that words and formulations have a life of their own that is (no doubt only obliquely) related to some universal or other— which is to say that they view the usual human construct as inadequate but do not blame the inadequacy on the absence of the ideal. Words mean what they mean. There is probably something out there that means what it means. The business of thinkers is to find some way of recording the discrepancy between here and there, of holding in the forefront both the facts of words and stories and the potential of the facts that lie behind and beyond them. The use of both textual parody and the dialogue between a know-it-all and a neophyte is a way of trying to determine in the midst of indeterminancy fixed perimeters in the uncertain dialogue of intense thinking.

The *Consolation*, long acknowledged as one of Chaucer's most important sources, holds the position of privileged text, the position which Homer and Sophocles hold in Lucian, and which the works of the classical philosophers hold in Boethius. It provides the world that the events of the poem call into question, intruding itself especially in the *Knight's Tale, Troilus and Criseyde*, and the *Nun's Priest's Tale*. Boethius is mentioned by name in the *Nun's Priest's Tale*. In *Troilus* there are two long passages—Troilus' hymn to love and the soliloquy on free will —which are close adaptations of corresponding passages in the *Consolation*. In both *Troilus* and the *Knight's Tale*, there are passages of varying lengths which echo passages and topics in the *Consolation*: fortune, happiness, justice, order, providence. The *Nun's Priest's Tale*, like *Troilus*, alludes to Boethius' discussion of the relation between foreknowledge and free will, the famous Augustinian-based conclusion to the *Consolation*. All three works in entirely different ways, as we shall see, parody orthodox medieval views of God's providential plan for man. But what makes the kinship of the *Consolation* with these works greater than these points of comparison suggest is that all are Menippean satires—dialogical, unyielding presentations of the world's multifariousness.

To recognize that an author's work belongs to a particular literary genre is, of course, only the first step. The main problem —understanding the meaning implicit in his handling of the conventions—is the problem I will be dealing with in the remaining chapters.[58] I will remark here that Chaucer's range in the three chosen works is startling. In Lucian, for example, a careful analysis of any one of the Menippean dialogues yields a center from which his other dialogues can be investigated with calmness. The variations have to do with the subject matter, not with a new attitude of the writer. But in Chaucer each narrator is so brilliantly individualized that we have the impression, as we move from one work to another, that we confront a new mind whose way of using this form is characteristic only of this narrator and this story. The attitude toward the *Consolation* embodied in the text varies, as we shall see, according to each narrator's vision.

2

Lucian as Menippean Satirist

Lucian's works provide a focal point for assessing the traits of Menippean satire, not only because numbers of complete dialogues, labeled Menippean, survive, but also because his interest in philosophy and philosophers and the problems and abuses of both makes his works an obvious parallel to and possible source of Boethius' *Consolation*.[1] Which of Lucian's individual works are classified as Menippean satires varies from critic to critic, but the rough rules of thumb that dictate different writers' selections are (1) Lucian's use of prose and verse in the work, (2) the appearance of Menippus as a character, (3) the tradition that Menippus had written on a similar topic, and (4) the imprint of Cynic philosophy upon the work.[2] Thus, *Zeus Rants* has notable interludes of verse. *Menippus*, which recounts Menippus' visit to Tiresias in Hades; *Icaromenippus*, which recounts his visit to Zeus in the heavens; and seventeen of the *Dialogues of the Dead*, where he wanders around Hades holding conversations with the great, all employ Menippus as protagonist. *Philosophies for Sale* and *Menippus* are thought to be based on Menippus' works the *Sale of Diogenes* and *Necyia*. Finally, *Zeus Catechized* and the *Downward Journey* use the cynically oriented Cyniscus as protagonist.

That Lucian had concerned himself with Menippus as philosopher is evident in the *Fisherman*.[3] We hear that Menippus has refused to take part in the other philosophers' furious attack on Lucian for selling them in the marketplace in a previous dialogue, *Philosophies for Sale*. The philosopher Menippus is also mentioned in the *Double Indictment*, where the figure of Dialogue complains in horror that he had heretofore been reserved for the writing of philosophy. He whines before the court: "Then [Lucian] unceremoniously penned me up with Jest and Satire and Cynicism and Eupolis and Aristophanes, terrible men for mocking all that is holy and scoffing at all that is right. At last he even dug up and thrust in upon me Menippus, a prehistoric dog, with a very loud bark, it seems, and sharp fangs, a really dreadful dog who bites unexpectedly because he grins when he bites" (3: 147). In this passage, Lucian in effect claims for himself the invention of the satiric dialogue, and whether he is accurate or not, it is certain that the model and its themes finds its way into Boethius and thence, by routes direct and indirect, into Chaucer.

Common Menippean traits in Lucian's works are violent alterations of tone between seriousness and joking, dislocation of probability in logic and narrative, and a travesty of all that is decorous: social hierarchies, religious customs, culture's laws. Tragic and epic scenes, themes and characters, in particular, are frequent objects for delighted attack.[4] The most profound travesty, however, is turned on human efforts to create philosophical systems, man's highest and most absurd method of imposing artificial and false orders on a chaotic reality, where there can be only questions and no answers, or false answers which delude the unwary. In contrast to prescriptive satire, which proposes a norm from which it attacks the deviations of its objects (e.g., the ideals of the gentleman for Horace, ancient Roman virtue for Juvenal), Lucian's satire attacks or parodies the concept of the norm itself. Thus, while all satire attacks human pretensions, his Menippean satire is distinctive in that it does so in a context which suggests no absolute standard. Lucian seems to have no interest in changing anything, or in making anything better. He attacks with Cynic contempt man's desire for the things of this world—power, riches, pleasure—but he does not go on to the Cynic conclusion: withdraw and live in a jar. Instead, with a kind of endless, gleeful energy, he attacks any established order of things and the monolithic complacency of those who promote it.

Critics have been uneasy about this apparent irresponsibility. Paulson, for instance, in distinguishing between Lucian's satire and that of the Roman satirists, writes that while Juvenal and Horace might agree to the travesty of sacrosanct institutions, they require some pieties, "would never allow man to wander free of all other men's thought the way Lucian seems to do."[5] Reardon comments in a similar vein: Lucian, he says, "quite lacks any serious base; his blood is compounded of venom, champagne, and printer's ink. The mere play of intelligence is all that counts for him, regardless of its object; he is unanchored, a free-playing brain, an unattached piece of clockwork. Sustained intellectual effort simply is not his line."[6] On the surface, Lucian seems to want only to poke good-natured fun at the world's enormous contradictions, to say that all men's efforts are funny and pointless. His world is a world with no exit, no goal, because whatever myth, whatever custom, whatever theory, whatever profession, in other words, whatever ideal men dedicate themselves to in act or language is absurdly and comically inadequate. The narrator himself takes the view that the world keeps going, but the reasons for that are not evident. Here in this life, there are questions but no answers that do not propose new questions, masks but no significant reality beneath them, quests but neither victory nor defeat, only something else which reveals a new form of idiocy itself needing investigation.

Yet underlying this freewheeling mockery is a serious question, namely, What is Utopia for man?[7] The scoffing narrator who dismisses what other men—in particular, lawgivers, poets, and philosophers—propose nevertheless attempts with great expenditures of exuberant digressiveness to define a viable way of thinking and ultimately acting which is not constantly being impeded by the world's absurdities: its theories, its categories, its restrictions on the intellect. In *Menippus* and *Icaromenippus*, the vehicle for this searcher's investigations is a dialogue recounting a fantastic journey in the course of which he tries to find an answer to his problem. Intent on getting things straight, on laughing at all misconceptions around him, and on pointing out their foolishness, Menippus wanders into a world whose terms Lucian draws from the writings of other men. Through this character, Lucian parodies their norms without providing any of his own. If Menippus' single-minded search for Utopia is totally inconclusive, therefore, his energetic determination to find one gives unity and, in Lucian, a good deal of laughter to the often chaotic surfaces of Menippean satire.

Lucian's *Menippus* opens with the protagonist parading up and down in delighted satisfaction, carrying a lyre and dressed in a felt cap and lion skin. A surprised friend stops him to inquire into this getup, and Menippus launches into an account of his recent journey to Hades. By way of preliminary, he tells the friend that he had discovered in the course of growing up that the authorities on the good life conflict. In particular, he had discovered that poets' accounts of the gods' activities and men's laws disagree about the delightful pursuits of adultery, quarreling, and theft. He turned to the philosophers for explanation, but they contradicted one another endlessly and moreover could not practice what they preached. He decided therefore to visit Tiresias in Hades and with the help of a Babylonian seer turned to a course of esoteric disciplines—diet, ceremonies, and incantations—as a preparation for the strange journey. After various adventures in Hades, he finally managed to corner the squeaky-voiced Tiresias, afraid of Rhadamanthus, to ask him the meaning of life. Tiresias told him to ignore the formulations of the philosophers, to attend to the present and to laughter, and to take nothing seriously. With this answer, Menippus returned by a shortcut to earth.

In the opening of this dialogue, the philosphers are attacked for the uselessness of their contributions to human efforts to understand, for the obsession with their own theories that blinds them to the contradictory nature of their words, for the discrepancy between their words and deeds, and for their failure to assess the conclusions to be drawn from the existence of so many contradictory schools of thought. In the central episode, the pretensions of earthly power, greatness, beauty, and wealth are mocked with Cynic glee: "So, with many skeletons lying together, all alike staring horridly and vacuously and baring their teeth, I questioned myself how I could distinguish Thersites from handsome Nireus, or the mendicant Irus from the King of the Phaeacians, or the cook Pyrrhias from Agamemnon; for none of their former means of identification abode with them, but their bones were all alike, undefined, unlabelled, and unable ever again to be distinguished by anyone" (4: 97–99). The trivial occupations to which the penury of death drives the once powerful occasion greater mockery: "But you would have laughed much more heartily, I think, if you had seen our kings and satraps reduced to poverty there, and either selling salt fish on account of their neediness or teaching the alphabet, and getting abused and hit over the head by all comers, like the meanest of slaves. In fact, when I saw Philip of Macedon, I could not control my laughter. He was pointed out to me in a corner, cobbling worn-out sandals for pay! Many others, too, could be seen begging at the cross-roads—your Xerxeses, I mean, and Dariuses and Polycrateses" (4: 103). In the conclusion of the dialogue, the rich are attacked for their oppression of the needy and are condemned by a tribunal to spend life on earth for 250,000 years in the bodies of donkeys "bearing burdens and being driven by the poor" (4: 107).

The narrative pattern of *Icaromenippus* is similar to that of *Menippus*. It opens with the protagonist muttering to himself; he is stopped by a friend who is puzzled, and Menippus rewards his friend's curiosity with an account of his recent trip to Olympus. It all began, he explains, with his perplexity over the cosmos, its source, its purpose, the haphazardness of the stars' scattering, the being of the sun, the multiplicity of the moon's shapes, and so on. He turned to the philosophers once more, choosing them by their dourness, by the paleness of their faces, and by the length of their beards, paid his money, and waited; but they did nothing for him but flood him with "first causes, final causes, atoms, voids, elements, concepts, and all that sort of thing" (2: 277). What he found hardest to accept, however, was that none was capable of agreeing with another; even their own statements were contradictory, yet they expected to win him as a disciple. In desperation, he made himself wings and flew to Olympus. After a stop on the moon, he arrived at the gates and was admitted. He heard Zeus' fear that he had become unpopular with men, watched him overhearing the prayers that come up from earth, and attended a banquet with the gods. His journey came to a climax with the divine tribunal which condemned the philosophers to death. Menippus was then deprived of his wings and returned to earth by Hermes.

In this dialogue, we see intensifications of the central themes in *Menippus*. Here, the search for the good life is linked to the mind's life rather than merely to man's daily living; the attack on the philosophers is more concentrated. They are attacked not only by Menippus and the Moon, but also by Zeus: "There is a class of men which made its appearance in the world not long ago, lazy, disputatious, vainglorious, quick-tempered, gluttonous, doltish, addlepated, full of effrontery and to use the language of Homer, 'a useless load to the soil.' Well, these people, dividing themselves into schools and inventing various word-mazes, have called themselves Stoics, Academics, Epicureans, Peripatetics and other things much more laughable than these" (2: 317). In this dialogue too, more clearly than in *Menippus*, it is not only the philosophers and their theories that are attacked, but all men's efforts to make any kind of theoretical organization of their lives. There is a vision here of the wondrous futility of all human games, not only the games that men play with language, myth, and theory, but even with the social conventions that they are heir to. Menippus mocks and amuses himself with the agonizing efforts—efforts either desperately honest or deliberately false (it makes no difference)—of men to make something out of the incomprehensible and unmalleable reality which surrounds them.

Menippus describes to his companion the laughable confusions of human life as he looked down from the heavens: "Although the doings of kings [adultery, murder, conspiracy, oath-breaking, treason against kin] afforded me such rare amusement, those of the common people were far more ridiculous, for I could see them too—Hermodorous the Epicurean perjuring himself for a thousand drachmas, the Stoic Agathocles going to law with his disciple about a fee, the orator Clinias stealing a cup out of the Temple of Asclepius and the Cynic Herophilus asleep in the brothel. Why mention the rest of them—the burglars, the bribe-takers, the money-lenders, the beggars? In brief, it was a motley and manifold spectacle" (2: 295).

Menippus goes on to include his friend in his wonder at this folly:

> It is as if one should put on the stage a company of singers, or I should say a number of companies, and then should order each singer to abandon harmony and sing a tune of his own; with each one full of emulation and carrying his own tune and striving to outdo his neighbor in loudness of voice, what, in the name of Heaven, do you suppose the song would be like?
>
> FRIEND
>
> Utterly ridiculous, Menippus, and all confused.
>
> MENIPPUS
>
> Well, my friend, such is the part that all earth's singers play, and such is the discord that makes up the life of men. Not only do they sing different tunes, but they are unlike in costume and move at cross-purposes in the dance and agree in nothing until the manager drives each of them off the stage, saying that he has no further use for him. After that, however, they are all quiet alike, no longer singing that unrhythmical medley of theirs. But there is the play-house itself, full of variety and shifting spectacles, everything that took place was truly laughable. (2: 297–99)

Asked by the friend what the cities and the men most resembled, Menippus replies: "I suppose you have often seen a swarm of ants, in which some are huddling together about the mouth of the hole and transacting affairs of state in public, some are going out and others are coming back again to the city; one is carrying out the dung, and another has caught up the skin of a bean or half a grain of wheat somewhere and is running off with it; . . . the cities with their population resembled nothing so much as ant-hills" (2: 301).

Yet in spite of the mockery, there is an exuberant vitality about all of this—another important trait of Menippean satire —which precludes any bitterness. The good-humored naïveté of the attack provides a kind of brotherhood of mutual interest. "If you think," Menippus continues in the above diatribe, "it is belittling to compare men with the institutions of ants, look up the ancient fables of the Thessalians and you will find that the Myrmidons, the most warlike of races, turned from ants into men" (2: 301). As here, the satire loses its strong vituperative thrust by an immediate burst of counter energy, which alters the course of the feeling. We are jerked from our complacent laughter at the foibles of the human race into having to contemplate without any suitable connecting terms the relation between ants and heroism. Similarly, Zeus' order to annihilate the philosophers is suddenly blocked by his memory of a prior decree. To the gods, he says: "It shall be as you will; they shall be annihilated, and their logic with them." But the condition follows at once: "However, just at present it is not in order to punish anyone, for it is the festival-season, as you know, during the next four months, and I have already sent about to announce the truce of God. Next year, therefore, at the opening of spring the wretches shall die a wretched death by the horrid thunderbolt" (2: 321). We suspect that by that point something else may have happened. But Menippus, at peace with his moment in time, is not at all concerned over the delay; he rushes off gleefully at the end of the dialogue to convey the news of the decree to the philosophers of the Porch.

This character—who is given a definable philosophy, mania, quest, or point of view with which to probe and momentarily improve the confusion of purposes, aims, noises in the cacophany of life—is set in opposition to various minor characters who attempt to defend or speak for the world he has entered. This prosecutor, in contrast to the defendants, has a pragmatic concern with the logicality of the present moment. Menippus dead explores Hades from pillar to post; alive, travels to see it and Olympus. He does not examine the befores and afters of things, nor assume any responsibility for their complexity. He merely probes analytically whatever comes under his gaze in the given conditions. It is the minor characters who feel responsible for coming to terms with the contradictions of time, matter, and event.

For instance, in *Zeus Catechized*, which deals with the problems of fate and freedom, the Cynic protagonist probes philosophical assumptions based on myth. His interlocutor, the highly defensive Zeus, is led with his headful of Homer into repeated pitfalls by the modest Cyniscus, who says he wants nothing from Zeus but to ask him a question—he says he has noticed that men do not generally get the wealth they ask of the gods anyway: "You certainly have read the poems of Homer and Hesiod: tell me, then, is what they have sung about Destiny and the Fates true, that whatever they spin for each of us at his birth is inevitable?" (2: 61). Zeus at once affirms the truth of their description and goes on to say that the gods too are subject to the Fates. Cyniscus concludes then that there can be no possible point in men's sacrificing to the gods. Zeus accuses him of sophistry and says that men sacrifice to honor what is superior. Cyniscus counters that a sophist would say that the gods are not men's superiors: "Really they are fellow-slaves with men, and subject to the same mistresses, the Fates. For their immorality will not suffice to make them seem better, since that feature certainly is far worse, because men are set free by death at least, if by nothing else, while with you gods the thing goes on to infinity and your slavery is eternal, being controlled by a long thread" (2: 69–71).

To Zeus' assertion that the gods' eternity is blissful and happy, Cyniscus retorts with the story of the crippling of Hephaestus, the crucifixion of Prometheus, the shackling of Cronos in Tartarus, and the enslavement of gods in the houses of men. Even their temples on earth are subject to destruction and their statues melted down. Zeus attempts to describe the noble relation of the gods to Fate by saying that Fate works through them. This statement draws forth the observation that the gods then are to Destiny as the drill and adze are to the carpenter, who certainly deserves all the respect. Zeus is not averse to men's honoring the Fates, but says that the gods deserve honor too, as they foretell the future. Cyniscus points out that it is useless to know what is fated, as it cannot be changed, and that the gods' oracles are frequently too ambiguous to be enlightening or to enable anyone to imagine that even the gods understand what they are talking about.

When Zeus tries to show that he is a good fellow because he allows Cyniscus to speak in this fashion and does not hit him with a thunderbolt, Cyniscus replies that he can hit him only if it is fated, that Destiny still deserves all the praise or blame.

Anyway, he goes on, thunderbolts tend to hit innocent trees, stones, shipmasts, and an occasional traveler, not guilty men robbing temples. This thought leads him to ask why the good are punished in this life and the guilty rewarded. Zeus asks whether he does not know that there are absolute rewards and punishments after death. Cyniscus admits his ignorance but wonders whether a bad deed done unintentionally is punished and a good deed also done unintentionally is rewarded. Zeus denies that either is. Then, Cyniscus points out, there should be no reward or punishment at all, "because we men do nothing of our own accord, but only at the behest of some inevitable necessity, if what you previously admitted is true, that Fate is the cause of everything" (2: 85). Zeus refuses to have anything further to do with him, and leaves Cyniscus thinking on the hard lot of the Fates ungraced by Destiny at their birth and forced to the enormous labor of attending to the details of everything that happens.

The desacralization of myth is a constant feature of these satires. In *Dialogues of the Dead*, Menippus runs across Tantalus, and asks: "Why are you crying, Tantalus? Why do you stand beside the lake lamenting your lot?" Tantalus replies: "Because, Menippus, I'm dying of thirst." The barrage of questions follows: Are you too lazy to bend down? Why do you need a drink? You have no body. Are you afraid of dying of thirst? I see no Hades beyond this one (7: 37–39). And if the Homeric inability to produce a logical version of torture in death amuses him, so much the more do mythic versions of prophets. Tiresias, in heroic pose in spite of having been reduced to a skeleton, attempts to fend off the questions of Menippus, which are characterized by that mixture of seriousness and levity that is an earmark of Lucian's dialogues: "It's difficult to tell now, Tiresias, whether you're blind, as our eyes are all alike—empty, with nothing but sockets. Indeed, you can no longer tell which was Phineus, or which was Lynceus. But I do know you were a prophet, and the only person to have been both man and woman. I heard that from the poets. So, for heaven's sake, tell me which life you found more pleasant—when you were a man, or a woman?" (7: 45). Tiresias answers that being a woman was more pleasant, as women have mastery over men and do not have to fight wars, stand guard, argue in parliament, or be cross-examined in court. Menippus counters by citing the bitter words of Euripides on the lot of women, but overcome suddenly with practical curiosity, wants to know whether Tiresias was barren, whether he had a womb, what the exact physical process was of his becoming a man again. Tiresias' peeved attempt to preserve the proprieties of his, at this point, nonexistent position, only draws Menippus' disgusted retort: "So you still keep to your falsehoods, Tiresias? That's just like you prophets; you're habitual liars" (7: 49).

The minor characters—like Zeus, Tiresias, and Tantalus in the works just cited—take little comfort in the probings of the protagonist no matter how helpful; but they are not strong enough to override or alter the terms of the protagonist's arguments, assumptions, or generally unmatchable energy. Their function, gods and men alike, is to maintain the sense of the spectrum of time and the terrible complexity of things. For instance, in *Dialogues of the Dead*, Menippus, the scoffing representative of the totality of logical perception, looks at an unidentifiable skull of Helen which Hermes has to pick out for him. Staring into the skull's eyeholes, he remarks: "Was it then for this that the thousand ships were manned from all Greece, for this that so many Greeks and barbarians fell, and so many cities were devastated?" Hermes' gentle retort pulls us back into the rewards of the fleeting moment: "Ah, but you never saw the woman alive, Menippus, or you would have said yourself that it was forgiveable that they 'for such a lady long should suffer woe.' For if one sees flowers that are dried up and faded, they will, of course, appear ugly; but when they are in bloom and have their color, they are very beautiful" (7: 23). The minor figures of the gods, unlike the protagonist, are conscious of history, of before and after, of cause and effect.

The minor characters in Hades have a similar awareness, for they remain attached to bodies that experience pain and pleasure, and they both delight in the presence of and lament the absence of the things of this world. The groans of Croesus, Midas, and Sardanapalus for their lost wealth are obvious reminders (*Dialogues of the Dead*, 7: 19), as is the lament of the souls in Charon's boat: "(ONE) Alas, my wealth! (ANOTHER) Alas, my farms! (ANOTHER) Alackaday, what a house I left behind me! (ANOTHER) To think of all the thousands my heir will come into and squander! (ANOTHER) Ah, my new-born babes! (ANOTHER) Who will get the vintage of the vines I set out last year?" (*Downward Journey*, 2: 39). Diogenes' question to Alexander—"Didn't the wise Aristotle even teach you to realize the insecurity of the gifts of fortune?"—brings the retort: "Wise Aristotle! Why, he's the arch-knave of all flatterers. Let me be the sole authority on him, with all his requests for gifts. . . . But I did at least get one thing from his wisdom—grief for those things you've just enumerated, for I think them the greatest of goods" (*Dialogues of the Dead*, 7: 71–73). Perhaps most memorable is Achilles' answer to Antilochus' charge that it was ignoble to say to Odysseus: "I would rather be the serf in the house of a landless man than king of the dead." Achilles replies:

> But in those days, son of Nestor, I still had no experience of this place, and, not knowing which existence was preferable, I preferred that miserable empty shadow of glory to life itself; but now I realize that glory is useless, however much men hymn its praises, that among the dead all have but equal honour, and neither the beauty nor the strength we had remain with us, but we lie buried in the same darkness, all of us quite alike, and no one better than the other, and I am neither feared by the Trojan dead nor respected by the Greeks, but there is complete equality of speech and one dead man is like another, "be he mean or be he great." That's why I'm distressed and annoyed at not being a thrall alive on earth. (*Dialogues of the Dead*, 7: 155–57)

As here, the minor figures are all troubled by some insistent problem created by themselves, by the scoffing inquirer, by the conditions of the universe. In the *Downward Journey*, Charon is troubled by the leaks in his boat, and he must ask all who enter to strip off their flesh to lighten the load. Hermes is troubled by an escaped tyrant whom he has to pursue and compel to descend to hell. He gets roundly berated by Charon and Clotho for arriving late with his charges. Hermes is further troubled by the Cynic characters' failure to weep after they finally get in Charon's boat. He tries to preserve the tradition by insisting that the happy cobbler, Micyllus, shed a tear. Obligingly the ironic Cynic laments: "Alas, my scraps of leather! Alas, my old shoes! Alackaday, my rotten sandals! Unlucky man that I am, never again will I go hungry from morning to night or wander about in winter barefooted and half naked, with my teeth chattering for cold! Who is to get my knife and my awl?" (2: 41). In these dialogues set in Hades, the examples of the discontent with the nature of death, with the inability of the draughts of Lethe to blot out the memory of life's joys, are legion.

In the dialogues set in Heaven, the discontents of the gods and their vulnerability to change and outside influences show a universe hardly more satisfactory. *Zeus Rants* opens with the panic-stricken Zeus trying to call together a council of gods, who at first do not take him seriously, then prove too numerous and too big to fit into the meeting place. His fear is aroused by a temple crowd's quick acceptance of the Epicurean Damis' proof that there are no gods, and that even if there were, they would have no interest in men; the Stoic Timocles tries to refute Damis, but with no success. Zeus is horrified by the possibility that this may cause the gods to lose glory, honor, and sacrifice smoke, all of which can come only from worshipping men. The god Momus, the divine scoffer, as Damis is the human, further disturbs Zeus by pointing out that what Damis says is true: the gods make no serious efforts to help men. At the end of the dialogue, even when the divine power to produce early darkness enables Zeus to bring the debate to a swift end, with the laughing Damis leaving Timocles in nominal possession of the battleground, Zeus is left musing: "I myself had rather have this man Damis alone on my side than possess a thousand Babylons" (2: 169). In the *Council of the Gods*, Zeus proposes a housecleaning to get rid of all unnecessary gods, gods that have somehow crept into Heaven without the proper qualifications. Momus, again acting as prosecutor, points out that no one's lineage is pure—not even Zeus'. The possibility for a norm of judgment dismissed, the whole issue is quickly swept under the table.

While the flaws in the minor characters are assessed by the

practical-minded know-it-all, the dialogues are balanced in such a way that he too is ironically assessed. This scoffer appeals to the schoolboy heart in all of us, and we identify with him as long as we are able, but a full reading of the works places him also in the context of the all-too-human. In *Icaromenippus*, a part of Menippus' desperate need to seek Olympus for an answer to his questions about the cosmos is his disgust with the philosophers' descriptions. Yet as the dialogue opens, he is busily describing it for himself: "It was three thousand furlongs, then, from the earth to the moon, my first stage; and from there up to the sun perhaps five hundred leagues; and from the sun to Heaven itself and the citadel of Zeus would be also a day's ascent for an eagle travelling light" (2: 269). The friend's request launches Menippus into an account of his journey to Olympus which is as full of moonshine as the accounts of any of his rejected philosophers: the most preposterous of their theories would hardly match the balderdash that Menippus himself brings back. If his journey is reality, then the theorizing of men who merely stand on the ground is a positive relief, a view we are forced to take in the midst of our laughter. The profound comic wisdom of the Menippean dialogue is that he who rejects all theories is automatically caught up by virtue of his humanity in propounding other, equally objectionable theories, for such is the condition of life.

The structure of *Menippus* too is balanced in the same kind of ironic counterpoise. The Cynic's preliminary searches for the good life are exactly like anyone else's. He is the epitome of that human trait which is a central cliché in Menippean satire: man, whatever his attempt to transcend his preconceptions, always fails. For all Menippus finds in Hell is what he takes with him into Hell to find. Studying with the—as it seemed to him— useless philosophers to arrive at an answer, he had concluded earlier: "They speedily convinced me that the ordinary man's way of living is as good as gold" (4: 81). In Hell, Tiresias tells him the same thing: "The life of the common sort is best, and you will act more wisely if you stop speculating about heavenly bodies and discussing final causes and first causes, spit your scorn at those clever syllogisms, and counting all that sort of thing nonsense, make it always your sole object to put the present to good use and to hasten on your way, laughing a great deal and taking nothing seriously" (4: 107–9). All Menippus' effort has only taught him again what he already knew. But in the meantime, Menippus, after his return, cavorts about on earth more pleased with his costume—the cap of Odysseus, the lion skin of Heracles, and the lyre of Orpheus, which his Babylonian guide had suggested he wear to get by the guards at the frontier of hell—than with the revelations of death. He has received no new answer, but because the space of his mind has been preempted with new images, he is happily unaware of his failure.

Though the Menippus-figure comes to a conclusion that effectively shuts out anything but his opinion, the irony of his position, as well as the discrepancy between his proposals and those of the minor characters, leaves the satire open-ended. On the one hand, because the major mind we witness has perfect confidence in its point of view, all counter positions appear ridiculous; all men but him appear to be absurd prisoners of their own hermetically sealed constructs. On the other hand, because the doubt and uncertainty in the minor characters we encounter undermines our confidence in the views of the protagonist, as does his own inadvertent treading of ways similar to the ones he dismisses, we have the sensation that we too are freed. If the minor characters can doubt him and his confident assessment of things, then so can we. This freedom does not relieve us of the tantalizing necessity to search for another answer, but it certainly frees us from the smugness of the protagonist.

If one level of Lucianic satire is provided for us by the author's positing a clueless but many-faceted universe, the other is provided by a profound delight in the indomitable inclination of men, and of the gods they create to rule them, to make constructs out of the futile spectacle, to busy themselves with that tiny little corner of the cacophany of creation which is theirs, to dedicate an amazing energy and interest to doing something about the problem they find before them, even when the problem is by the nature of its being insoluble.

The profound satisfaction that Lucian's Menippean satire

gives is the enormous sense of freedom it creates by transcending the restriction of pedantic traditions, conventions, and categorics. The despair it could create is the despair of belonging to a species that has no attainable goal. From this extreme position, it is as if man's destiny were to live in a hell in which he is constantly inspired by his nobler self to find the ideal way of action and thought that will make the world a Utopia, yet must enter upon this search without having been provided with either the capacity to imagine the accurate answer or the materials suitable to achieve this end. We do not, in fact, often fall into this despair because of this satire's exceptional support of the individual's right to search for new ways out of a cosmos that does not trouble him or support him with anything other than the absolutes of his own construction. Because of this freedom there is an edge to the laughter which this satiric form arouses that delights the heart. For it asserts that we cannot destroy ourselves or each other with our rigid formulations, habits, and theories. We are always free. In the mind, we encounter no fate that we ourselves have not first named and given power to defeat us. We sense in Lucian an arcane and magnificent faith that we have always the option—though we will undoubtedly never use it—of going where the true gods are.

Many hard things are said about Lucian: that he is a second-rate writer, that "he had no ideas."[8] But of course in this genre, which has as brilliant a potential as any literary form in Western civilization, the "idea" is that no idea holds total validity: what it suggests is that we ought to remain intellectually free in the face of our traditions, conventions, customs, heritage, even our own prior assumptions. The reader will feel or not that this is a profounder assertion to make to the earth than the presentation of a so-called "original idea." For those to whom this relentlessly honest satire is satisfying, the illustration of Lucian's success is contained in this story told by Maurice Hutton in his introduction to W. H. Tackaberry's excellent work on Lucian: Luigi Settembrini, supporter of the Italian Resorgimento, professor of Greek at Calabria, was imprisoned in a small, filthy cell along with common criminals by the Neopolitan government for his Italian sympathies. He wrote: "My body and my clothes are soiled; it is of no use to try and keep clean; the smoke and the dirt make me sickening to myself; my spirit is tainted; I feel all the hideousness, the horror, the terror of crime. Had I remorse, I should think that I too was a criminal. My spirit is being undone; it seems to me as if my hands were also foul with blood and theft. I forget virtue and beauty."⁹ To remind himself of their existence once more, he made the Italian translation of Lucian.

It is to be remarked that Hutton, in spite of serious efforts to write a suitable introduction to Tackaberry's work, did not understand. He finds it a paradox that such saintly men as Settembrini and Tackaberry should turn for balm to the "levity of Lucian," "to the scoffs and gibes, not less characteristically pagan than superficial." He can think of only two possibilities: (1) their concern as intellectuals for their direct opposite and (2) their Christian charity. To another writer's justification of Settembrini's choice—"the purity of Lucian's style and his gentle irony"—Hutton can only say that he is not confident of the purity, and gentle irony is to be found in greater Greeks than Lucian. He comments a little earlier: "To select Lucian as an antidote to evil seems an eccentricity parallel with that which has made Horace the last companion of martyrs. In the latter case the world assumes the companionship to be merely the happy associations of boyhood; but we do not learn to love (or hate) Lucian amid the diversions of the schoolroom."¹⁰ It is too bad we do not, for Lucian would teach us early what we must struggle to learn late: the nature of intellectual freedom.

3

The Consolation of Philosophy
as Menippean Satire

While it is universally agreed that Boethius' *Consolation of Philosophy* is a Menippean satire, the secondary material that surrounds it (surprisingly mild in view of the work's fame in the Middle Ages) is confined largely to the study of Boethius' influence and his sources in other philosophers and to various historical problems the text raises (e.g., the Christianity of Boethius; his part in the events that led to his downfall).[1] When these studies attempt to account for, rather than to assume, the work's importance to medieval writers, only one of the two explanations put forward deals in any way with its form. Perhaps most often we read that the immense, widespread appeal of the *Consolation* was caused by its being a popular compendium of commonplace philosophical ideas written in a dialogue of alternating verse and prose passages. Because there were familiar ideas here for all tastes, cast in an easily digested form, the work made pleasant reading and therefore found a place among the great books of the world. This explanation, however, is hardly adequate to account for the interest accorded to the *Consolation* by such minds as those of Dante, Jeun de Meun, and Chaucer.

We might as well admit that if the stated ideas of the *Consolation* are frequently not original, the way of combining them is.[2] In making his conventional world out of a pastiche of allusions to other men's works, Boethius merely adheres to the demand of the genre he is using—Menippean satire. Paul Turner, writing of the kind of scholarly criticism Lucian's works have engendered, points out: "Detailed investigation of Lucian's sources has shown that he deliberately tried to include the maximum amount of literary materials in his works. One scholar has completed a list of Lucian's quotations, allusions and reminiscences, which cover fifty-five closely printed pages."[3] The same sort of study can be made of any Menippean satire. Boethius' sources, for instance, have been said to include Seneca, Virgil, Horace, Ovid, Juvenal, Plato, Aristotle, Cicero, the Stoics, the Cynics, and the Neo-Platonists.[4] To conclude, however, that Boethius' work is then nothing but an unoriginal compilation is to miss the central need of the form, a place of discourse whose conditions are instantly recognizable to any listener or reader, and whose assumptions the ironies of the dialogue can engage and elaborate.

The second common explanation for the *Consolation's* popularity ignores the form of the work altogether and relies heavily on the historical circumstances with which tradition surrounds the writing of the *Consolation*. Here, the text is seen as perpetually popular because it is a monument to the courage of Boethius. His suffering led him to question the existence of divine justice, a problem which is a part of the most intense experience of all men. According to this view, his ability to write the *Consolation* in spite of his own personal difficulties gives the text its enduring appeal. But this attempt to see the text as the mythic account of the "triumph of the innocent man punished" is scarcely satisfying. There is no dramatic conclusion to the work that brings the philosophical explanation to bear on the historical predicament. Book 3 has no relevance to the historical predicament at all; and even the end of book 2 must be juggled a bit to make it apply. Book 5 arises more or less naturally out of the questions Boethius asks Philosophy, but a man who had just celebrated the crowning success of his life amidst the cheers of family, friends, and country would ask the same questions. Even the tone of the text denies that despair is its center. If the *Consolation* had intended to record that act of courage by which a man had overcome his suffering, we could only comment that the suffering has been lost in the shuffle. We have only to place the *Consolation's* rather cheerful, logical speeches against the impassioned and beautiful outbursts of Job, for example, to doubt the explanation. Certainly, in regard to suffering, Stewart is right: the *Consolation* "smells of the lamp."[5]

That there is no time lag between the experience and the fiction causes further trouble. In order to account for the dialogue between Boethius and Philosophy, even under these historical auspices, it must be said that the text is a fictional re-creation of the process of man's working his way out of despair; but the practical objection is that there was no time, had the despair to be worked out been the one mentioned in the opening of the *Consolation*: Boethius' imprisonment by Theodoric. Boethius was never released from prison; he was put to death in the same year. The text seen as a natural development in the relation between experience and fiction will not fit, for example, in the same category as the *Divine Comedy*. Yet most readers would agree that the experience described is an assimilated experience and would agree with Gibbon when he writes: "The sage who could artfully combine in the same work the various riches of philosophy, poetry, and eloquence, must already have possessed the intrepid calmness which he affected to seek."[6] The truth is that this identification of the central myth of the *Consolation* as the "triumph of the innocent man punished" rests on the tradition that Boethius wrote the whole of the *Consolation* after he was put in prison. It is more probable that he took a partially completed manuscript to prison with him into which he saw, assuredly with a certain grimness, that he could splice to advantage an account of his downfall. Thus, while an account of the writer's suffering was included in the final version of the book, and is dealt with theoretically at some points, one man's triumph over his personal suffering does not explain the book's form, and only incidentally explains its pervasive impact.

We turn with relief from this complicated and progressively less efficient theorizing to the form of the *Consolation*'s fiction. The critical silence that surrounds this subject no doubt stems in part from the perhaps startling superficial differences between the extant Menippean satires and the *Consolation*, differences which make the critic fight shy of looking for underlying similarities. The obscenities of the *Satyricon* and the rambling potpourri of the *Marriage of Philology and Mercury* seem to hold no common ground with the classic, intellectual severity of the *Consolation*. Mras, in his article on Varro's Menippean fragments, attempts to get over the rather imposing hurdle of such differences in subject matter by saying that Boethius made a kind of transcendent use of his inherited form: Boethius is "einer der seltenen Fälle, wo es dem Nachahmer gelingt, sein Vorbild zu übertreffen und die von seinem Vorgänger einge- schlagene literarische Richtung zu veredeln."[7] Yet such differ- ences occasion us no difficulty with more familiar forms. Both *Tom Jones* and *Emma* are novels; the different matter upon which the writers' comic perceptions are exercised is not suffi- cient to destroy the underlying fact that both belong to the same genre. To feel that the *Consolation*, the *Marriage*, and the *Satyricon* have nothing in common is to take matter at the expense of form. As the preparation for discussing Chaucer's three works, I shall analyze the Menippean qualities of the *Consolation*, for to judge by Chaucer's use of it—a major sub- ject I shall be pursuing in the final six chapters of this study—he saw Boethius' work not only as a textbook for classical philoso- phy but also, and much more important, as the culmination and fulfillment of an ironical mode of containing and assessing the realities of human thought and experience.

While the satire of the *Consolation* is of the same order as that of Lucian's works, Boethius chooses a different ground for his investigations. Instead of the descriptions of the universe proposed by Homer, we have those proposed by Plato and Aris- totle. Instead of a Ranting Zeus, we have an Unmoved Prime Mover, and the mythical names which appear are used merely as incidental poetic equivalents of this same God. Instead of a journey to Olympus or Hades, the journey through space and time, we have a journey through philosophical propositions and theories, a journey whose bounds are not the four dimen- sions of physical perception, but the infinite dimensions of the mind. The immediate effect of the change from poetry to phi- losophy is to steady the tone. Travesty of the decorous, the chief satiric technique of Lucian, is not in evidence. The tone of the work does not alter startlingly between seriousness and joking. Philosophy, Boethius' dignified version of the Menippean pro- tagonist, has a mind which indulges in only a cryptic form of irony. Boethius, of course, like the usual lower member of the

Menippean dialogue, finds nothing funny, nor after book 1, prose 4, are his speeches ironic. While there are alterations in point of view, we do not shift radically from one to the other as we must do in Lucian and Seneca. In fact, our problem is to grasp the shifts that do occur rather than to understand that under the shifts there is the consistent intellectual pattern, which Frye speaks of as native to the genre. But the sequence of the journey on which Philosophy takes Boethius is quite as full of seeming irrelevancies as the earlier Menippean satires, and the goal is quite as unexpected to the character struggling with his historical necessities. There is no inevitable sequence in the subjects she discusses (fortune, happiness, evil, providence and fate, chance, foresight and freewill), nor does Boethius ever reach his "home," the goal promised a number of times, partly because he keeps asking questions, partly because "home" for man is the recognition that he lives in time, that the dialogue will continue, that there will be insights, but no final answers.[8]

The dominant Menippean theme—man's amiable habit of making constructs and theories for delight and protection, inadequate though they may be in the midst of chaos—remains central as a theme, but Boethius, by switching his cosmos from Greek poetry to Greek philosophy, complicates the intellectual terms under which we must consider it. Instead of a dominant character speaking for the simplest of philosophies (the Cynic or one equally uncommitted to confronting the problem of the universe intellectually in language), we have Philosophy, spokeswoman par excellence for the master tradition of philosophy and its theoretical explorations of the limits of language. Of course, it is easier to see the relation of Menippus and his fellow Cynics to the minor characters around them in perspective than it is to see the relation of Philosophy to Boethius. But there is, nevertheless, the same underlying Menippean attempt on the part of Philosophy to establish her own way to a Utopian vision of life and thought in the *Consolation*, the same doubt in her listener about the feasibility of ignoring the way created by the chaotic demands of time and the images of his perception and knowledge. Finally, there is the same ironic suggestion that no one, neither the masterful Philosophy nor the struggling

Boethius, is capable of attaining absolute knowledge, only capable of knowing that the mind must be kept free to continue its search.

The topoi and themes we find in Lucian are instantly recognizable in the *Consolation*: the alteration of prose and verse, citations from Homer (bk. 1, pr. 4, pr. 5; bk. 2, pr. 2; bk. 4, pr. 6; bk. 5, m. 2) and Euripides (bk. 3, pr. 6, pr. 7), and attacks on the world views associated with poetry, false philosophy, material goods. In the opening of the *Consolation* (bk. 1, pr. 1), Philosophy, seeing the Muses standing around Boethius' bed inspiring his elegiac poetry, cries out: "Who let these theatrical tarts in with this sick man? Not only have they no cures for his pain, but with their sweet poison they make it worse. These are they who choke the rich harvest of the fruits of reason with the barren thorns of passion. They accustom a man's mind to his ills, not rid him of them."[9] She drives them away without mercy.

She is as contemptuous of the false philosophers and their sects as are Lucian's Cynics. In the opening of the *Consolation*, she dismisses the partial visions of the thinkers who have torn off pieces of her dress and gone off thinking they had all of her.

> Did I not often of old also, before my Plato's time, have to battle in mighty struggle with arrogant stupidity? And in his day, was I not beside his teacher Socrates when he won the prize of a martyr's death? And after him the crowd of Epicureans and Stoics and the rest strove as far as they could to seize his legacy, carrying me off protesting and struggling, as if I were part of the booty, tearing my dress, which I wove with my own hands, and then went off with their torn-off shreds, thinking they possessed all of me. (Bk. 1, pr. 3)

Later, Philosophy sneers at that prime butt of Menippean satire, the *philosophus gloriosus*. A disinterested observer puts a false philosopher to the test:

> He had insultingly attacked a man who had falsely assumed the title of philosopher, not for the practice of true virtue but simply from vanity, to increase his own glory; and he added that he would know he was really a philosopher if he bore all the

injuries heaped upon him calmly and patiently. The other adopted a patient manner for a time and bore the insults, and then said tauntingly: "Now do you recognize that I am a philosopher?" To which the first very cuttingly replied: "I should have, had you kept silent." (Bk. 2, pr. 7)

Much of book 2 is directed to attacking those who concern themselves with material possessions and worldly goods. These attacks are similar to Lucian's and share some of the topoi of his dialogues. Fortune's speech in the *Consolation* contains an image of the goods as the clothes which Fortune provides naked man and then takes away when she chooses.

> When nature brought you out of your mother's womb, I accepted you, naked and poor in all respects; I supported you, and, ready to be kind to you, even pampered you with my wealth, and over-indulgently spoiled you—which is precisely why you are now so angry with me. I surrounded you with every kind of affluence and splendour within my power. Now I am pleased to draw back my hand. You should thank me, as having enjoyed the use of what was not yours, not complain as if you had lost something of your own. (Bk. 2, pr. 2)

In the parallel passage in Lucian, Menippus, staring at piles of undistinguishable skeletons, remarks:

> So as I looked at them it seemed to me that human life is like a long pageant, and that all its trappings are supplied and distributed by Fortune, who arrays the participants in various costumes of many colours. . . . And often in the very midst of the pageant, she exchanges the costumes of several players; instead of allowing them to finish the pageant in the parts that had been assigned to them, she reapparels them, forcing Croesus to assume the dress of a slave and captive, and shifting Maeandrius who formerly paraded among the servants into the imperial habit of Polycrates. . . . Some, however, are so ungrateful that when Fortune appears to them and asks her trappings back, they are vexed and indignant, as if they were being robbed of their own property, instead of giving back what they had borrowed for a little time.[10]

Philosophy (bk. 2, pr. 7) describes the small part of the earth which a man's fame touches by pointing out that the whole of the earth is no more than a pinpoint in the universe, that according to Ptolemy only a fourth of the earth is inhabited, that when deserts and marshland are subtracted, hardly any room is left at all. "Now," she says, "is it in this tightly-enclosed and tiny point, itself but part of a point, that you think of spreading your reputation, of glorifying your name? What grandeur or magnificence can glory have, contracted within such small and narrow limits?" In the parallel passage in *Icaromenippus*, Menippus is contemplating the vanity of wealth and power, but the point of view about the insignificance of the individual's material desires in the scheme of things is the same: "And when I looked toward the Peloponnese and caught sight of Cynuria, I noted that a tiny region, no bigger in any way than an Egyptian bean, had caused so many Argives and Spartans to fall in a single day. Again, if I saw any man pluming himself on gold because he had eight rings and four cups, I laughed heartily at him too, for the whole of Pangaeum, mines and all, was the size of a grain of millet" (2: 299).

As the other side of these attacks, Boethius also touches on the common Menippean theme in his discussion of wealth, the superiority of the simple life to that of the rich (bk. 2, pr. 5); its most memorable expression is found in the following meter, which Chaucer later adapted for his poem "The Former Age." The elevation of the simple life that we find here and at the end of Voltaire's *Candide* and Lucian's *Menippus* is not a nostalgic elevation of primordial innocence but a metaphoric presentation of what the satire takes as intellectual man's most pressing need: the maintaining of a place where he is free to begin his thinking without unnecessary restrictions.

In addition to these Cynic themes, the *Consolation* employs three major concerns of Menippean satire which we were examining in the preceding chapters. These are (1) the search for a Utopian life, (2) the contrast between views from an eternal present and a series of transitory moments, represented in the stances of two stock characters whose colloquy establishes the parameters of the dialogue, and (3) the comic and ironic assessment of the views of both these characters, an assessment leaving the issues we may designate as "content" without resolution.

The Consolation of Philosophy

The whole aim of the dialogue is to establish an ideal way of thought. Philosophy accuses Boethius of having left the paradise he had earned under her tutelage, his "city and country":

> When I saw you weeping in your grief I knew at once that you were wretchedly banished; but how remote was that banishment I should not have known if your speech had not told me. But how far from your homeland have you strayed! Strayed, not been driven, I say; or if you prefer to be thought of as driven, then how far have you driven yourself! . . . Surely you know the ancient and fundamental law of your city, by which it is ordained that it is not right to exile one who has chosen to dwell there? No one who is settled within her walls and fortifications need ever fear the punishment of banishment: but whoever ceases to desire to live there has thereby ceased to deserve to do so. (Bk. 1, pr. 5)

The aim of her subsequent words is to reestablish the reality of this place for him once more. Later she promises to provide him with wings to take him to his country:

> For I have wings swift flying
> Which can ascend the heights of heaven;
> When your quick mind has put them on,
> It looks down on the hated earth,
> Passes beyond the sphere of measureless air.
> .   .   .   .
> If the road bring you back, returning to this place,
> Which you now seek, forgetful,
> "This," you will say, "I remember, is my native land,
> Here I was born, here shall I halt my step."
> But if you like to look upon
> Earth's night that you have left,
> Those tyrants wretched peoples fear as fierce
> You will see as exiles.
> (Bk. 4, m. 1)

Philosophy's attacks on the traditional Menippean targets are a part of her effort to reestablish this "country." She attacks the Muses because they draw the passively receptive poet into their totally integrated world and inspire his words. Her objection is to this tradition of human passivity, whereby the poet is only a mouthpiece for energies behind him, not to poetry per se: she herself sings most of the meters. She feels that Boethius is not exerting himself, merely wallowing in a despair created by sordid images. Poetry (language, rhetoric) is good only insofar as it proceeds from the active principle of the mind and makes a didactic point. When it is properly subordinated and totally rational, it makes a satisfactory momentary pause in the midst of difficult logical arguments: "So let us use the sweet persuasiveness of rhetoric, which can only be kept on the right path if it does not swerve from our precepts, and if it harmonizes, now in a lighter, now in a graver mood, with the music native to our halls" (bk. 2, pr. 1).

As Philosophy dismisses the poetry of Boethius, the irrationality of the heart's despair, so too she dismisses his public profession. After Boethius' account of the political machinations that led to his downfall, Philosophy attacks the world of empire, whose laws ideally should regulate the intercourse of societies and nations and allow the individual to participate in a harmonious whole. For her, empire is at best a challenge, if indeed she accepts the Platonic maxim Boethius attributes to her: "It was you who established through the words of Plato the principle that those states would be happy where philosophers were kings or their governors were philosophers" (bk. 1, pr. 4). At its worst, as she mentioned earlier, empire is a destroyer of philosophers; she cites the ancient martyrs—Anaxagoras, Zeno, and Socrates—and the more recent—Seneca, Soranus, and Canius (bk. 1, pr. 3). She further negates any vision, ideal or otherwise, based upon the practical necessities of human political relations, by dismissing the importance of bodily exile, the alienation from the city or country or society which had been the individual's *raison d'être* (bk. 1, pr. 5). Only the mind and its "country" matters.

The one central image she draws from the practical political world reflects the contempt she feels for it; when the actions of other men become intrusive, her followers should retire into a castle capable of withstanding all sieges and from the wall laugh at the marauders below: "If ever they range against us and press about us too strongly, Wisdom our captain with-

draws her forces into her citadel, while our enemies busy themselves ransacking useless baggage. But we are safe from all their
mad tumult and from our heights we can laugh at them as they
carry off all those worthless things; we are protected by such a
wall as may not be scaled by raging stupidity" (bk. 1, pr. 3).
The choice of this image betokens an absence of sense of responsibility for world order, a refusal to accept the heavy weight of
ruling and meditating on how to hold together the diverse and
many-faceted impulses of human societies. In this, she is quite
as indifferent to the unavoidable problem as any Cynic.

The impregnable castle under siege as a metaphor for her
Utopian world of the mind is, however, an accurate image for
the disjunction between the mind's eternity and the body's chaotic temporality. The "castle" is the place of stasis and security,
a vantage point without obstructions, a place where conflicts
may exist without the unpleasant penalties of death, negation,
or temporal validation. In the first half of the *Consolation* (bk.
1, m. 1–bk. 3, pr. 9), it is from this vantage point that she rejects all worlds whose harmony, unity, and peace must rest in
some source outside the individual, the only place Boethius can
find his country. Having dismissed his poetry and his official
commitments, she dismisses, in books 2 and 3, his concern with
the goods of this world. Picking up a hint from Boethius' lament
about the loss of his possessions, she attacks all things a man
might strive to acquire, arguing that they draw an expenditure
of energy on false causes. Her basis for dismissing them is that
they cannot be possessed (bk. 2, pr. 4) or controlled (bk. 2, prs.
5–7); they cannot bestow sufficiency, power, respect, fame, or
joy—rewards they deceptively hold out (bk. 3, prs. 1–9). In the
second half of the *Consolation* (bk. 3, m. 9–bk. 5, pr. 6), the
Castle of Reason is the place of security in which she may theo-
rize about the nature of things without concern for time's need
of sequence and consistency. The forceful and active commitment to the world of the mind, to intelligible constructions and
ideas, provides the keynote to Philosophy's visions of Utopia.

Boethius, her interlocutor in the dialogue, is eager to share
her enthusiasm but not always convinced. He is carried along
in most of the dialogue by the rationalistic energy of his men-

tor, but his account of his downfall establishes him clearly in the context of history. He is a man who can be hurt by pain, outraged by injustice, and embittered by the ironic failure of his efforts, a man caught up in life in every sense of the word— in continuance, activity in the face of disorder, a concern with act and result in immediate as well as larger contexts. Like the lesser figures in Lucian's Menippean satires, Boethius establishes the sense of time, the context which permits us to see the seemingly impervious and triumphant protagonist in perspective.

In book 1, Boethius regrets the loss of his power, his goods, his life of service and study. In book 2, the book of Fortune, his four reactions of significance are all concerned with his awareness of time and act as a counter to the great flights of rhetoric being loosed against him by Philosophy. He protests that her arguments are effective only as long as the music lasts (pr. 3). He admits that the continuing love of his family anchors him away from the storm (pr. 4). In prose 5, he fails to follow her argument that nothing material can be possessed by man and delights in the beauties of fair fields even if they are not his. Finally he confesses that the one thing he always wanted from Fortune was fame, to have deserved well of the state (pr. 7). While Philosophy admits that this desire is the "last infirmity of noble mind," she pounds him into the dust with proofs of fame's insignificance, its short duration, its narrow scope. All of book 2, in fact, except for a few lines in proses 3 and 4 which present material related to Boethius' life, is characterized by Philosophy's delight in her ability to lay out the absurdities of believing in the temporal goods of Fortune and by Boethius' inability to absorb himself wholeheartedly in her self-sufficient flights above time.

Book 3, the book of the *summum bonum*, avoids Boethius' temporal problems, and he therefore follows along where he is led; but at the end, when Philosophy proposes that "Since God is good, evil is nothing," he objects: "Are you playing a game with me, weaving an inextricable labyrinth with your arguments, since at one time you go in where you are going to come out again, and at another come out where you went in? Or are you folding together as it were a wonderful circle of the simplicity of God?" (pr. 12). At the beginning of book 4, he pulls the discussion back to his own temporal problem: "Why is it then that the innocent suffer and the evil prosper?" In prose 5, after having been shown in the first part of the book that the good are actually powerful, successful, and rewarded and that the evil are weak, failing, and punished, Boethius, nevertheless still struggling with the problems of time, holds onto the notion of popular fortune and demands to know whether only random chance decides material rewards in this world. "But as it is, my belief in God as governor increases my astonishment. Since he frequently grants delights to the good and unpleasant things to the wicked, and on the other hand frequently metes out harshness to the good and grants their desires to the wicked, unless the cause is discovered, why should his governance seem to be any different from that of random chances?" (bk. 4, pr. 5). Philosophy immediately includes this question in its largest context to say that it is a part of the problem whose facets are as difficult to quell as the many heads of the Hydra; she mentions Providence, fate, predestination, chance, and freedom. But when, in the face of her previous description of fatal order, she insists that men have free will (bk. 5, pr. 2), her constructs break down for him, and time suddenly leaps to the fore again with its possibilities and contingencies.

Boethius at this point makes a final bid (bk. 5, pr. 3) for the demands of man thinking in time. He argues that if there is freedom in time, then the foresight of God is a logical impossibility. If God, who cannot be mistaken, foresees the event, then it must occur, and man is tantalized by options where there is no possibility of choosing. He thinks of problems he has been willing to put out of his mind. The divine system of rewards and punishments, which Philosophy has explicated in book 4, prose 6, breaks down, and Boethius concludes that prayer is quite useless. The remainder of the book is dedicated to Philosophy's explanations. In these remaining proses of the book, Boethius has little but monosyllables. There is no doubt, however, that the question of prose 3 gives Philosophy a run for her money. The *Consolation* ends with the prisoner's silence. He is thoroughly trounced, at least verbally, by the engulfing power of his mentor's explanations.

The irony directed against Boethius is readily apparent. Like

Zeus in *Zeus Catechized*, Tiresias and Tantalus, for instance, in the *Dialogues of the Dead*, and Claudius in Seneca's *Apocolocyntosis*, Boethius is an unquestionably important figure who is the obvious butt of the protagonist's joke. This neophyte, whose experience we initially respect for a great variety of reasons, is judged comic, foolish, unseeing, or inadequate by a set of standards set up by the protagonist as the only respectable ones in the world. Stated bluntly, Boethius in Philosophy's eyes has proved to have unfortunate similarities to the *philosophus gloriosus*. He had spent his life, by his own report, dedicated to employing the precepts of philosophy in his intercourse with men. Confronted, however, by the experience of his downfall, his philosophy deserts him completely. His dilemma is not without remedy; Philosophy has enough sympathy to come to him, and we see him in the course of the work go over some of her major precepts.

Philosophy—like Menippus, Seneca's Narrator, and in a different way, Gulliver's kings and Candide's instructors—is outside nature's laws. Her immunity to the natural requirements faced by ordinary human beings is apparent in her allegorical name and in Boethius' description of her timeless and immortal appearance at the beginning:

> There seemed to stand above my head a woman. Her look filled
> me with awe; her burning eyes penetrated more deeply than
> those of ordinary men; her complexion was fresh with an ever-
> lively bloom, yet she seemed so ancient that none would think
> her of our time. It was difficult to say how tall she might be,
> for at one time she seemed to confine herself to the ordinary
> measure of man, and at another the crown of her head touched
> the heavens; and when she lifted her head higher yet, she
> penetrated the heavens themselves, and was lost to the sight of
> men. (Bk. 1, pr. 1)

In all her discussions with Boethius, as I pointed out earlier, she shows the same unbounded enthusiasm and energy as Menippus and his fellows for attacking world views that do not coincide with her own, the world views that acknowledge the burden of time.

Like the Lucianic protagonist, she takes the pragmatic view of things. Hers is the rationalistic mind which sees things only as they are in a timeless present, which has the ability to penetrate and exclude all inconvenient data. Her whole system of argument depends upon the positing of a world of the eternal present that supersedes the demands of temporality. The worlds of Boethius she attacks in the first part of the *Consolation* depend in significant ways on time, on man's necessity to live his life with language, man, and materials. What she tries to convey to Boethius is a point of equilibrium at which the destructive power of time and its minions ceases to have any effect. This effort is to be seen in various guises in many Menippean dialogues, but the presentation of this effort is especially apparent in Boethius' portrayal of Philosophy. Her attacks, like Menippus', bear resemblances to the Cynic view of existence, and like his, do not lead to the Cynic conclusion "Railing at life from a 'tub' is best," but rather to an energetic interest in exulting in her own view of things. In the second half of the *Consolation*, which begins with book 3, meter 9, she proposes instead of poetry, government, and material possessions, a series of worlds born through the creative power of the mind, whose terms shall be imagined and established by herself, albeit with references to her major disciples.

With this meter we encounter one of the three great shifts in perspective in the *Consolation*. The names I give the four sections of her argument—Cynic (bk. 2–bk. 3, pr. 9), Platonic (bk. 3, m. 9–bk. 4, pr. 5), Aristotelian (bk. 4, pr. 6–bk. 5, m. 1), and Augustinian (bk. 5, prs. 2–6)—are not intended to indicate Boethius' literal sources for these sections, but rather techniques and points of view to which the sections allude. The analogies between Lucian and the first section have already been discussed. The Platonic section begins with a paraphrase of Plato's *Timaeus*, and two proses of the discussion on evil contain a paraphrase of the *Gorgias*. The Aristotelian section ends with an allusion to Aristotle's definition of chance. The debate about the relation of foreknowledge and free will in the final section of the *Consolation*, which contains one indirect allusion to the *City of God* (bk. 5, pr. 4), is a debate always associated with Augustine. The Platonic section makes continual use of dialectic like the Platonic dialogues which embody the "open" system of Plato's philosophy. The Aristotelian section proposes a highly schematic organization for the universe like Aristotle's "closed" system. The final section moves back to the "open" system of Augustine.[11] Again it must be said that Boethius is original. The chief point of his moving from system to system is to portray Philosophy's knowledge of, but at the same time, freedom from, the confinement of any system. Boethius' technique of allusion has driven many scholars into a search for his exact sources. This search has yielded little agreement because Boethius is selecting certain outstanding features of the systems to which he alludes, not reproducing specific texts. His work echoes other writers' ideas—this kind of echoing is a recurrent feature of Menippean satire—but the center he establishes is his own.

In book 3, meter 9, Philosophy proposes the Platonic image of the world as the projection of God's thought. Her proposals here hardly coincide with her proposals so far. In the first section we have been subjected to a Cynic *contemptus mundi*. In effect, Philosophy tells Boethius that the material world and its activities are unworthy of any serious man's interest. He is to recognize it but hold it and its offerings at a distance. While her advice is directed to teaching Boethius how to handle intellectually the discrepancy between soul and body, spirit and matter, both remain acknowledged facts of human existence. But in the Platonic section, Philosophy rejects man's inevitable subjection to time and material and substitutes a world of total mind. Her unvoiced suggestion is that if God can think a beautiful world into time and space, then so can she and so can man. We float in a void along with Boethius, for she has set about ignoring man's difficulty in transcending the demands of his body and his worldly experience.

In the last three proses of book 3, she employs the syllogism to mirror her recommended combination of energy and stasis. This is her first variation on the theme of the supremacy of mind, for the syllogism bears to the Platonic Idea the same relation that the world bears to the mind of God. Prose 10, particularly, is full of geometrical analogies. Using the propositions 'God is good' and 'God is the One,' she establishes irrefutably that all things begin and end in God and that the world is governed by goodness. These are her answers to questions which Boethius was not able to answer in book 1. She ignores the unpleasant implications of the tautology of the syllogism 'We can only prove what we assume.' In this phase of her argument, in order to have a beginning point, she accepts without need of proof such Platonic statements as "For the universe did not take its origin from diminished and unfinished beginnings, but proceeding from beginnings whole and completely finished it lapses into this latest, exhausted state" (bk. 3, pr. 10). A cyclical view of history, which underlies Cynic philosophy both in Lucian and in Philosophy's own first section, would argue that there is neither progression nor decay, only Fortune's ups and downs. To Philosophy's next sentence, "But if, as we have just shown, there is a certain imperfect happiness in a good that perishes, it cannot be doubted that there is some enduring and perfect happiness," Boethius could have objected, as did Alexander in Lucian (7: 71–73), that man's reconciliation with the frail goods is his only hope of happiness. Instead, however, he courteously attempts to follow her.

In the first half of book 4, Philosophy employs her second variation on the image of book 3, meter 9, the world of definition, the linguistic mirror of the secure world she proposes. With these terms, she satisfactorily excludes any possibility for the existence of evil. God, who is omnipotent, is good; he cannot be or do evil. Thus, evil is nothing. This conclusion is to ignore all the pain and agony men have ever endured.

When Boethius rejects this Platonic world of the mind as interesting, but useless to his human needs (bk. 3, pr. 12; bk. 4, pr. 5), Philosophy shifts ground completely into what is, roughly speaking, the Aristotelian section of the *Consolation* (bk. 4, pr. 6–bk. 5, pr. 2) and proceeds to classify and subordinate the powers rampant in the universe as providence, fate, and chance. In her new method of approaching the relation of God and the universe, she now picks on a different aspect of the implications in the image of book 3, meter 9, the world as the

projection of God's thought. Instead of suggesting that man has
the freedom of God to imagine a universe, she now suggests
that he is a cog in a completely determined world order. God as
he thinks is called providence, and the projection of this
thought into time is called fate:

> For providence is the divine reason itself, established in the
> highest ruler of all things, the reason which disposes all things
> that exist; but fate is a disposition inherent in movable things,
> through which providence binds all things together, each in its
> own proper ordering. For providence embraces all things to-
> gether, though they are different, though they are infinite; but
> fate arranges as to their motion separate things, distributed in
> place, form and time; so that this unfolding of temporal order
> being united in the foresight of the divine mind is providence,
> and the same unity when distributed and unfolded in time is
> called fate. (Bk. 4, pr. 6)

She has told Boethius that all men are dedicated to the search
for good, God, and happiness—not only the enlightened but
also the unimaginative who mistake material possessions for
their highest happiness. Even the evil are, in their desperate
and futile way, engaged in this search. Nothing, in fact, escapes fatal order.

> So it is that although all things may seem confused and disor-
> dered to you, unable as you are to contemplate this order,
> nevertheless their own measure directing them towards the
> good disposes them all. . . .
>
> . . . .
>
> For a certain order embraces all things, so that that which has
> departed from the rule of this order appointed to it, although it
> slips into another condition yet that too is order, so that noth-
> ing in the realm of providence may be left to chance. (Bk. 4,
> pr. 6)

And later in her discussion of chance, she confirms this picture
of total order: "We may therefore define chance as the unexpected event of concurring causes among things done for some
purpose. Now causes are made to concur and flow together by
that order which, proceeding with inevitable connexion, and

coming down from its source in providence, disposes all things in their proper places and times" (bk. 5, pr. 1).

The fortunes of men are no exception to the rule: the course of fate "also binds the acts and fortunes of men in an unbreakable chain of causes, which since they start from beginnings in immovable providence must also be themselves immutable. For things are governed in the best way if the simplicity which rests in the divine mind produces an inflexible order of causes, and this order constrains with its own immutability things which are mutable and would otherwise be in random flux" (bk. 4, pr. 6). Though the optimistic suggestion of the preceding section (bk. 3, m. 9–bk. 4, pr. 4)—that the creative glory of God whose thought forms the universe in the same instant it conceives it is the pattern of freedom men in their prolonged struggle with time and material must attempt to emulate—is now replaced by a totally deterministic assessment of man's place, Philosophy's spirit is in no way dampened. Fate is seen as an incitement to heroic activity (bk. 4, pr. 7, m. 7), whose commitment, we are tempted to say with Ker of the fated events at Ragnarök, "is perfect, because without hope."[12] "For it is placed in your own hands," Philosophy tells Boethius, "what kind of fortune you prefer to shape for yourselves" (bk. 4, pr. 7).

The most startling of her shifts in point of view occurs in the final section of the *Consolation* (bk. 5, prs. 2–6), the Augustinian part of the work. In the first section of the *Consolation* Boethius gives a kind of helpless acquiescence to Philosophy's Cynical attacks on material goods. In the Platonic section of pure mind, he is entertained, but finds her proposals inapplicable to his problem. In the Aristotelian section, the determinism that her description of the all-embracing fatal order projecting from the mind of God implies arouses interest rather than repulsion. But when he asks one more theoretical question which will establish irrefutably his secure place in a universe where all is fated, she throws him for a loop. He asks: "But in this close-linked series of causes, is there any freedom of our will, or does this chain of fate also bind even the motions of men's minds?" (bk. 5, pr. 2). Presumably, if she had said, "No, men do not have free will," the matter would have ended there.

But instead of confirming the picture of the universe that she has drawn in the preceding section, she slips to a new norm of argument. She avoids the determinism Menippean satire abhors and focuses once again on the dualism which, if it knows man to be the creature fated forever to live in time with nothing better than occasional flickering visions of peace and of a divine order whose eternity is not troubled by temporal difficulties, also knows him to be in some strange way free. "Freedom there is," she said, "for there could not be any nature rational, did not that same nature possess freedom of the will. For that which can by its nature use reason, has the faculty of judgement, by which it determines everything; of itself, therefore, it distinguishes those things which are to be avoided, and those things that are to be desired." She in effect pulls the rug out from under Boethius' feet, and the frantic question of the next prose embodies his fear. He is outraged by the logical contradiction between foreknowledge and free will, by the realization that he is in reality committed to time and progression and that if all of this action and thought is divinely foreknown by an omnipotent God who obviously cannot err, there is no possibility that he can be free.

The idea that Philosophy must counter is the idea that foreknowledge imposes necessity on the occurrence of future events. After a certain amount of recasting in which she merely repeats Boethius' arguments and questions, she first sets out to show that knowledge is determined by the mind of the knower, not by the object known. Sense, imagination, and reason, all possessed by man, know an object in different ways—sense by touch, imagination by memory, reason by the awareness of the universal. Intelligence possessed only by divine beings comprehends an object in yet a different way, and she launches into her famous distinction between eternity and time. Man living in time has the past behind him and the future before him, but God in his eternity is not troubled by necessities that govern the sequence of things. "Eternity, then, is the whole, simultaneous and perfect possession of boundless life, which becomes clearer by comparison with temporal things. For whatever lives in time proceeds in the present from the past into the future, and there is nothing established in time which can embrace the whole space of its life equally, but tomorrow surely it does not yet grasp, while yesterday it has already lost. And in this day to day life you live no more than in that moving and transitory moment" (bk. 5, pr. 6). God embraces all time in his eternal present; and he sees events occurring before him in the temporal present as coexisting with past and future events. Therefore, God's knowledge (*providentia*, not *praevidentia*, she points out) imposes no necessity on these events.

Not the least indication of her energy, her solution to the challenge creates a brilliant new version of the relation of man and God, which is quite unlike the image underlying the preceding section, where there is no other possibility than total determinism, where the relation of fate and providence and all similar pairs are linked in inextricable bondage, no more separable than form and content. The new image is an accurate portrayal of the binary opposition between the timeless moment and time, a classic feature of the Menippean dialogue. Her description of the relation between time and eternity is, of course, representative of her relation to Boethius from the beginning. Her battle cries, self-mastery, divine happiness, being, eternity—all exhort to states of timelessness. Her techniques, proposition, syllogism, definition, the image of fatal order, are all ways of embodying the transitory, of abstracting it into the definiteness of a Utopian eternity. Nevertheless, this final solution is an admission that man's reality is time and all that involves, and though the end of the *Consolation* is beautiful, it is also a practical reminder of the theoretical quality of her advice. It cannot solve the problem of man's everlasting dilemma: the struggle between the weight of his body, the unalterable sequence of his moments, and his perpetually unsatisfied yearning for that experience where the dance and the dancer are one. Boethius, like the usual Menippean character concerned with time, remains suspended with new thoughts, no answer to his quandary, and an irrefutable proof of his intellectual ignorance.

The ironic assessment of Philosophy runs along the same lines as that of Menippus. Boethius portrays in her the same egocentrism that amounts to the position 'The thing that is done under my aegis is right; the same thing done under anyone else's is wrong.' Menippus attacks the philosophers for the absurdity in their descriptions of the universe, yet his own is hardly better. While his determination to see for himself how things are is commendable, what he is capable of seeing is absurd too, a point Lucian drives home by calling the dialogue *Icaromenippus* rather than *Daedalomenippus*.[13] In the *Consolation*, Philosophy attacks Boethius for consoling himself with poetry, but she herself goes on to console him with it. She attacks Fortune's goods as totally useless in book 2, yet in book 3 finds them and man's liking for them useful in demonstrating man's natural desire for the good which is God.

In book 2, she attacks Boethius' concern with fame (pr. 7), yet in book 4, when she comes to tell him how to meet Fortune, all her examples are drawn from actions that betoken a concern for the heroic life of man: "And therefore a wise man ought not to take it ill, every time he is brought into conflict with fortune, just as it would not be fitting for a brave man to be vexed every time the sound of war crashed out. Since for each of these the difficulty is itself the occasion, for the latter of increasing his glory, for the former of further fashioning his wisdom" (bk. 4, pr. 7). The following meter on the epic heroes of old ends:·

Go then, you brave, where leads the lofty path
Of this great example. Why in indolence
Do you turn your backs in flight? Earth overcome
Grants you the stars.

(Bk. 4, m. 7)

Philosophy has the Menippean authority figure's tendency to say what fits the situation before her; she does not worry overly about her contradictions of previous statements. The demands of time fit awkwardly into the ways of eternity.

The wrenching shifts in her modes of argument (Cynic, to Platonic, to Aristotelian, to Augustinian) suppose a mind delighted by categories but indifferent to mere temporal demands of logical consistency. While no one has, so far as I know, been so unkind as to say so directly, Philosophy is in every argument she utters pulling small pieces off the philosophical systems of the philosophers she alludes to. What separates her from those she attacks in her opening remarks to Boethius is not her method but her attitude, her awareness that all theories and systems should remain inferior and subordinate to the principle of the free, exploring mind. The knowledge of the systems is essential, but to be piously bound by them would be to confine free intellectual potential within a deadening pedantic determinism.

The juxtaposition of two characters speaking for two conceptions of time and limitation provides the same kind of irony as that of Lucian's dialogues. Philosophy operates with magnificent freedom in terms of her own timeless symbols and propositions. The overmastering tautological structure of human paths to knowledge that takes Menippus into Hades only to find what he already knows dominates everything that Philosophy says. She can prove what she sees or assumes, discover what she posits, find what she looks for. But she is not bound by any restriction these activities impose, since she can shift ground when she wishes. Boethius juxtaposes with this world of Philosophy one man's personal experience, chaotic, uncertain, impenetrable. Greatly overmatched, he nevertheless does not succumb. He is merely silent, a state of suspension which in both Lucian and Chaucer is common to the end of this dialogue.

The facets of Menippean satire in the *Consolation* which we have just examined are all linked to a concern at the heart of the genre, the paradoxical relation between freedom and limitation, or as the pair is so often called in Chaucer, experience and authority. On the surface, Boethius represents in his namesake the inborn limitation of the mind of the individual, and in Philosophy its aspirations toward freedom. Philosophy stands as the direct opposite of the prisoner's consciousness, a spirit whose movement is impeded neither by walls nor by intellectual limitations of any sort. In the course of the five books, the imagery used in the presentation of the dialogue reflects these roles. Boethius is a prisoner, whose bodily movements are hampered, a patient, whose bodily functions are impaired, a pupil, whose mind is hemmed in by ignorance. The darkness-light imagery of the meters reflects the same relation. The present state of Boethius' mind is represented by darkness; the state to which he will move, by light. The idea is simply represented in the natural image of the sun driving away the night or the wind driving the clouds from before the sun, and complexly represented in Platonic references to the philosopher's search for the sun out of the cave and to the doctrine of reminiscence. Philosophy, in her role as freedom, is hindered neither by prison, illness, ignorance, nor darkness. She is the natural force that will dissolve the prison, the doctor who will cure the patient, the teacher who will instruct the pupil, the wings which will lift man from darkness to light.

But there is an ironic awareness that this freedom is had at the expense of another kind of limitation. Her freedom can be offered only at the cost of a relentless paring away of the graspable alternatives which, at any given moment, do not interest her. Her "castle," like any Utopia or Paradise, is also a prison. Drawing on the quintessence of various philosophical conventions, she says what it is traditional to say in the face of the loss of material goods and unjust suffering. This involves her, on the one hand, in the uttering of the commonplaces by which man survives experience too difficult, complex, and terrifying to master; on the other, in the presenting of certain syllogisms, which, because they exclude irregularities and exceptions, operate in the same calming fashion as the commonplaces. In excluding alternatives, in concentrating on what is always true, given the conditions she employs at the moment, Philosophy speaks from the bottom of ruts so deep that for a mere mortal it is all but impossible to look out. Her theories, inherited and acquired, which at first sight appear merely neutral, perforce impose certain patterns on the mind, certain ways of thinking about experience that exclude other ways. Their tendency is toward authoritarianism, toward rigidity and a forbidding of flexibility. Because Philosophy's words are created out of this world of tradition and inherited knowledge, she may, at any given moment, be said to represent the limitation imposed by the paucity of citable paths to knowledge.

Boethius is, of course by contrast, ironically associated with freedom, which under her control, he gradually loses. He has had an experience he finds himself unable to account for. He exists in the uncertainty of time. But because the experience is new to him, it suggests possibility and a path away from the formulations of all of his previous mental endeavors. His own discovery that this experience of his downfall means that he is free is recorded in the end of his prayer in book 1, meter 5, where he contrasts the order of nature with the disorderly control fortune exerts over the life of man. In the course of his discussion with Philosophy, he hears in the Cynic section that he should not concern himself with Fortune's goods, in the Platonic that true happiness is God, in the Aristotelian that not only is man's life governed by laws as firm as those of nature but also that even by struggling there is no possible way of avoiding the order they impose, in the Augustinian that he is free to make choices *sub specie aeternitatis*. For him the various phases of the argument raise the implicit question, How is man ever to learn anything new when those who mean to help him exult at such length on subjects so remotely related to his questions? Or, How is man to understand the relation between his own experience and the words of the authorities of the past when, as perhaps not the least of his troubles, he is compelled to frame his questions in their terms? Only they will speak to him, it is true, but he is forced out of an original understanding of his predicament by having to use their words to describe it. Viewed as the final dialogue of man's intellectual life, at that moment the only dialogue in which he is capable of engaging, the argument yields the recognition that all we can hear is an elaboration of the past that drowns whatever small originality there may be in the experience of the present.

The dramatic and philosophical relationships by which the dialogue represents the themes—limitation and freedom—set up contrasts, depths, shadows, and overtones which to the ironic eye suggest two opposing visions of the life of the mind. In one light, Boethius' relationship to Philosophy verges on the tragic. Boethius is desperately serious, has, in fact, no one else to turn to; she wanders insensitive and indifferent among such delightfully impressive philosophical problems as appeal to her. This juxtaposition of a man whose constructs have fallen to pieces and a figure whose constructs are infallible and inexhaustible provides the outer extremes of two worlds whose momentary meeting can be maintained only by a force which dominates the incipient explosion.

This sense that disparate elements are being held together by a titanic expenditure of energy is an aspect of the work's being that parallels its positing a speaker with absolute authority and absolute worlds. Whatever rug we lift, we find the basic blocks of its structure uneven; nothing lies beneath us in natural repose. The dialogue takes place between beings of different realms, the human and the supernatural. This supernatural figure, however, is not divine (the normal supernatural opposite for man), but only "the love of wisdom," a quality of the human mind. Because of this strange collocation, the "dialogue" threatens constantly to spring apart into two monologues, with Boethius as tormented man wanting to address God, and Philosophy as the voice distilled from the titanic efforts of man to think, wanting to address pure mind. The dialogue exists only because of that ultimately wistful and poignant courtesy the members of the Menippean dialogue show toward one another.

The discrepancy in their aims adds a significant dimension to the definition of tragedy found in book 2, prose 2, the passage so often cited as the medieval definition of tragedy: "What else is the cry of tragedy but a lament that happy states are overthrown by the indiscriminate blows of fortune?" The definition belongs to Fortune, not Philosophy, and certainly should not be regarded as Boethius' conception of the matter, since it figures only as a minor fraction of the total philosophical conception that informs the work.[14] The tragic sense imbedded in the *Consolation* arises in Boethius' perception of man's perpetual failure. The failure that matters is not his inability to stay at the top of Fortune's wheel but his inability to translate his experience of whatever cast into something intelligible and complete. In a very broad sense, the tragic sense that pervades the book is that common to the Menippean dialogue, the knowledge that man is not provided with images or words that are adequate to contain his electrifying inklings of reality.

Boethius' awareness of this dilemma that lies at the heart of Menippean satire is much more apparent than Lucian's because Boethius uses his own name for the minor character in the work. In the trilogy of dialogues that confronts us in the *Consolation*, Boethius takes the lower position. In the inner dialogue he is, of course, the subordinate of Philosophy. While his questions change the course of the argument, he at no point rises to any kind of transcendent position in relation to her. In the frame dialogue, which is established by the elegiac lament that opens the work and is the only point at which we see him independent of Philosophy, he represents himself in the subordinate position also, as the victim of circumstances over which he has no control, namely, as we learn later (bk. 1, pr. 4), his condemnation, banishment, and imprisonment by the Roman Senate. The strange authorial acceptance of the lower position impinges upon us without hindrance because the fiction of the frame dialogue is not fully realized. We know that the author speaks to us, as authority, of an experience he had as the subordinate of Philosophy. But there is no dramatic realization of the frame dialogue, no controlling voice at the end which says: "I had a strange experience the other night." There is no recognition of the time lag between the experience and its recording in writing. The result is that the inner dialogue emerges as the stronger, proved by most writers' tendency to take Philosophy's words as the unironic views of Boethius. As Boethius emerges from these roles into the dialogue that he implicitly carries on with us, he remains a kind of apologist for his relation to his own training. This intermingling of author, author-character, and persona—all in the subordinate position—has the aesthetic effect of focusing our attention on the ironic complexities and limitations set up by the phases of our inescapable experience with tradition, the self, and the human attempt to formulate experience in words.

In this same trilogy of interlinked dialogues that make up *Menippus* and *Icaromenippus*, the free voice of the protagonist dominates without consistent hindrance. Menippus in the frame dialogue tells a friend about his experiences with various characters with whom he spoke on his marvelous journey; he is unquestioned protagonist in both frame and inner dialogues. Though the gods of Olympus are stronger than he, he has a freedom from the demands of the universe which they lack. Lucian maintains his separate identity as author and may, of course, be said to carry on a third dialogue with us as his subordinates. While he directs a great deal of good-natured irony at Menippus, Menippus remains his spokesman; Lucian accords only incidental sympathy to the minor characters and their struggles. The friend is a convenience for Menippus' storytelling. The minor characters of the inner dialogue too are stock figures, representing one point of view. The philosophers are subjected to uninhibited attacks; the dead and the gods are allowed only momentary rights as they attempt to speak for the problems of time. Boethius in his subordinate role is, by contrast, a fully developed character with a family, friends, enemies, interests, duties—in other words, a historical past. As the speaker for time, he lays much stronger claims on our attention than do any of Lucian's minor characters.

The Menippean thrust of the *Consolation* remains the same as in Lucian; the protagonist's views prevail, but in the *Consolation* they prevail with the ironic awareness that the supernatural protagonist's freedom is Other, not available to man, who though he can imagine it, cannot experience it, except as he writes to contain it. Boethius' acceptance of the lower position portrays the Menippean recognition of man's inability to formulate his own experience. This device of the subordinate author leaves intact the philosophical relativism of Philosophy and acknowledges man's need for the piecemeal constructs of innerly consistent, if mutually contradictory, worlds, his need of a frame of mind under whose auspices he can at least temporarily dismiss without apology all that is unexplainable. The *Consolation* thus recounts Boethius' ironic, but nevertheless total, resubmission to the orthodoxy whose possibility is established by the egotism of logic, the absoluteness of whose views excludes whatever would turn its self-contained, static worlds into a world of flux, process, and uncertainty, or even into a world forced to admit their existence. Thus, in the *Consolation*, instead of an uninhibited attack from a detached point of view on human constructs, myths, morals, laws, customs, and theories—the kind of attack which makes up the major portion of the Lucianic dialogue—we have a portrayal of man's dialectical necessity to accept these constructs, to organize, to order, to insist that the universe can be understood as a graspable entity. The circus arena is as comprehensive as in Lucian, but there is only one ring, the act is a single one, and it is rather more apparent in the end that this is the place where man will exist as long as he thinks.

As in Lucian, however, the comic view prevails. Viewed as only one dialogue among many possible ones on the earth—as a Menippean dialogue, this is its status—the *Consolation* is full of what Bakhtin calls "reduced laughter."[15] We watch Boethius attempt to relate himself to Philosophy and her amicable pedantry, her overemphasis, her exuberance. He asks about evil and suffering, and she proposes to improve his digestion. But in making the effort to come down out of her world to include the prisoner in her wholeness, she provides at least an ambiguous comfort. There is pathos as well as irony in her decision to employ the ways of time. These methods of the dialogue are toys to her, but the human mind of Boethius, in submitting, is bound to these methods absolutely and has in fact no other means of proceeding. If there is an offhand quality in her remarks, none of which, from her coign of vantage, are vitally necessary, if one thing implies another, if everything is the same thing, at least she continues to speak, to set up a dialogue in time, where the prisoner must exist.

While Boethius must struggle unsuccessfully with the concepts she throws at him and attempt to wrest a connected meaning out of them that will satisfy his linear understanding in time, he is at least allowed space for the struggle. Comprehending all, she throws down bits, whereas Boethius, comprehending nothing, struggles to pick up the bits in a frantic effort to comprehend the whole. He fails, but he has at least been allowed to fail in the light. If a superabundance of interest, help, and active interference from his gods is as distressing to the fragility of man in the end as silence and total indifference, it has at least the value of suggesting that his search has a goal, even if he can never attain it, even if he must tenuously and frustratingly discourse with his overly helpful Philosophies as long as he thinks.

The Boethian dialogue—an archetypal image of the mind's struggle to come to terms with chaos and certainty, freedom and limitation—is an exploration which portrays what the mind must perpetually contend with as it fights to forge its meanings. In Boethian terms, man does not face a dead God, or a cosmic indifference, but a continual stream of friendly information and concern from all sources able to advise him. The representation of this process has played its part, too, in holding readers. The drama of the dialogue adds another dimension to the definition of the *summum bonum* given in book 3. Man's greatest happiness is that the symbolic entity here called Philosophy will come to him. Beyond the body's torment and the mind's despair, Boethius voices the profound Menippean belief that there is an unexpected splendor in the nature of things which not only rescues man temporarily and allows him to proceed, but also urges him to soar triumphantly to the joys of creating a world where much that matters in the chaos of primary experience ceases to exist. The sense that joy and possibility pervade the universe in mysterious ways is not uncommon in great books. Athena comes to Odysseus, Virgil and Beatrice to Dante, Prince Arthur to the knights of the *Faerie Queene*. If divine grace—or, to put it another way, man's profound conviction that something in the universe is good and wants him to live in happiness—explains the presence of Philosophy as it does that of Athena and Beatrice, human hope that better worlds are possible explains the courteous attention of Boethius. This sense in the *Consolation* that the mind of man is allowed to participate on whatever ironic basis in this triumphant freedom has been one strong factor in creating its reputation.

For the practicing medieval writer, the appeal of the *Consolation* was also technical. The work provided a brilliant, provisionally nonheretical model for containing, without necessarily espousing, the perception of the essential chaos of all matters in the universe. Lucian, who draws Menippus' attitude from his own consummate intelligence, highly trained in logic, created in his spokesman a character who can never have been regarded as anything but a symbol of archheresy by the Establishment.[16] Boethius, on the contrary, drawing Philosophy's words from the master philosophers who had preceded him, palliated to a large degree the extraordinary perception Menippean satire insists on. In the Boethian dialogue, the befuddled "I" embodies the human awareness of the inescapability of chaos; the all knowing Other, the capacity to ignore it and concentrate on theoretical ways of thought which support the existence and possibility of escape, of a resting place where in freedom and light, the power of superior thought transcends pedantry and tyranny (not, of course, chaos). The cento-like quality of Philosophy's speeches, which engage only briefly the writings she draws on, nevertheless proclaimed the possibility for live statement in the face of lost texts, inaccessible books, insuperable ignorance, and a lack of time to master all that is there. Finally, the ironic counterpoise of the dialogue, which precludes the possibility of the descent into mere "preaching," of whatever brilliance, gave the assurance of the total valence of intelligence and its capacities for speculation and of a power which could not be stultified by the dead weight of ecclesiastical, social, or civil pedantries.

In an early work, *De interpretatione*, Boethius had announced that as his lifetime task he would translate the works of Plato and Aristotle, write commentaries on them, and then reconcile their differences.[17] While philosophers generally have pronounced Plato and Aristotle incapable of being reconciled, the *Consolation* would seem to contain the key to Boethius' vision. The reconciliation exists by means of anamorphic selection. Particular questions raise one philosopher's answers into the limelight; when the question changes, then another set of answers is called for. The reconciliation is achieved through the imagining of an intellectual space large enough to contain whatever systems are put into it. What is listed under *A* does not invalidate or even disturb what is listed under *B*. It is the imagined world of the encyclopedist, not of a school, that we encounter in the resolution. Many medieval writers experimented with the Menippean counters and structures given such memorable expression in the *Consolation*, but none with such dazzling enthusiasm and success as Chaucer.

4

Fortune, Happiness, and Love in *Troilus and Criseyde*

The Menippean characteristics of *Troilus and Criseyde* most
frequently discussed are the mixed genres, tragedy and comedy
with their attendant high and low styles, and the oppositions in
world views and ideas, most notably the opposing views of love
and of freedom.[1] Muscatine, for instance, calls *Troilus* "a comedy and a tragedy of universal and timeless dimensions," and
goes on to say that the "poem is neither simple in structure nor
homogeneous in style. Rather than being linear in design, it is
composed of patterned contrasts, encompassing a great diversity of moods and tone, often abruptly juxtaposed."[2] Later he
writes (in an excellent description of the demands that Menippean satires make on the reader): "The *tertium quid* created by
the interplay of these styles and these philosophical positions is
best called a genre unto itself, for the result is a qualitative difference from romance or novel that requires a different kind of
attention from the reader. It needs what S. L. Bethell in a similar context has called 'multiconsciousness,' the simultaneous
awareness of different and opposite planes of reality."[3]

Troilus and Criseyde is generally considered to be the most
Boethian of Chaucer's poems; but this is not to say that Chaucer can be shown to espouse particular philosophical positions
presented in the *Consolation*. For one thing, the eclecticism of
the Latin work militates against the certain isolation of a point
of view—a necessary first step were specific philosophical influence to be the primary basis of a comparison between the
two authors. The *Consolation* is a dramatic dialogue in which
the author is not the main speaker and the protagonist Philosophy presents as her subjects of discourse allusive summaries of
major classical philosophical systems; moving from locus to lo-

cus, she draws on Cynic, Platonic, Aristotelian, and finally Augustinian ideas. To conclude, in view of this eclecticism, that Boethius was an Augustinian because the section based on a problem posed by Augustine is last in the sequence is about as certain as concluding that Lucian was a Platonist because in *Philosophies for Sale* Plato brings the highest bid. For another, because the *Consolation* is a Menippean satire, the attitude toward ideas is more important than the ideas themselves; they are treated as free-floating entities, metaphoric attempts to name the unnameable. What Philosophy supports, therefore, is not a system, but the right of the mind to make and to move through systems; to discard and imitate systems; to stay ineluctably and creatively free to think with the brilliant minds of the past.[4] *Troilus*, as a Menippean satire, shares with the *Consolation* an investigation of the mind's ability to formulate concepts and interpretations and yet remain free of the implications of these formulations. This investigation is apparent both in Chaucer's portrayal of his characters and in the formal structure of the narrative.

What the designation "Boethian" for *Troilus* means in the context of Menippean satire is that Chaucer uses the *Consolation* as inserted text (a text whose presence continually implies an alternate world view) more frequently and with greater deliberation in this poem than in any other of his works.[5] Troilus' speech on Love (3. 1744–71) is a close reworking of book 2, meter 8, in the *Consolation*; his speech on free will (4. 958–1082), a close reworking of book 5, prose 3, the prisoner's bitterest outcry against Philosophy's cheerful philosophizing. There is evidence that Chaucer added both passages to his completed manuscript.[6] Pandarus' words on Fortune are direct summaries of the major comments Boethius makes on this subject in the *Consolation*. Criseyde's speech on happiness draws on a major passage in book 2, prose 4, and also the general problem of book 3. Chaucer, using a structure which is more complicated than that in the *Consolation*, since it has a consistently present frame dialogue (the narrator and the old story), alludes verbally to the *Consolation* in passages that make the dialogue between Pandarus and Troilus a direct imitation of that between Philosophy and Boethius. In this chapter, I shall be dealing with the relations between the *Consolation* and the speeches on Fortune, happiness, and love and on the place the three main characters hold in the Menippean dialogue.

Troilus shares with the *Consolation* an investigation of that high idealism, nowhere else so strong in Chaucer's poetry, based on the concept of universal love which sees man potentially safe in the context of strong human and divine support. The *donné* of both the poem and the *Consolation*, the law under which mortals live—as powerful a law in Menippean satire as the law which puts them in the midst of an incomprehensible universe —is that they will care about each other. We see Boethius' love for justice, for the rights of innocent men and the Senate, not to mention for his wife, sons, and father-in-law. We see Philosophy's concern and love for Boethius. We read Philosophy's description of the celestial love controlling, creating, and caring for the universe (bk. 2, m. 8; bk. 4, m. 6). But above all, the *Consolation* makes the strong affirmation, much like love, that man's intellectual tradition, his collective historical achievement, contains the way to truth and provides eternal sanctuary transcending the toils of chaotic experience. *Troilus* focuses most intensely on the extreme form of this care, the love of man and woman. They love each other in the face of all evidence to the contrary, despite their contempt (Troilus), their frustration (Pandarus), their fearfulness (Criseyde), their exclusion (narrator). The words "Love is he that alle thing may bynde, / For may no man fordon the lawe of kynde" (1. 237–38) could be taken as the poem's epigraph. But there are other dimensions to this love and care in the poem. Troilus' concern for humankind in the high moments of his love, Pandarus' friendship for Troilus, the narrator's obsessive care for his characters, even Deiphobus' efforts to gather together friends who will support the cause of the supposedly threatened Criseyde, illustrate the mortal propensity for getting involved with the responsibilities and joys of other human beings' problems.

In *Troilus*, the relation between this idealistic concern and indifferent events is more profoundly ironic than in the *Consolation*, where we are not forced to witness Theodoric's decision, Philosophy's failure, and Boethius' death. In *Troilus*, whose final books do contain the events of the aftermath,[7] we face the effects of the decree which sends Criseyde to the Greeks; we face Pandarus' failure and Troilus' death. The idealized love of the narrator and Troilus establishes heights from which they fall. The narrator's desperate efforts do not affect his inherited story's end. Pandarus, in spite of all his care, succeeds in having given Troilus a love whose disappointments are even more frightening than his own. Events move on and drag the characters into the maelstrom, leaving them to react with whatever reserves their minds possess. But before the final failure, the characters, especially in their Boethian speeches, attempt to project upon the unintelligibility of things a scheme whereby their concern for one another may, if not keep them safe, at least give them the illusion that they have found a way of understanding human life. As Stroud points out, the poem is "a philosophical 'quest' in certain respects parallel to the *Consolation*."[8] The portrayal of their attempt to explain the conditions of existence, to be happy in the face of a universe that is, to say the least, uncooperative, is the profoundest Menippean quality the poem and the philosophical work share.

The most energetic contriver of schemes for happiness is Pandarus. As Chaucer portrays him, we have a conflation of three stock figures from Menippean satire: the friend, the scoffing authority figure, and the manipulating god. Boccaccio's story, of course, gave Pandarus the role of friend; Chaucer complicates his function in the poem by giving him the role of the Philosophy figure in the dialogues with Troilus and that of the *deus* figure in his manipulation of the action. The poem begins and ends with Pandarus playing the part of sympathetic friend, the listener who does not interfere. In the intervening episodes, he rises to the positions of the other two figures.

At the end of book 1, it is apparent as the poem moves from dialogue to action that Pandarus becomes the *deus* figure, the "creator." Chaucer describes his preparations thus at the end of book 1:

For everi wight that hath an hous to founde
Ne renneth naught the werk for to bygynne
With rakel hond, but he wol bide a stounde,
And sende his hertes line out fro withinne
Aldirfirst his purpos for to wynne.
Al this Pandare in his herte thoughte,
And caste his werk ful wisely or he wroughte.
(1. 1065–71)

The last two lines echo the passage in the *Consolation* where Boethius describes the fatal order of the universe projected from the mind of God by comparing it to the artist's plan, which, in due course, he then executes in time: "For ryght as a werkman that aperceyveth in his thought the forme of the thing that he wol make, and moeveth the effect of the work, and ledith that he hadde lookid byforn in his thought symplely and presently, by temporel ordenaunce; certes, ryght so God disponith in his purveaunce singulerly and stablely the thinges that ben to doone."[9] Pandarus goes on to excite, threaten, and cajole Criseyde, encourage and propel Troilus, invent schemes and elaborate illusions, inspire letters, arrange "chance" meetings, play with astronomy. For Pandarus, the affair between the two lovers is an art work; it pleases him as the artists' creation pleases the artist.

In this role of creator and god, he is, like his prototypes, concerned to give his charge exactly what he wants. In Lucian's *Philosophies for Sale*, Zeus and Hermes give each of the philosophers at the auction a chance to show off his wares before all comers, and each peacefully allows himself to be sold as a slave in order to get the attention of those who would otherwise ignore him. Lucian satirically implies that the philosopher's highest aim is, at whatever cost, to get hold of a listener. Nature in the *Parlement of Foules* wishes to give the birds their mates, which is, in merely mortal eyes at any rate, the highest aim of birds. Pandarus, of course, wishes to give Troilus Criseyde. The *deus* figure's adoption of the unnecessary rigmarole of auction, parliament, or courtly love procedures—after all, Lucian's philosophers will show off, birds will mate, and those desperately in love more often than not overcome invisible obstacles and find their way to the one they love—is to elevate the ordinary and produce that comic, delightful, and charming exploration of things that lies at the heart of Menippean satire.

The unnecessary quality of Pandarus' *deus*-like contrivance establishes the basis for the comedy in the first two and a half books. As Chaucer has adapted Boccaccio's story, there is no external reason whatsoever for a secret affair. Both Troilus and Criseyde are unmarried, and Criseyde, as the ease of her social intercourse with the sons and daughters of Priam at the house of Deiphobus shows, is of a social class suitable for a king's son.[10] Criseyde herself is hardly without immediate passionate interest in Troilus, as her words indicate: "Who yaf me drynke?" (2. 651), and later, "Ne hadde I er now, my swete herte deere, / Ben yold, ywis, I were now nought heere!" (3. 1210–11). But when Pandarus encounters Troilus, he is obsessed with the notion of secrecy. A total innocent in love, Troilus has no experience to tell him how human mores organize, direct, and materialize this wondrous feeling. The new lover finds it unthinkable that anyone has loved before him and that the stale customs of those about him could possibly have any constructive course to offer as an outlet for his feelings. Pandarus, like the obliging god, arranges a secret affair, rather than a state marriage, to meet Troilus' desire. Troilus further regards Criseyde as unattainable, and Pandarus, obligingly again, strings out the procedure of approach as long as he can, the most elaborate of his plans being the meeting at Deiphobus' house.

In the dialogue scenes with Troilus, Pandarus fills the role of mentor in the basic Menippean dialogue. Like Philosophy, he appears at the sufferer's need and takes on the responsibility of helping him overcome his difficulties. Various echoes of the *Consolation* make his identification with Philosophy automatic. Like Philosophy to Boethius, he cries "Awake" as Troilus appears to faint (*Consolation*, bk. 1, pr. 2; *Troilus* 1. 729ff.). Like Philosophy, he is described as physician, and Troilus, like Boethius, is described as a patient (for instance, 1. 857, 1086ff.). Pandarus' love of proverbs parallels the objective, maxim-like language of Philosophy; the proverb in its homely way is a method of universalizing and explaining the individual instance of human experience. In his role as the Philosophy figure, as in that of Menippean god, Pandarus is intent on helping Troilus realize his quest. But while the *deus* figure is concerned to give the preoccupied one exactly what he wants (the obfuscation created by his elaborate contrivances is intended to add ceremony to the character's otherwise unimpressive aims), the mentor figure establishes a system antithetical to that adhered to by his interlocutor; his purpose is to place the quest in as direct and objective a light as possible.

The other system which Pandarus as "Philosophy" is intent upon establishing for Troilus in the dialogues of the three major phases of the story (before the affair, during the affair, after the affair) is based on the recognition of flux and change as the given condition underlying all human endeavor. His vision, like that of many of his Lucianic prototypes, is that of the Cynic. In the dialogue of book 1, where he is attempting to rouse Troilus from his despair, he echoes Fortune's words (bk. 2, pr. 2):

> "Than blamestow Fortune
> For thow art wroth; ye, now at erst I see.
> Woost thow nat wel that Fortune is comune
> To everi manere wight in som degree?
> And yet thow hast this comfort, lo, parde,
> That, as hire joies moten evergon,
> So mote hire sorwes passen everechon.
>
> "For if hire whiel stynte any thyng to torne,
> Than cessed she Fortune anon to be.
> Now, sith hire whiel by no way may sojourne,
> What woostow if hire mutabilite
> Right as thyselven list, wol don by the,
> Or that she be naught fer fro thyn helpynge?
> Paraunter thow hast cause for to synge."
>   (1. 841–54)

Pandarus creates a stage set for the particular view he is trying to establish for Troilus at this moment. In arguing that Fortune's being bad to Troilus is grounds for thinking that it will soon be good, he—in the way of the Menippean authority—banks on the belief that Troilus will look only to the next moment in his life, not to the whole pattern implied. Prolonged consideration of the monotony of the ups and downs of Fortune's wheel might well make Troilus despair altogether. Pandarus' stanza on contraries, some lines later ("For thilke growND that bereth the wedes wikke / Bereth ek thise holsom herbes . . ." [1. 946ff.]), has much the same import. In Pandarus' view, change is unavoidable and so are the collocations of good and evil.

In book 3, after the lovers' first consummation, he once again warns Troilus of the ephemeral nature of earthly goods and evils. Like his Menippean prototype, the message he takes from his observations is not withdrawal but knowledgeable confrontation, which involves an awareness of the dangers of being happy with any of the goods of Fortune. The first four lines of this warning echo the *Consolation*, book 2, prose 4:

"For of fortunes sharpe adversitee
The worste kynde of infortune is this,
A man to han ben in prosperitee,
And it remembren, whan it passed is.
Th'art wis ynough, forthi do nat amys:
Be naught to rakel, theigh thow sitte warme;
For if thow be, certeyn, it wol the harme.

"Thow art at ese, and hold the wel therinne;
For also seur as reed is every fir,
As gret a craft is kepe wel as wynne.
Bridle alwey wel thi speche and thi desir
For worldly joie halt nought but by a wir.
That preveth wel it brest al day so ofte;
Forthi nede is to werken with it softe."

(3. 1625–38)

In his conception of Fortune, Pandarus accepts a theory about a universal force outside himself with whose ways human beings can attempt to come to terms. He has no illusions about either its beneficent or malevolent interests in human life. He maintains only that thoughtful consideration may preserve happiness for a time, but he recognizes that worldly joy is hung on a fragile and easily breakable thread.

In addition to the authority's objective, cynical view of

things, Pandarus possesses his prototype's even more important
trait, the ability to switch to a new norm of argument when circumstances demand, a switch, however, which violates his
charge's need for consistency.[11] In book 4, when the change
Pandarus considers inevitable occurs—Parliament's decree
forces Criseyde to leave Troy—he laments with his friend
about Fortune's power.

> "Who wolde have wend that in so litel a throwe
> Fortune oure joie wold han overthrowe?
> . . . .
> Swich is this world! forthi I thus diffyne,
> Ne trust no wight to fynden in Fortune
> Ay propretee; hire yiftes ben comune."
>
> (4. 384–92)

But he instantly proposes an alternative. With fine Menippean
indifference to the complexity of his interlocutor's real desire,
he moves to a new norm which will counter the effect of
change: substitute another woman who is firmly based in Troy.

> "This town is ful of ladys al aboute;
> And, as to my doom, fairer than swiche twelve
> As evere she was, shal I fynde in some route,
> Yee, on or two, withouten any doute.
> Forthi be glad, myn owen deere brother!
> If she be lost, we shal recovere an other."
>
> (4. 401–6)

Pandarus' suggestion willfully misses Troilus' feeling for Criseyde even further, if possible, than the Eagle of the *House of
Fame* misses Geoffrey's feelings about the flight he arranges into
the heavens, or, for that matter, at least as far as Philosophy's
explanations about order miss Boethius' human feelings about
his downfall and disorder.

The shocked Troilus adroitly points out that Pandarus does
not give up his own love even though it is unrequited, that he
preaches what he does not practice. (This is another characteristic of the Menippean authority figure; witness Philosophy on
the subject of poetry.) Pandarus, then shifting to another alternative, seizes on Philosophy's final words on Fortune, which

demand men's heroic confrontation of events, and attempts to make Troilus act in the face of change, to take Criseyde to another city.

> "Thenk ek Fortune, as wel thiselven woost,
> Helpeth hardy man to his enprise,
> And weyveth wrecches for hire cowardise."
> (4. 600–602)

These words echo the passage where Philosophy tells Boethius that it lies in his hands to form for himself what Fortune he pleases and the following meter where she illustrates her injunction with the stories of Greek heroes who found the path of high renown (bk. 4, pr. 7, m. 7). These words in the *Consolation* are not Philosophy's most profound words on Fortune, but they are the only ones which attempt to help man live with its powers. The lesson that Pandarus has accepted to the full is that the human will has the capacity to make a way in a universe without order. Troilus again refuses to accept this suggestion in its entirety.

By book 5, Pandarus' role narrows once more to that of friend. Unchallenged creator of the action for the first three books, he feels the events of book 4 intrude across his authority. The "house" he has erected is violated; indifferent forces come into play and take away his momentary divinity. After the decree, Troilus wants nothing done and so destroys Pandarus' role as "god"; he will not accept Pandarus' antithetical views on how to handle his relation with Criseyde and so destroys Pandarus' role as Philosophy. The one Menippean trait that remains to the end in Pandarus, the first and obviously also the last, is the courtesy to listen. When they face the emptiness of Criseyde's absence, he tries to hold things together a little by playing the part of the sympathizer. He says what he thinks Troilus wants to hear: Criseyde will come back, dreams have no meaning, or he hates Criseyde. Pandarus, with his constructions, has inadvertently created havoc in the life of Troilus. He attempted to make him happy in the ways that matched both his exuberant inventiveness and his Cynic knowledge of the transitoriness of the world. He encouraged a long summer affair. Both the approach of winter and a different conception of a relation with a woman cause his projections to fail.

As Chaucer portrays Pandarus, he is ironically deprived of his major roles by the artificiality of the courtly love scheme he imposes and by the personal element that remains inextricably intertwined with his endeavors. Pandarus presides over only a "game." The limits of his influence are much narrower than those of Philosophy in the *Consolation* because the terror of the problem he proposes to remedy is so much smaller. Whatever uncertainty is set up by love—and in Troilus that happens to be a great deal—there is no moment so fraught with the potential for joy as the moment of falling in love. The worst experience that Troilus has, the personal experience commensurate with Boethius' betrayal by the Senate and subsequent imprisonment, is the experience at the end of the poem when he thinks that Criseyde has betrayed their love. This experience of the worst is not the one that produces in Chaucer's poem a Menippean authority that offers comfort. Pandarus becomes, because of the diminution in the problem he handles, a parodic Philosophy, who can handle only the first phase of Troilus' double sorrow. The personal element in Pandarus' undertakings makes him also a parody of the *deus* figure, and makes his creative artifact ultimately unsuccessful. Because he is deeply involved in the same problem he attempts to solve for Troilus—a hopeless love for a woman—he is not "other" like the Olympian divinities of *Philosophies for Sale*, who have no desire to expound philosophical theories, or like Nature in the *Parlement of Foules*, who has no desire to mate herself, or like the harmonizing God of the elements in the *Consolation* (bk. 3, m. 9), who, being the One, has no impulse to partake of the interaction of the Many.

The artificiality of Pandarus' adopted roles creates a certain unpleasantness beneath the comedy. There is an implicit hint that the affair Pandarus creates is a vicarious (and, as far as Criseyde is concerned, vicious) outlet for his own frustrations. While his own hopeless affair is grounds for Troilus' doubting the efficacy of his advice (1. 622–23) and grounds for Criseyde's teasing (2. 98), the scene that opens book 2 suggests bitter per-

sonal knowledge. As Pandarus rolls and turns in his greenness
on May 3—the day, as John P. McCall has shown, of prostitutes
and unbridled sexual license[12]—Chaucer alludes to the myth of
Tereus, Philomela, and Procne, a myth of rape, murder, and
bloody silencing.

> Pandarus, for al his wise spechc,
> Felt ek his part of loves shotes keene,
> That, koude he nevere so wel of lovyng preche,
> It made his hewe a-day ful ofte greene.
> So shop it that hym fil that day a teene
> In love, for which in wo to bedde he wente,
> And made, er it was day, ful many a wente.
>
> The swalowe Proigne, with a sorowful lay,
> Whan morwen com, gan make hire waymentynge,
> Whi she forshapen was; and ever lay
> Pandare abedde, half in a slomberynge,
> Til she so neigh hym made hire cheterynge
> How Tereus gan forth hire suster take,
> That with the noyse of hire he gan awake.
>   (2. 57–70)

Although every direct statement that Pandarus makes about
his reason for helping Troilus indicates that it is because he
loves him, this passage prefacing his first move calls up the dark
and chaotic depths of sexual passion. Pandarus' aim is to transmute desire by creating a state of artificial order with the courtly
love rituals, one of whose purposes, as Andreas Capellanus makes
evident, is to control the natural violence of desire.[13] But even if
Troilus fares better than Criseyde with Pandarus, the unpleasantness is all-pervading. Pandarus acts the voyeur with them
both as they make love that first night. The narrator hints that
after Troilus leaves, Pandarus takes Criseyde in that high state of
physical excitement and has sexual relations with her (3. 1574).
His disregard for filial obligations cannot quite be ignored. Before he knows whom Troilus loves, he offers his sister at once,
and of course is only too happy to seduce his niece for Troilus
with one of the most disreputable means of human persuasion,
what might be called the conditioning of the trapped beast.

The speeches that Chaucer gives to Pandarus on Fortune reflect his amoral disengagement from and objective view of events. The speeches contain straightforward quotations from and allusions to the *Consolation*, but they ignore the whole universe of moral structures, all the implications and complexities that surround these passages in the *Consolation*. For this character, Chaucer uses Boethius' text as a gold mine of proverbs. Pandarus' speech in book 1 is quoted from the speech of Fortune herself (bk. 2, pr. 2), where her self-centered, devil-may-care attitude represents the most limited view of things that Boethius presents. The general moral of Pandarus' speech in book 3 is also drawn from the second book of the *Consolation*: earthly joys are transitory; nothing man wants of worldly things will ever provide him a sense of permanent happiness. Pandarus' view of life is the view of the surface; he investigates no deeper significance in things. Change is the only certainty. The way of living with this fact, as his final comment about Fortune reveals ("Fortune favors the brave," taken from bk. 4, pr. 7), is to face up to what one wants. The passages are cited accurately without the overt verbal and thematic alterations that create either the burlesque or the philosophical parody in the Boethian speeches of Criseyde and Troilus. The worldly wisdom of the keen-eyed, genial cynic has served him; unfortunately, it has not served others. One of the subjects of the poem is the danger created by those, like Pandarus, who play in the interstices of the world's illogical components but lack the ability to do anything if the conditions change and actual events intrude, an inability which provides the lull that marks the moment in which, for good or for evil, the human struggler escapes from the authority figure in the Menippean dialogue.

Criseyde is the most hesitant of the characters in her projection of a mode of thought and action that will lead to happiness. In the unenviable position of pawn in both her historical setting and in the Menippean dialogue, she is the scapegoat upon whom the crowd may wreak its fury at Calchas' desertion, the substitute "prisoner" whom they may exchange for Antenor. In the Menippean dialogue, she is the object of Troilus' quest and the necessary but undifferentiated piece in Pandarus' game. She has no real place of her own, only the place, the experience, that Pandarus creates for her with Troilus. Living on the fringes of things, she tries to keep attention away from herself. The secret affair under Pandarus' deft manipulations holds the attraction of a "safe" adventure, admittedly a contradiction in terms.

While Pandarus' master machinations provide a kind of human quest for her—namely, a better life with the love of Troilus—their dialogue takes place by the consent of the game in which they admit each other's fakery, rather than by the necessity that underlies the Menippean opposition. In Pandarus' elaborate playing and leaping about in the scene where he tries to get her in the mood to hear of Troilus' love, he takes a hard look at her to feel out exactly how to speak:

> Than thought he thus: "If I my tale endite
> Aught harde, or make a proces any whyle,
> She shal no savour have therin but lite,
> And trowe I wolde hire in my wil bigyle;
> For tendre wittes wenen al by wyle
> Thereas thei kan nought pleynly understonde;
> Forthi hire wit to serven wol I fonde."
> (2. 267–73)

She reacts in kind after he has told her of Troilus' love:

> Criseyde, which that herde hym in this wise,
> Thoughte, "I shal felen what he meneth, ywis."
> (2. 386–87)

Pandarus proceeds on the note of *carpe diem*, but this brings only a bitter lament from Criseyde, which climaxes in the words:

> "What! is this al the joye and al the feste?
> Is this youre reed? Is this my blisful cas?
> Is this the verray mede of youre byheeste?
> Is al this paynted proces seyd, allas!
> Right for this fyn? O lady myn, Pallas!
> Thow in this dredful cas for me purveye,
> For so astoned am I that I deye."
> (2. 421–27)

Having failed with the traditional approach of the seducer, Pandarus adopts more disreputable means of subduing her. He implicitly reminds her of her precarious state in Troy. He threatens not to return, and then with great violence, to kill himself in front of her. Frightened by the kinds of exclusion his act may lead to, she gives in to his demands.

> She gan to rewe, and dredde hire wonder soore,
>
> And thoughte thus: "Unhappes fallen thikke
> Alday for love, and in swych manere cas
> As men ben cruel in hemself and wikke;
> And if this man sle here hymself, allas!
> In my presence, it wol be no solas.
> What men wolde of hit deme I kan nat seye:
> It nedeth me ful sleighly for to pleie."
>
> (2. 456–62)

As Pandarus finds this approach effective in keeping her subdued to his plans, he later threatens her with the supposed malice of Poliphete and the jealousy of Horaste. Criseyde, here and later, like other mortals trapped by a situation they cannot handle, puts a good face on a bad situation, promises Pandarus that she will do what he asks, and turns to find what good he can offer her, namely the love of a man whom she can respect.

In the circumstances that surround Criseyde, she lacks the opportunity for the experience in the immediate present, in the center of life, where the significant Menippean dialogue can take place. Events always throw her into the backwash. Calchas' departure only puts her in the situation where something terrible might happen to her. The experience of falling in love with Troilus could be the startling real experience it is for him at the festival of the Palladium, and is indeed couched in a phrase to suggest it: "Who yaf me drynke?" (2. 651). But Pandarus has created the frame of mind in which she catches her first sight of Troilus, not the opportunity, if it can be called that, to acquire the dignity of that final isolation when she cleanly stakes herself against the unnerving demands of the experience. And, of course, the narrator, apologizing for the wrong reason ("For I sey nought that she so sodeynly / Yaf hym hire love, but that she gan enclyne / To like hym first" [2. 673–75]), hints in his obscure way at the falseness of her entry into loving Troilus. The decree of Parliament (book 4) that she must be exchanged for Antenor is a blow that might have thrown her into the center of things. But she is not present for the news; she hears of the decree by rumor, and Pandarus rather than Troilus comes to see what is to be done. As always, she merely tries to keep out of harm's way, out of that moment when she is forced to experience the worst. She promises Pandarus to console Troilus, promises Troilus that she will return, does all the things she is supposed to do, hoping that the external events of the world accurately provide the authoritative voice her uneasiness can obey in safety.

After the exchange, Criseyde finds herself among the Greeks, in the tenuous safety of a tent, instead of a house, under the protection of a but recently concerned father, instead of Pandarus and the sons of Priam. Diomede's insistent and obvious advances provide for her a parody of the security formerly offered her by Troilus. A kind of ironic pathos results, for in these humiliating circumstances she does attempt to find a recognizable way of life. Nothing larger is open to her. On the night of the ninth day of her absence, she says:

> "But natheless, bityde what bityde,
> I shal to-morwe at nyght, by est or west,
> Out of this oost stele on som manere syde,
> And gon with Troilus where as hym lest."
> (5. 750–53)

But her father will not help her (694–95); she is afraid to go across no-man's-land alone (701–7). No Greek will take her back for fear of the Greek agreement with her father; no Trojan would meet her for fear of Priam's agreement, which has led to the recovery of Antenor. Troilus is incapable of making practical plans for meeting her to help her come back, help which, even if she had been Eurydice, would not have been amiss. Too fearful, missing the pseudodialogue with Pandarus

("And this was yet the werste of al hire peyne, / Ther was no wight to whom she dorste hire pleyne" [727–28]), on the tenth day she begins to speak to Diomede, until at last:

> Retornyng in hire soule ay up and down
> The wordes of this sodeyn Diomede,
> His grete estat, and perel of the town,
> And that she was allone and hadde nede
> Of frendes help; and thus bygan to brede
> The cause whi, the sothe for to telle,
> That she took fully purpos for to dwelle.
>
> (1023–29)

Criseyde's major Boethian speech (3. 813ff.),[14] which deals with happiness, reflects her uneasy conviction, apparent in all her decisions, that anything mortals can desire is too fragile to bear its own weight. The speech appears in the prelude to the consummation scene. Pandarus, creeping through the trap door, wakens her to say that Troilus is dying of the wrench her unfaithfulness with Horaste has given him. At this unreasonable charge, she breaks forth suddenly in a lament for the state of human happiness.

> "O God!" quod she, "so worldly selynesse,
> Which clerkes callen fals felicitee,
> Imedled is with many a bitternesse!
> Ful angwissous than is, God woot," quod she,
> "Condicioun of veyn prosperitee;
> For either joies comen nought yfeere,
> Or elles no wight hath hem alwey here.
>
> "O brotel wele of mannes joie unstable!
> With what wight so thow be, or how thow pleye,
> Either he woot that thow, joie, art muable,
> Or woot it nought; it mot ben oon of tweye.
> Now if he woot it nought, how may he seye
> That he hath verray joie and selynesse,
> That is of ignoraunce ay in derknesse?
>
> "Now if he woot that joie is transitorie,
> As every joie of worldly thyng mot flee,
> Than every tyme he that hath in memorie,

Fortune, Happiness, and Love in *Troilus and Criseyde*

The drede of lesyng maketh hym that he
May in no perfit selynesse be;
And if to lese his joie he sette a myte,
Than semeth it that joie is worth ful lite."
(3. 813–33)

The speech is a cento of maxims from the *Consolation*. The Latin prose from which the first three stanzas of her speech are drawn is the culmination of Philosophy's simple remedies for Boethius' misery at his downfall (bk. 2, pr. 4). Boethius laments in the words that Paolo and Francesca made famous: the worst unhappiness is to have been happy. Philosophy offers four points to show him that he is not in as miserable a condition as he thinks. She tells him first, that he still has the most precious part of his possessions, an honored father-in-law, a loving wife, distinguished sons. Secondly, the state of his happiness has not actually changed: at any moment in human life, happiness is always mixed with unhappiness; some are rich, but ashamed of low birth; some noble, but miserable in their poverty; some lament their childlessness, others their children. Third, she says, man's attitude toward his estate decides his happiness. She points out that the place he calls exile is the homeland of some men, and continues with words Hamlet makes famous: "Nothing is good or bad but thinking makes it so." She tells him, fourth, that true happiness lies only in what cannot be taken away, such as the mastery of self. Because Fortune's goods are easily taken away, they are associated with two kinds of evil, even when possessed: men are either in the precarious position of not knowing their mutability or in the agonizing position of fearing their departure. Her fifth point is that since the soul, the immortal part of man, leaves earthly goods at death, it is obvious that their values are limited.

The outline of the Latin prose is likely to waken only a glimmering recognition in the reader thinking of Criseyde and her speech. Her platitudinous beginning—worldly happiness is mingled with bitterness—is lifted out of Philosophy's third point: attitude determines happiness. Her designation of worldly happiness as "false felicity" comes from book 3 of the *Consolation*, where Boethius dismisses all things earthly for the true happiness which is God. When she laments that the anguish of the condition of happiness is that joys neither come all together nor remain always, she alludes to Philosophy's second point: happiness and unhappiness are the twin elements of human existence. Her second and third stanzas come from Philosophy's fourth point: true happiness has no connection with fortune's goods. She concentrates on the joylessness of ignorance and the fearfulness of knowledge that attends those who possess the goods. These stanzas, an outburst about the impossibility of happiness in this world, probably seem, upon first encounter, unnecessarily elaborate. The feeling is not due purely to our seeing the speech in the ironic context created, on the one side, by Pandarus' lie, on the other, by the joy of the consummation scene which follows immediately; rather, we have the impression that in some way we are being asked to face emotion in excess of the occasion. Criseyde's soliloquies and laments often, be it noted, make such demands on us.

The exaggeration, which has the effect of belittling her anguish, is readily discernible when we compare her situation with Boethius'. Her sorrow is caused not, as Boethius' is, by a loss of her place in the world—not by a loss of freedom, authority, and the right to be heard—but by someone else's jealousy over her nonexistent relations with an unknown man. Not despair, but disappointed exasperation causes her to speak. For confirmation that this belittling is a part of the intended effect, we have only to think of the different effect of the speech had it occurred as she faced the fury of the Trojans after Calchas' desertion of Troy. The diminution can also be seen in the philosophical bases of the speeches. The underlying idea of the Latin prose is that there is a permanent good superior to the feeble attractions of the things of this world. What underlies Criseyde's speech is a sense of continual change. The permanent good is mentioned only as a theory that certain clerks hold. The statements she takes from points two and three of the Latin argument are only clichés; what she takes from point four is its least important subdivision. Her speech is a burlesque of the speech in the second book of the *Consolation* because Chaucer has her employ the grand philosophical idea for the trivial.

The this-worldly orientation of Criseyde's speech contrasts

ironically with book 3 of the *Consolation*, where Boethius makes the search for happiness equivalent to the search for God and the *summum bonum*. The man who has happiness has the highest good and becomes God. That his illustrious state is not attainable by possession of any of the goods of this world— riches, power, honor, fame, pleasure—is made abundantly evident in the first nine proses and meters of the book. But the pro cess by which happiness is to be achieved is not explained in so many words. The only inkling we get of the transition between the definition of the false shadows of happiness in the first nine proses and the definition of the state of true happiness in the last three proses is meter 9, sometimes called a summary of the *Timaeus*. The meter contains a poetic definition of God's power. He is the sower of earth and sky, who sets time in motion, who projects the universe from his mind in his own beautiful and eternal image, who releases the world soul to create the movement of the parts and fills the whole with lesser souls and lives. To be God, then, to be happy, to partake of the highest good, is to be able to create, to be able to place an imagined construction in actual time, to project a universe. This supreme creative act is a central pattern for the joyful intellectual projections which Menippean satire supports. But Troilus, not Criseyde, attains this state.

In the last stanza of Criseyde's speech, we see that Chaucer has given her an implicit creative projection to define what little possibility for happiness she feels.

> "Wherfore I wol diffyne in this matere,
> That trewely, for aught I kan espie,
> Ther is no verray weele in this world heere.
> But O thow wikked serpent, jalousie,
> Thow mysbyleved and envyous folie,
> Why hastow Troilus mad to me untriste,
> That nevere yet agylt hym, that I wiste?"
>   (3. 834–40)

Here we have the suggestion of the paradise image.[15] Jealousy is the metaphorical serpent which has tempted Troilus out of the garden of Love. This image gives us what, in her thinking, takes the place of the world of eternity and the ideas of perma-

nence which lie behind book 2, prose 4, and book 3, meter 9, in
the *Consolation*. For the love that she and Troilus share is associated in her mind with the idea of Paradise, the place of the
walled garden. In various ways Chaucer suggests that for Criseyde, the giving up of freedom for love is the move into a paradise of beauty which eliminates any cause for fear. The image is
first established in the long scene after Pandarus' initial revelation of Troilus' love. Criseyde sees herself and her present life in
the image "untied in the pleasant pasture" ("unteyd in lusty
leese" [2. 752]). She is without fear of being checked in any
way. The following stanza registers a reversal of mood ("To
what fyn lyve I thus?" [757]), in which she restlessly desires a
way. Her mood vacillates between loving and not loving until
she hears the song of Antigone, a pure pastoral lyric in celebration of the paradise of love (827ff.). The ecstatic joy which the
song describes captivates Criseyde. Antigone remarks on the ex-
clusiveness of the real experience and suggests its absoluteness,
its extraworldliness, by her comparison: "Men mosten axe at
seyntes if it is / Aught fair in hevene . . . / And axen fendes is
it foul in helle" (894–96). Light fails all around them, the ladies
leave, and the nightingale sings to Criseyde alone in the darkness. This scene marks the transition from one image to another: the freedom of the pasture to the comfort and magic of
the enclosing paradise.

The idea of love as an enclosed place of absolute happiness is
constant for Criseyde. In the early stages of hers and Troilus'
love she feels that love has opened the gate to all joy (3. 468–69).
Troilus frequently seems to her a wall of steel and a shield. Nor
does she give up the idea later when she hears that she must go
to the Greeks:

> "For though in erthe ytwynne be we tweyne,
> Yet in the feld of pite, out of peyne,
> That highte Elisos, shal we ben yferre
> As Orpheus with Erudice, his fere."
>
> (4. 788–91)

The suggestions in this passage are complex. Paradise is a state
after death now. The story of Orpheus and his love contrasts

ironically with Troilus and his love, as Troilus has not even come to her after the session at the Parliament. That Criseyde speaks the words at this point suggests a futile hope that Troilus will eventually exert himself like Orpheus and rescue her from hell, even if only temporarily, so that they may dwell in the Elysian fields at least in an afterlife. There are sufficient references to her fear of the Greeks throughout the poem to suggest to the reader that she feels that to move to their camp is to move to hell. In her final letter she asks: "How myght a wight in torment and in drede / And heleles, yow sende as yet gladnesse?" (5. 1592–93) Of course, Troilus' love is not hers of the constructed paradise, and he does not understand. He "looked back" to their love before he could make a decision about rescuing her.

Criseyde's Boethian speech on happiness registers her momentary disappointment and her persistent fear of what has seemed to prove (and proves definitively later) to be only too fragile a place of safety. Chaucer, by reducing Boethian ideas to platitudes in order to make a trivial distinction, conveys her irritation at the world's falseness. The speech is not to belittle Criseyde; rather, it conveys to us with a certain sadness her opinion of man's attempts to recognize and actively contain the beauty of this world. In her, Chaucer touches only tentatively upon the godlike happiness of creating a world of joy, for even before the consummation of Troilus' and her love, he has her sense its destruction. She cannot believe for very long; she has too keen a sense of the chaos whose powers ultimately invade life. Her words on Fortune, which seem to echo Pandarus' last words on the subject, are, in fact, distinct from his:

> "Thus maketh vertu of necessite
> By pacience, and thynk that lord is he
> Of Fortune ay, that naught wole of hire recche;
> And she ne daunteth no wight but a wreeche."
> (4. 1586–89)

Her words suggest confrontation by patient waiting, the avoidance of the action that events demand, survival by confinement of one's attention to the immediate.

Admitting no deterministically established power over the destinies of men, she lacks a frame within which to see herself as significant, as definite, or as someone who is able to make a total positive commitment. She attempts to avoid her knowledge of chaos and achieve some greater happiness by passively accepting Troilus' love in the safety of Pandarus' contrivances. When these fail, she eventually drifts into the substitution of Diomede for Troilus. But the extraordinary lack of clarity in her last letters, where she can neither beg Troilus for help nor attack him for his passivity, indicates her dilemma. She has no opponent against which to struggle, no belief in a set of perpetual, unchanging laws which circumstance and chaos cannot alter. She drifts reluctantly on the uncertain streams of chance, clutching whatever momentary assistance is offered her in the establishing of a way.

Troilus, a figure of some complexity in the paradigm of the Menippean dialogue who falls in with Pandarus' plans for most of the story as his subordinate, begins with the objective know-it-all vision himself. At the Festival of the Palladium in book 1, he is a scoffer at love, at the trials of mere creatures reacting to the fleeting joys of time. His falling in love with Criseyde changes his view, and he accepts the Cynical Pandarus as mentor. Like the narrator with his authority, the old story, Troilus is only too happy to accept Pandarus' suggestions and contrivances so long as they give him what he wants; but he rejects them when the events of book 4 bring about the departure of Criseyde and show Pandarus incompetent. Troilus is left to his own human attempts to find a higher and more satisfactory dialogue. He fails and in the epilogue moves back again to the vision of the objective authority, laughing now at all human emotion.

> And down from thennes faste he gan avyse
> This litel spot of erthe, that with the se
> Embraced is, and fully gan despise
> This wrecched world, and held al vanite
> To respect of the pleyn felicite
> That is in hevene above; and at the laste,
> Ther he was slayn, his lokyng down he caste.

And in hymself he lough right at the wo
Of hem that wepten for his deth so faste.
(5. 1814-22)

Except that the narrator, terribly disconcerted at this point and also now finding himself without his guiding authority, inappropriately gives Troilus his alternative for a moment—a Christian heaven—Troilus' indifference is as great as that of Menippus (*Icaromenippus* 2. 295ff.), surveying the meaninglessness of the earth. Troilus, in his spiral, samples the delights of both the Menippean sufferer and his objective opponent. If Yeats' saddened perception was that we cannot have the joys of youth and wisdom at the same time, Chaucer's was that we cannot have love and laughter together, human love (both spiritual and sexual) and philosophical laughter which finds a pinnacle where it is immune to mutability.

Within the span of the love story, the most beautiful of the three characters' philosophical quests for happiness is Troilus'. His conception of the auspices under which he lives is stated most clearly in his Boethian Hymn to Love, the culminating description of the effect his relation with Criseyde has had on him.[16] It is meant to record his feeling during the three years of his happiness, and it immediately precedes the account in book 4 of the breakup of his illusion that perfect joy can last forever. Dramatically, it is presented as the song he sings over and over to Pandarus in the garden, as the summation of the feeling that grows out of the awareness of the beauty and goodness of Criseyde. But for all its heartfelt joy and delight, it, like the free will soliloquy, is a philosophical parody of its Boethian counterpart. That is, the speech is used to ends quite as serious as those of the Latin text, but the context, and hence the point, is different. The reverberations in the juxtaposition echo throughout *Troilus* and behind the assumptions which underlie the *Consolation.*

The Latin meter (bk. 2, m. 8), on which Troilus' hymn is based, is the most important single section in book 2 of the *Consolation*—more important even than the two proses, Fortune's speech (pr. 2), which Pandarus cites, and the discussion of earthly happiness (pr. 4), which Criseyde burlesques. This final meter provides the basis for the general philosophical assumptions which, in retrospect, inform the whole of Boethius' views on the relation of God to the universe. The arrangement of the lines in the Latin text is determined by Philosophy's intent to argue and persuade. She begins by offering obvious examples of concord in nature which all men, whatever their philosophical leanings, can assent to. She concludes with the statement that this concord is caused by a force called Love, whose function is to act as the virtuous power controlling, informing, and ordering nature (and by implication, Fortune) and human society.

> That the world with stable feyth varieth accordable chaungynges; that the contrarious qualites of elementz holden among hemself allyaunce perdurable; that Phebus, the sonne, with his goldene chariet bryngeth forth the rosene day; that the moone hath comaundement over the nyghtes, whiche nyghtes Esperus, the eve-sterre, hath brought; that the see, gredy to flowen, constreyneth with a certein eende his floodes, so that it is nat leveful to strecche his brode termes or bowndes upon the erthes (*that is to seyn, to coveren al the erthe*)—al this accordaunce of thynges is bounde with love, that governeth erthe and see, and hath also comandement to the hevene. (P. 340)

She immediately leaps to the negative position to support her contention; if some force did not keep them together, they would fall apart. She then suggests that harmony in human relationships is caused by the universal power of love:

> And yif this love slakede the bridelis, alle thynges that now loven hem togidres wolden make batayle contynuely, and stryven to fordo the fassoun of this world, the which they now leden in accordable feith by fayre moevynges. This love halt togidres peples joyned with an holy boond, and knytteth sacrement of mariages of chaste loves; and love enditeth lawes to trewe felawes. (Pp. 340–41)

These lines enforce the examples from nature. There are, according to all men's observations, some signs of peace and concord in human relationships; it is not difficult to accept love as the possible cause. But the examples from human relations are less valid than those taken from nature and are well saved for the second group. Fear, self-seeking, custom, and convenience can be thought almost as quickly as love to play their part in alliances, friendships, and marriages.

The concluding lines of the meter take care of the possible objection to the idea of the all-pervasive control of Love by providing a culprit for the discord, the uncertain soul of man. Love's failure is that it cannot control the "animus," the mind and heart: "O weleful were mankynde, yif thilke love that governeth hevene governede yowr corages" (p. 341). The contrast of the perennial symbol of order, the movement of the heavens, with what is the most easily blamed of the symbols of disorder, the human mind, brings into the Latin poem and the book a new level of awareness. The jarring note in the love and peace of the universe is the human mind and heart, which does not achieve its potential. The cause of man's unhappiness is not Fortune's mutability but man's own inability to think and feel in harmony with the universe which surrounds him and of which he is physically a part. For all its seeming innocence, however, this complaint has an ambiguous impact. On the surface, it is the regret that man cannot align his soul to the order and love that embraces all else; below the surface, since the events of his life, his Fortune, are included in this All, the mind's separation is the loophole that allows man his only freedom.

Chaucer completely rearranges and adapts the meter for Troilus' song:

"Love, that of erthe and se hath governaunce,
Love, that his hestes hath in hevenes hye,
Love, that with an holsom alliaunce
Halt peples joyned, as hym lest hem gye,
Love, that knetteth lawe of compaignie,
And couples doth in vertu for to dwelle,
Bynd this acord, that I have told and telle.

"That that the world with feith, which that is stable,
Diverseth so his stowndes concordynge,
That elementz that ben so discordable

Holden a bond perpetuely durynge,
That Phebus mote his rosy day forth brynge,
And that the mone hath lordshipe over the nyghtes,—
Al this doth Love, ay heried be his myghtes!

"That that the se, that gredy is to flowen,
Constreyneth to a certeyn ende so
His flodes that so fiersly they ne growen
To drenchen erthe and al for evere mo;
And if that Love aught lete his bridel go,
Al that now loveth asondre sholde lepe,
And lost were al that Love halt now to-hepe."

(3. 1744–64)

Chaucer's rearrangement destroys the argument of the meter as an argument, for he merges the first and second groups of examples and avoids the concluding lines of the Latin poem. He begins Troilus' hymn with the theorem, Love's power is universal, for it rules earth, sea, and sky, society and fellowship, and causes couples to dwell in virtue. In his second and third stanzas, he turns back to the beginning of the Latin poem to describe Love's power over the laws of nature. In these rearranged lines, there is a complete alteration in basic assumption: human love becomes as certain as the order of nature. Instead of the Boethian argument, we have a lyric poem which celebrates the beauty of personal feeling, where human love accounts for order, not order for human love. Troilus does not attempt to find truth, to persuade of truth. He expects assent before he begins. His concern is only to voice the magnificence and importance of the effect his human love has on his understanding of things. His examples are not points of departure for journeys into philosophic constructs, but elaborate celebrations of his basic emotion. This intense emotional joy in a single individual's experience is not something that can be called on at will, such as the experience the Latin text deals with initially—the order of nature, and Love as the moving force behind it—but Troilus' joy is recognizable to anyone who has loved. The important change, however, is that a feeling gives rise to the song, not what most would take to be an unambiguous scientific observation.

Chaucer's alteration creates a parody of the Latin poem by

proposing another way of looking at the universe. While logic and scientific insight validate Philosophy's words, emotion and, at this point, obliging events validate Troilus' position. Troilus' hymn celebrates earthly love rather than the love synonymous with the universal power that keeps the stars in their paths. This change does not, as is sometimes supposed, create philosophical burlesque, as in Criseyde's Boethian speech, where the great idea is applied to a trivial episode. The sum total of Troilus' being is caught up in this love, and like Boethius, he celebrates both human and universal love. But compared to the logic of Boethius' poem, Chaucer's first stanza has the cart before the horse. The hymn is, in its way, the grand triumph of the pathetic fallacy: because I love, not only men, but all nature loves and could not exist without sharing this feeling.

Troilus' last stanza, a substitution for the last three lines of the Latin poem, pushes the logical aberration apparent in the rearrangement of the first three stanzas to a conclusion that makes intelligible the shift in emphasis. The result is that the speech does not belittle Troilus' love as it would if it were burlesque, but uses the *Consolation* to send our comprehension of it and him to the highest peaks that Chaucer attains in the poem.

> "So wolde God, that auctour is of kynde,
> That with his bond Love of his vertu liste
> To cerclen hertes alle, and faste bynde,
> That from his bond no wight the wey out wiste;
> And hertes colde, hem wolde I that he twiste
> To make hem love, and that hem liste ay rewe
> On hertes sore, and kepe hem that ben trewe!"
> (3. 1765–71)

These last lines, a wish and a prayer, are spoken from what Troilus takes to be the perfect safety of the favored votary. He not only assumes that he has attained the exquisite position whose inaccessibility to men's heart and mind Philosophy laments; he also prays that others may be "twisted" into it. In the divine happiness he experiences, he projects a world in which man is no alien exception to the order of things. He becomes the

Boethian happy man par excellence; he partakes of godhood as his happiness in his human love links him to the harmony of the spheres ("Omnis igitur beatus deus" [bk. 3, pr. 10]). His love gives him a freedom in action, a freedom to shape, mold, and improve his surroundings in a way that he has never had before. His every action, we hear as the book ends, beautifies and orders the lives and manners of all who approach him.

While Chaucer's presentation of Troilus in this speech as the Boethian happy man creating a universe infused by love heightens to a startling degree our perception of the intensity of Troilus' feeling, it also heightens our fear of his hybris at having invaded the realm of the gods. For a moment in this hymn, Troilus has the freedom of Dante's "ie'm la sua volontade è nostra pace." But this is a freedom and joy for angels in Boethius (bk. 5, pr. 2) and the superior dead in Dante—for those, in a word, not subject to dependence on the material vicissitudes of time and change, on the inadequate or misunderstood symbol, on the inevitable participation in those universal lurches that dislocate the patterns which men use to interpret their lives. Chaucer's substituting the stanza of joyful satisfaction for the warning contained in the last lines of the Latin meter supports the sense of unreasonable joy that Troilus feels here.

Troilus has experienced to the full the total joy of which man is capable; he abjures his soul's freedom to contemplate objectively the love he has been given. In this speech, he does not make the logically necessary distinctions, does not defend himself with proverbs like Pandarus, or hedge himself in with man-made devices for insuring a measure of safety like Criseyde. We are tempted to think here that his commitment to the oneness of things is natural: what Fortune gives him is pleasant. But the same attitude is apparent later in the free will soliloquy, where what events offer him is unpleasant: the exchange of Criseyde for Antenor. There he is equally eager to commit himself to his projections of wholeness by refusing to act in such a way as to meddle with what he is given. But the net result of his decision in both instances is to deny himself any insight into the demands of the freedom that his humanity imposes upon him.

Troilus' relations to the other two concepts we have been investigating in this chapter—fortune and happiness—show an identical attitude. His words on Fortune also represent his total trust in the force of outside powers. Fortune is a goddess upon whom his unhappiness may be blamed when he does not have Criseyde and who may be praised when he is happy. In book 1, he had complained:

> "For wel fynde I that Fortune is my fo;
> Ne al the men that riden konne or go
> May of hire cruel whiel the harm withstonde;
> For, as hire list, she pleyeth with free and bonde."
> (1. 837–40)

After the decree in Parliament in book 4, Troilus retires to his room to mourn in the same vein:

> "Fortune, allas the while!
> What have I don? What have I the agylt?
> How myghtestow for rowthe me bygile?
> . . . .
> Have I the nought honoured al my lyve,
> As thow wel woost, above the goddes alle?"
> (4. 260–68)

The allusions to Fortune which Chaucer gives Troilus indicate his necessity to believe in an outside force controlling his destiny, and his unwillingness to act as if he is free.

The references also reveal another trait in Troilus, a tendency to combine unlike concepts in patterns without any awareness of their dissimilarity. The Boethian Fortune affects men's material and physical lives, but she does not bring love or friendship, both being beyond her power. Only dull sublunary lovers with souls of sense should pray to Fortune about their love. Troilus' addresses to her indicate an inability to distinguish between body and spirit, between the ephemeral and the eternal, between the real and the ideal. The lack of interest in distinguishing gives him a touch of the godlike, but it also marks him for tragedy. Unwilling to accept these ancient dualisms, he constructs intellectual patterns out of irreconcilable concepts. As long as these hover ill-matched, but uncomplaining, he is safe; when the absolute tensions of Parliament's decree exert their force, the dualisms drift apart. The payment exacted for insisting that they must stay together is total despair.

The image of Troilus' projection of happiness, the ordered harmony of the universe, is consistently natural. He expends upon his world of love, the joy and belief that the Boethian God gives to the Creation. He believes that his love is perfect and harmonious, that man's effort has no part in it. He is committed in his totality to this conception of things from the moment of his first loving Criseyde until his death. Troilus' sense that all things are inevitable, pure, and orderly, contrasts with the projections of Criseyde and Pandarus. Pandarus' image is a house, a man-made construct. Criseyde's projection for happiness, a garden with artificial walls, is half natural, half man-made. For Pandarus, in other words, happiness is a state one creates. For Criseyde it is in part what one finds, in part what is made by others. But for Troilus, happiness is what one finds. The same attitudes are apparent in these characters' dealings with love and Fortune.

The insertion of the *Consolation* as privileged text behind the characters' speeches in *Troilus* functions to create the simultaneously present angles of approach to philosophical problems characteristic of Menippean satire. The placement and ramifications of the *Consolation*'s theories contrast with those of the Chaucerian characters. The latter's theories, in turn, with their differences in placement and application, call those of the *Consolation* into question. In the end, the presence of multiple views in the poem dramatizes both man's continual attempt to make something meaningful out of life's events and demands and the impossibility of finding any solution in an undecipherable universe. The presence of the privileged text helps to give multiplicity and its attendant irony an unbreakable hardness of absolute "thereness." Because of the technique, no matter what the pileup or collapse of conflicts, the irony, as Elbow puts it, "stays said"[17] in *Troilus*.

In their Boethian speeches, the characters may be seen to read the *Consolation* in the same idiosyncratic way as they read the universe. Pandarus' specific statements on Fortune are in exact accord with those in the *Consolation*, but there are worlds of matter in the Latin text that Pandarus does not touch upon. His abstracted words treat the text as a purely man-made entity without sacrosanct implications or necessary contexts, from which bricks can be taken at will. His words on Fortune, like his proverbs, exemplify the most elementary method of codifying a human experience that has no discernible order behind it. His is the least ambitious of the efforts to see into reality, and he is least concerned with forces outside himself, partly because he recognizes them in all their unknowableness. In making Criseyde burlesque the *Consolation*, Chaucer has her treat it as half serious, half alterable. In effect, she thinks that it says some good things but that they are in the wrong order and have the wrong emphasis. The half commitment, or the total commitment in the circumstances of artificial safety, is the earmark of her attitude toward life. She fears the trust men inadvertently put in the thin crust of things, a too delicate mask to chaos. Troilus' philosophical parody of the *Consolation* treats it as an understanding ally; the borrowings are adapted to fit a context. His relation to the Latin text is natural, though logically inaccurate; no stresses and strains undercut the work's validity for him. Of the three characters, he seems to have the most profound philosophical conception of things because the demands of categories and a realistic appraisal of his situation are excluded from his consideration.

On this side of the irony, the *Consolation* operates as an unbending and ominous standard, a standard which the characters do not reach. What Chaucer omits from their Boethian speeches is the suggestion already implicit in book 2 of the *Consolation* of an eternal, unchanging world; all versions are variants, of course, on the world of the mind: self-mastery, being, providence, eternity. There is, as far as Chaucer's characters are concerned, no happiness apart from this world, no higher order to which Fortune is a minion, no love without human objects. Love perceived as the force that rules the universe falls into the category of a glorious revelation for Troilus only, a feeling he experiences at the height of his joy. But even with him Chaucer reverses the importance of the personal and universal views of love, the personal having the larger portion of attention. Happiness is associated purely with the limited experience of persons basking in the light of good Fortune. When Fortune smiles, the lovers are happy and so is Pandarus; when she frowns, they are unhappy.

Their inability to manufacture an informing principle transcending the immediacy of events in which they are caught up is in a sense the characters' failure. Pandarus fails to see, has no need to see, any larger patterns of moral and ethical dictates at work in the world around him and operates upon the chance of things. His blindness is caused either by a limited imagination or by a philosophic conviction about the nature of reality. Criseyde fails to discover the notion of a mind sufficient unto itself and can find happiness only in the fleeting comforts of earthly love. A woman of basically realistic perception, her fearfulness drives her into the necessity of believing that nothing threatens her. Pandarus and Troilus create a sense of safety and well-being for her; she is able to feel at times that this is a world with impervious walls. But the flimsiness of the illusion is seen in the ease with which it is knocked down, as is evident in the violence of her reaction to the report of Horaste and Troilus' distrust. To maintain her security in this world, she grasps at straws, Diomede being the last of these. Troilus fails to acknowledge the dichotomy between the gods and men and their respective perquisites and celebrates his earthly emotion in divine terms. His blindness is that of a man totally committed to and lost in his idealistic illusions of universal perfection, represented best in the Hymn to Love. In the course of the final books, his illusions are shattered, but not his love.

Yet the catastrophe the characters of *Troilus*, unlike those of the *Consolation*, have to endure in the course of the work allows us to move to the other side of the irony with some ease. Impinging events render ivory-tower theorizing suspect, perhaps useless, for all its delights. The characters' fragile efforts to frame their perceived reality in correspondingly altered terms exact some sympathy from us. When Criseyde maintains that there is no happiness in this world of things and does not revert to Philosophy's ideal of eternity, she is in one sense right. The idea that happiness is in the mind immediately suggests the figure of the weeping Stoic; man's body continually reminds him of the world, and theories that attempt to exclude it exclude the unforgettable. The proof in book 3 of the *Consolation* that men desire happiness, or the highest good, jumps from the negative value of material goods to the world of pure mind. In the realm of logical thought alone, the ascent to truth must be through images, and Criseyde's projection of the walled paradise which emerges from the allusions surrounding her is as true or as false an image of the goal of divine happiness as Boethius' image of the fountain which is the source and end of all rivers. In fact, for the purpose of conveying the feeling of joy, Criseyde's image is better. Here, as always, Philosophy dismisses the problem of feeling and concerns herself only with the structures of formal logic.

Again, with Troilus, we cannot say simply that Chaucer intended to condemn him because he did not arrive at Philosophy's view of things. Troilus' emphasis on personal love instead of universal love may, after all, be regarded as an effort to put first things first. It is a personal feeling like Troilus' which leads man to a theory that the fatal order of determinism may be informed by a force that is soft and beautiful, inspiring commitment, rather than demanding obedience and submission. The fact that Troilus' love was not momentary but lasted for three years, a period in which he felt the oneness of all nature and all men, suggests that his experience was that which provides the easy route to an intellectual concept of eternity and a beneficent God.

The proposed states of timelessness which the Chaucerian characters fail to rise to are, after all, only hypothetical ways of organizing and accounting for the manifestations of time. For all Philosophy's saying so, the concept of Fortune does not, in her Aristotelian section, attach itself well to the concept of the total oneness of the universe projecting from the mind of God. The statement that the fortunes of men are a part of fatal order is not the subject of proof, but merely an aside, listed as a subordinate category of the things controlled by fate: "And this ilke ordre constreyneth the fortunes and the dedes of men by a bond of causes nat able to ben unbownde; the whiche destynal causes, whan thei passen out fro the bygynnynges of the un-moevable purveaunce, it moot nedes be that thei ne be nat mutable" (bk. 4, pr. 6, p. 369). Philosophy, in the same prose, declines to discuss by what agency fatal order is implemented in time: "Thanne, whethir that destyne be exercised outhir by some devyne spiritz, servantz to the devyne purveaunce, or elles by som soule, or elles by alle nature servynge to God, or elles by the celestial moevynges of sterres, or elles by vertu of aungelis, or elles by divers subtilite of develis, or elles by any of hem, or elles by hem alle; the destinal ordenaunce is ywoven and acomplissid" (p. 368). Her final position on Fortune (bk. 4, pr. 8, m. 7) is the ancient one (Fortune favors the brave), framed by an existentialist who doubted the existence of overriding principles in the universe. For Philosophy to end in this way is, in effect, for Boethius to suggest that hypothetical systems are beyond man's power to integrate into his individual experi-ence.[18] In *Troilus*, we find the dramatization of this human in-ability.

One major reason for Chaucer's citing Boethius so frequently in the poem is to remind his readers of man's incessant struggle, the struggle profoundly celebrated in Menippean satire, to pro-ject upon the chaos of things a pattern of coherence which vali-dates his existence. The characters' views and the views of Bo-ethius' systems seem to be both true and both false. They are true as they are formulations of a perceived reality in the mind; one is more highly rationalized than the other. They are false as they are personal and idiosyncratic illusions which men, living and philosophic, construct in reaction to their efforts to per-ceive reality. In part, men cannot bear reality and make illu-sions to defend themselves. In part, they find it dull and create illusions for the purpose of entertaining themselves. In part, they find it tantalizing, an untranslatable experience for which, by some curious compulsion, they are driven to invent a language, in the hope that they may match it and solve the un-solvable. They fill time and space; they are not bored; but they do not succeed.

The technical reason for Chaucer's citing the *Consolation* is that textual parody, the invoking of an instantly recognizable and powerful alternate text, creates a dialogue in the mind of the reader; the text grafted in forms another dimension of a present in which varying time schemes and ideas penetrate each other without merging. What men have called the sacred mingles with what they have called the profane, the pagan with the Christian, the moral with the amoral and immoral, the past with the present. There is a mingling of styles high and low, of modes comic and serious. The new images and colors emerging from the superimpositions loom as potential human universals hitherto unrecognized. The juxtaposition of old and new texts offers to readers the possibility of acquiring a position of knowledge higher in the great silence of Menippean satire than they have been able to hold before.

5

Freedom in *Troilus and Criseyde*

*There is no need to show at length, that nature has no par-
ticular goal in view, and that final causes are mere human
figments.*

Spinoza

Whatever similarities or ironic dissimilarities can be shown
to exist between *Troilus and Criseyde* and the *Consolation*,
there is one way in which they differ totally. The *Consolation* is
a Menippean comedy, and *Troilus* is a Menippean tragedy. Menippean comedy portrays the game of flitting lightly from one
lily pad to another to avoid the ever-present threat of sinking in
the pond; Menippean tragedy portrays the fixation on an aspect
of a perishable leaf and the too-prolonged pause that tumbles
the searcher into the water. In the *Consolation*, Boethius, the
figure parallel to Troilus in the dialogue, follows Philosophy's
leaping from point of view to point of view, from system to system, with only one major outcry (bk. 5, pr. 3); but even then,
he is quickly silenced, and they move on together, as Aristotelian determinism gives way to Augustinian theology. Philosophy, in other words, succeeds in keeping her charge in tow; her
capacity to propose eternally new solutions remains undimin-
ished. We have a brilliant Menippean comedy. In *Troilus*, Pandarus, like Philosophy, is constantly moving from one position
to another in his effort to balance Troilus' unrealized desire.
But while Troilus follows where he is led for a time, he finally
refuses to take Pandarus' view that one woman is as good as another or that any action is better than total passivity. Troilus
freezes, the lily pad gives way, and he sinks into the water.

Troilus, in failing to adopt, if not Pandarus' direction, at
least his attitude, fails to appreciate the mobility of the human
intellect and the capacity of the human imagination to find
new ways out. The awareness that because nothing is know-

122

able, our joy must depend on our actively and imaginatively experiencing to the hilt any knowledge and power we possess, fails to impinge upon Troilus. In the face of the unignorable events that alter his situation, he insists on the validity of one formulation, one object, one way of having the joy he had during the three years of his love. He refuses to face the future, to investigate the loopholes for freedom in the contingencies of the present. The narrator in the frame dialogue makes an analogous refusal. We have a doubly focused Menippean tragedy.[1]

The earlier critics, especially Curry, argued that an oppressive sense of fate dominates the structure and philosophy of the poem.[2] But I propose to argue the reverse, to argue that the tragedy is created not by the definable presence of fate but by its unalterable absence and that it is the characters' unsuccessful struggle to overcome the latter horror which defines a major element in Menippean tragedy. The work embodies the moment when the Menippean satirist drops his support of men's royally energetic inclinations to make constructs, the moment when the satirist demonstrates the maxim of the child in the fairy tale: "The king has no clothes on."

In an important sense, fate holds in Troilus the same place it holds in the *Consolation*. It is a major concept but not one to be mistaken as a successful name of that which ultimately controls. It is the name of a facet of a theory made to explain—and men's explaining is the only way they have to defend themselves against the unintelligible—some part of what they encounter. In the *Consolation*, any given theoretical explanation may be deterministic, but Philosophy's ability to move unhindered from one theory to another provides the expected Menippean sense of intellectual freedom. In both works philosophical theories, professional (those of Philosophy) or amateur (those of Chaucer's characters), are projected over a series of events totally indifferent to men's conclusions. No new events, it is true, intrude in the *Consolation* to call Philosophy's proposals into question; she and Boethius remain safe in the castle of the mind. But underneath this theorizing there lurks Boethius' exile, unjust condemnation, isolation from his family and friends, and denial of the right to live his life as he has chosen. Philosophy's theories, alternatives to simple spiritual despair at the denial, do not in any way change these unpleasant and powerful realities. In *Troilus*, we have a horizontal, rather than a vertical, juxtaposition of events and theories which prove impotent to affect or explain these events. Chaucer's alteration of emphasis from theory to event makes possible the dramatization of the inadequacy of theories and explanations.

By focusing on the two hopeful but unsuccessful determinists, Troilus and the narrator, I hope to show that Chaucer's complete acceptance of Menippean satire's governing universal abstraction, freedom, forms the bedrock, the hard core, behind his presentation of characters and their acts in the poem. Fate or doom, so often spoken of in conjunction with this poem, has only the place of a major actor in freedom's play. Fate is the name of the culprit that both the narrator and Troilus propose to explain the chaotic depression that events in the story cause. But their proposal is the result of their human need for an overmastering authority that suspends their responsibility for exercising their freedom and their overwhelming sense of man's inadequacy to alter anything in a universe that, after all, does not align itself to their need for understandable meaning.

Troilus' bitter recognition that outside events can break up the experience that for a time created for him the miracle of transcendent splendor, meaning, and worth leads him in his six major scenes in books 4 and 5—the most important being the scene at the temple (4. 946ff.)—to struggle to believe that Criseyde's departure and his despair are as determined by the nature of things as he took his love to be. In each scene he fails to find the fate that supersedes his freedom. The narrator, in the same way, fights a losing struggle against the dictates of his "old story," whose power to subvert his deepest desire—namely, to protect Criseyde from her reputation for infidelity and to obscure the part that Troilus' passivity and (alas) hopeless idealism play in bringing it about—leads him into citing the Boethian hierarchies at sporadic moments to avoid assuming the poetic authority to comment with insight on the events he records. He too fails, for as the poem closes, his knowledge of the accountability he does not wish to accept rends apart his narrative structure. In the epilogue, his story and his fatal theories having failed him, he, and the conclusion with him, falls to pieces.

The principal passage in the poem that has led to the statement that fate dominates it is Troilus' Boethian soliloquy in the temple (4. 953–1082), a passage which Chaucer added to his already completed manuscript of the poem. It has aroused more attention than any other Boethian passage used by Chaucer in any of his works. A difficult speech, it has often laid Chaucer open to the charge of making an artistic blunder.[3] While I am convinced that the passage is an important illustration of the Menippean attitude toward theorizing, it is useless to deny that the elementary problem faced by every critic and reader— whether he or she condemns the speech or finds some way of justifying it—is that Chaucer makes it nearly impossible to wade through.

The prime difficulty is caused neither by the lack of appeal in the subject, nor by the total absence of dramatic relation to the events which immediately precede and follow it. It is caused by Chaucer's failure to reproduce for Troilus the involved intellectual desperation and dedication which Boethius gives to the problem he is trying to solve. When we find ourselves at the temple with Troilus, we are prepared for a short prayer; we are even prepared for a long one, Troilus' general preference, although we know him here to be under a pressure he has not experienced before. But we expect the prayer to be for guidance among various alternative courses of action, not a prayer which denies over and over the possibility of action. Troilus meanders along in a startling offhand way, wavering back and forth between the opinions on both sides of the question of those who, as he puts it irreverently at one point, "han hir top ful heighe and smothe yshore" (4. 996).

In the second half of the speech, where he does speak in first person and in the chair *exemplum* even lectures a hypothetical "you," he has jumped from the question of the fated will, which was troubling him to begin with, to the question of the foreseen will, which has only an incidental bearing on his problem. The increasingly fringe-like quality of his involvement with the subject stands in contrast to the Latin argument, where Boethius fights to clarify for himself the question of free thought with any tools he can lay hands on. Boethius, in this particular dramatic situation, rides the high ridge of an intense philosophical and human predicament. Troilus, by comparison at least, drowns in the stagnant pool of withdrawal from human commitment to conflict, both physical and intellectual. The parodic overtones in his speech make it as difficult to read as do the lack of dramatic tensions surrounding it.

If we examine the speech to find just what it is that separates it from the aims of Boethius in the same area, the main initial difference we discover is that the two speakers concern themselves with different kinds of freedom.[4] An examination of the Latin speech, as well as of any section in the *Consolation* for that matter, will show that Philosophy is deeply interested in only one kind of freedom: the freedom of thought. It is the existence of this freedom that Boethius questions at the beginning of book 5, prose 2: "But I axe yif ther be any liberte of fre wille in this ordre of causes that clyven thus togidre in hemself. Or elles I wolde witen yif that the destinal cheyne constrinith the moevyings of the corages of men" (p. 374). To this Philosophy answers that those are most free who set their minds on God; those who concern themselves with their bodies and the things of the earth are the captives of their own freedom.

Proving that freedom of thought exists is what Philosophy dedicates herself to in the concluding portion of the fifth book. Physical freedom, though mentioned now and again, is only a tangential concern. If Boethius had been deeply concerned by the problem of the existence of this freedom, he would have rebelled at the end of book 4, prose 6, where everything that moves in the world is proved to be a part of the order of fate; certainly it would have been made a part of the prisoner's question in book 5, prose 2. Because he is not directly concerned with the question of free acts, as might be expected, the words *fatum* and *libertas arbitrii* are never discussed in conjunction in the Latin text.

In contrast to the *Consolation*, the kind of freedom with which Troilus is concerned is freedom of action. The theme is enunciated at the beginning of his speech:

Freedom in *Troilus and Criseyde*

"For al that comth, comth by necessitee:
Thus to ben lorn, it is my destinee.

"For certynly, this wot I wel," he seyde,
"That forsight of divine purveyaunce
Hath seyn alway me to forgon Criseyde."
(4. 958–62)

He is concerned with the predetermined quality of physical events, in particular his impending loss of Criseyde, not foresight's hindrance to thinking or feeling. The contrast may be seen in the formulation of the two theses underlying the speeches: for Boethius, it is to prove that his mind is still free; for Troilus, it is to prove that the events of his life are still determined. The reversal of the thesis of Boethius' speech has a very profound effect on Chaucer's deployment of the material Boethius gives him. For instance, the new thesis defines for us the difference in the psychological necessity behind both speeches. In the *Consolation*, too much talk of logic and order—or, in other words, the threat of determinism—causes Boethius to struggle for freedom. In *Troilus*, the falling down of the walls surrounding the events of his life—or, in other words, the threat of freedom—causes Troilus to struggle for determinism.

Troilus' whole speech, in fact, is his effort to argue himself out of his uneasiness into a position of safety, safety being a state of affairs in which he need not exert himself into choosing an act that will enable him to keep Criseyde. He wants a continuation of the dream world of love, harmony, and beauty for which Pandarus has manufactured a setting. He wishes to attribute the authorship of his world to fate and God and not to its obvious author, Pandarus. He begins by citing the universal powers which make him unable to stop her departure. He decides that he is fated to lose her: necessity and destiny arrange it thus; providence has foreseen it. This list is indeed an impressive array of forces compelling him to acquiesce in Criseyde's departure. These lines are cast in the form of a statement, not of a doubt or a question.

He goes on to support his feeling by citing what, for his purposes, is a mind-lulling theory of the relation of men to God's

127

justice: God through his order disposes everything according to its merits by his predestination.

"Syn God seeth every thyng, out of doutaunce,
And hem disponyth, thorugh his ordinaunce,
In hire merites sothly for to be,
As they shul comen by predestyne."
(4. 963–96)

Troilus assumes not only that he is fated to lose Criseyde, but that a just God gives him what his merits deserve in depriving him of his beloved. This second condition is highly convenient for Troilus' game, as it averts any necessity for passionate anger (which might stir up action) against a God who rewards without seeing or creates men unable to merit reward. Men have, according to this theory, enough freedom to earn their judgment; the implication is that he, Troilus, has none in this case, because to lose Criseyde is what his acts have already merited. Patch remarks: "In other words Troilus wishes to indicate that he is not responsible for the present disaster, but he wishes to do so piously. There is a kind of self-pitying humility in his attitude. He will not trouble to blame anybody else, God or man, so long as it be acknowledged that he himself has been opposing unfair odds and that he has never really had a chance—with all due respect to the Creator's sense of justice."[5]

Feeling safe that his philosophy will not cause him to act, he embarks briefly on the subject of the debate between fate, which great clerks support, and free choice, which some men insist on. The latter theory, even if not the province of the "great" clerks, is a potential threat to his safety:

"But natheles, allas! whom shal I leeve?
For ther ben grete clerkes many oon,
That destyne thorugh argumentes preve;
And som men seyn that, nedely, there is noon,
But that fre chois is yeven us everychon."
(4. 967–71)

The closest that Boethius comes to mentioning a theory of the universe where freedom exists without fate is in a reference to Augustine's statement that Cicero in *De divinatione* dismissed predestination in order to save man's dignity (bk. 4, pr. 4).[6] This alternative poses a universe with different rules from those Troilus assumes to begin with. If there is only free choice, then there may be no ordained order. Troilus is not prepared for excursions into this thought, which, if accepted, would increase rather than decrease the responsibility to act, which he is trying to avoid.

Protesting that he does not know which sly clerk to believe (4. 971–72), he slips back at the beginning of the next stanza into his chosen universe of omniscient, omnipotent gods. But he avoids the obvious continuation of his subject, namely the debate between predestination (fate) and free will, the debate that centers on the problem of whether action or the ability to initiate action is possible. He turns instead to the debate about the conflict between foresight and free will.

> "For som men seyn, if God seth al biforn,
> Ne God may nat deceyved ben, parde,
> Than moot it fallen, theigh men hadde it sworn,
> That purveiance hath seyn before to be.
> Wherefore I sey, that from eterne if he
> Hath wist byforn oure thought ek as oure dede,
> We han no fre chois, as thise clerkes rede."
>   (974–80)

His change of course indicates that, again frightened by the nearness of his probing to the subject of his own action, a matter he does not wish to have to consider, he slips over to a safer one, which is only loosely related to his problem. I suspect that at this stanza, most readers' attention begins to wander uncontrollably.

This, the beginning of the main body of the speech, is a close adaptation of Boethius' outcry in bk. 5, pr. 3. Chaucer follows the first part of the speech exactly: (1) Troilus states the thesis that God, who cannot be deceived, foresees all; hence man has no free choice in either thought or deed (4. 974–94). (2) He thinks over the debate about the order of causes, whether God's providence causes the events to come or whether the events to come cause God's providence (995–1022). (3) He goes through the *exemplum* of the viewer and the man sitting in the chair; he concludes that the order of things is that true opinion in the viewer about the man's sitting depends on the sitting, rather than the sitting on the viewing. Nevertheless, the two things are interdependent (1023–43). (4) He applies the example to foresight and the event of future things, concluding that even if the things to come were the reason for God's foresight, it would make no difference to man and his free choice, since the things must come. He then dismisses as ridiculous the idea that temporal events can cause God's knowledge (1044–71). (5) He ends with the observation that when he, Troilus, knows a thing to be or to come, then it must be or come. The same must be true of God's knowledge also (1072–78).

Except for the intent which underlies it, the passage is very close to the Latin text. But this middle corridor leads Troilus to a goal different from that of Boethius. Boethius continues, going deeper and deeper into the contradiction between God's providence and man's freedom, until he is at last forced to cry out at the terrible alienation of man from prayer and a personal God. Troilus stops, passing out of the argument at this point, having satisfactorily convinced himself that he has no free choice (and therefore need not exercise it), and that events in the future are safely set up (and that therefore he has no need to attempt to influence their forming). In good logical fashion, he has proved what he assumed. But a paradox appears in the conclusion to Troilus' speech. Boethius, with only slightly more evidence than Troilus cites, saw that if what he assumed were true, then man would have no moral responsibility and prayer would be impossible. Troilus, quite unaffected by any of the logical consequences which the proof of his assumptions has just set up, concludes his soliloquy with a prayer to Jupiter:

> "Almyghty Jove in trone,
> That woost of al this thyng the sothfastnesse,
> Rewe on my sorwe, and do me deyen sone,
> Or bryng Criseyde and me fro this destresse!"
> (4. 1079–82)

Not only has Troilus' argument proving that everything is determined convinced him that he can pray; it has also convinced him that the future has alternatives, that not all is fated. Prayer too, after all, is a projection in which the one praying assigns attributes to his God. Troilus' imagined Jupiter is capable of creating a good solution as well as a bad. Troilus' ability to imagine that God is free provides in his imagination the inevitable corollary that there are forces other than fate in the universe. Willy-nilly, Troilus in his last stanza is in a position directly opposite to the one he began with, namely the conviction that for him everything is unalterably fixed.

The dramatic debate of the Latin text is in fact transformed by Chaucer into an inner debate. One side of the debate lies in the spoken words of the speech; its thesis is that there is a predestined order of events. The other, whose thesis is that man is free, runs in Troilus' head as he argues and acts as devil's advocate in the debate; its presence and power are indicated by the jumps in the argument, and in Troilus' lack of wholehearted commitment to the logical demands and consequences of his argument.[7] The silent opponent finally triumphs and releases Troilus from his initial and, to our minds, depressing assumption; it has made him free again. Of all experiences with freedom, the most magnificent is to be released from the oppression caused by what we ourselves assume. It is a freedom far beyond any that could be derived from the structures of formal argument. The effect here, of course, is semicomic. Troilus, for all his intellectual effort to deny himself freedom, is once again threatened with the pressure to do something about stopping Criseyde's departure for the Greek camp. Pandarus, speaking up at this point, attempts to get Troilus to act in freedom, to reject his relationship to Criseyde, to take her away, or at least to wait and see what happens in the interview with her.

The kind of change that occurs in Troilus' thinking is a clue to Chaucer's purpose in adding the speech. The philosophical argument—which involves the conflict of freedom and God's foreknowing, foreseeing, and foreordaining—is generally interesting only when it occurs to us that the formulations that can be rung upon it have nothing to do with our lives, but are only one of man's more exacting ways of playing God; that is, the debate is a way of creating cohesions and relationships between unlike things, hence of creating importance and meaning where none exists. Whether the artifact matches or mirrors or reflects some ineffable reality is not of as great an immediate interest as the revelation in a parallel situation: that where only mortar, stones, and cement once existed, we now have a cathedral. The debate has the attraction of all creative endeavors; it places new, three-dimensional constructs in time. We have only to think of Chaucer's two other passages on the subject of fate and free will, in the *Nun's Priest's Tale* and in the *Knight's Tale*, to see that it was as a method of structuring pieces of a known reality, not as a method of approaching truth, that the problem from time to time excited his interest. Instead of saying, "One day a fox caught a rooster," he greatly increases the triviality of the event for his mock heroic purposes by saying that fate had conspired on that day to create one of the world's great tragedies, a tragedy, moreover, foreordained in a dream. In the *Knight's Tale*, instead of saying, "One day Palamon and Arcite met at a grove and fought until Theseus and Emily came along and stopped the fight," he magnifies the total improbability of the meeting by explaining how destiny, the minister-general of providence, brought it all about. Troilus is involved dramatically in the human pastime which Chaucer lets the Nun's Priest and the Knight use on these other occasions. Troilus, instead of saying, "Without any of my own effort, I have attained a perfect love and do not wish to exert myself now that I seem about to lose it," jumps, in his fear, into philosophy, where he tries to re-create the clerks' three-dimensional realm to escape the freedom he possesses, an activity which, for him, rather exasperatingly results only in a cathartic release into the state of being free once more.

The Boethianism of Troilus' soliloquy is of a very special sort. There are no telling parallels in dramatic situation or philosophical conclusion. Boethius' words provide structured ways of thought about the raw realities of existence which Chaucer uses as a commentary on those separately apprehended realities. For the prisoner, Boethius, the speech in the *Consolation* is the climax of his effort to objectify his desperate sense of man's predicament. But to Philosophy, this ephemeral desire is insignificant; and the speech, within the Menippean intellectual system of the *Consolation*, is only a momentary flaming illumination of man's physical dungeon. In this Menippean satire man's freedom lies in the contemplation of the brilliant light shining forth from the great minds of the past. For Troilus, the speech in the temple, which shares so many words with the Latin book 5, prose 3, is merely a structure that he attempts to build for his protection in a universe which, he suddenly sees, offers no visible guidance whatsoever. Chaucer, with telling implications, here establishes an incongruity between the philosophical words and their application. The speech, in fact, provides an excellent philosophical parody of the speech in the *Consolation* and an even better parody of the uses of determinism.

Troilus' soliloquy on freedom is a part of a larger pattern apparent in books 4 and 5 of the poem, in which Chaucer presents Troilus' varied attempts to handle the catastrophic event which destroys his expectations of happiness, the exchange of Criseyde for Antenor. Each stage consists of three major phases: (1) Troilus becomes aware that all is not determined for his happiness (nor, of course, for his unhappiness, though he sometimes interprets it that way), and he experiences the chilling existence of freedom; (2) he withdraws from the threatening event and attempts to isolate and suspend his own relation to it; (3) through an outside agent, he experiences a sense of release from his obsession, where for a time, at least, things are in balance, momentarily contained, and provide a situation in which he is willing to choose an action. This pattern is repeated with variations three times in book 4 and three times in book 5. His soliloquy in the temple is the second stage in his progress to knowledge.

The first stage begins at the Parliament near the beginning of book 4, Troilus' elementary initiation to the conditions of freedom and chance in human life. Hearing that Calchas has arranged the departure of Criseyde, Troilus hesitates to withstand the exchange because of the need for secrecy. This has been one of the prime conditions of his and Criseyde's relation. He further hesitates to speak against it because of the conflict within himself between love, whose motives are selfish, and reason, whose motives are honorable; the latter suggests to him that he must ask Criseyde whether she wants to stay. Only Hector hits on the proper public grounds for attacking the proposal: Criseyde is not a prisoner and should not be used in an exchange of prisoners. But in the great outcry of the mob that Antenor be returned for the good of the city, a motive Troilus honors, Troilus again is silent.

Faced with this abyss, Troilus withdraws, the second phase of the pattern. Instead of acting by going to Criseyde with the news or deciding on an action contrary to the decree, he accepts the decision as irrefutable, as irrefutable as his love. In this state of emotional conflict, he withdraws to his room, where he experiences the naked shock of the reversal of his lot. Compared to a tree in winter, a dead image, and a wild bull, he vents his rage, which culminates in the conventional question of the reason for his birth. He questions the disposition of fortune, which so unfairly deprives a votary of his deserts, asks Love how he is to live without her, and compares himself to Oedipus. But he is not finished. He further addresses his spirit, his eyes, Criseyde, and fortunate lovers, whose prayers he requests. His thought turns to Calchas' vengeance and his new Greekness, which Troilus finds particularly irksome.

Pandarus' appearance begins the third phase of the pattern and puts an end to Troilus' isolation and withdrawal. Pandarus' simple presence changes the atmosphere from winter to spring, and he brings release into action in spite of Troilus' adherence to codes that provide grounds for hesitation. That Troilus' attempts to come to terms with the new situation are honorable is seen in his rejection or qualified acceptance of the main strands of Pandarus' advice: forget her and find another; or else take her away from Troy. The first, Troilus labels advice for a fiend; the second—the obvious act for a great lover—he rejects on a number of grounds: the war is fought over the abduction of a woman; the exchange involves his father's word and the good of the city; love demands secrecy. Pandarus' insistence that all laws are broken for love and his promise that he and all his kind will fight to the death to support his flight with Criseyde makes Troilus at least agree to a meeting with her. The three-phase pattern is repeated in the structure of the speech in the temple. Troilus states the thesis that he is fated to lose Criseyde, withdraws into the momentary safety of his theory that the human will is foreseen and fated, and releases himself with the illogical conclusion that he can pray to Jupiter, who has alternatives. Again, Pandarus leads him back into action.

The third stage of Troilus' confrontation with freedom occurs in his last night with Criseyde. Heretofore he has supported Parliament's decree as the way which must be accepted. Pandarus has had alternatives. In this scene, however, Troilus has the vicarious experience of seeing Criseyde advance his position.

> "My goyng graunted is by parlement
> So ferforth that it may nat be withstonde
> For al this world, as by my jugement."
> (4. 1297–99)

The plan she proposes is that she will return to Troy; that in the Greek camp she will convince her father she is happy in the city, will appeal to his greed by promising to send him goods from Troy, will prove his gods false to him. Her plan requires no effort from Troilus, and after her promise he acquiesces for a while, though with some doubt. But later, after they make love, his doubt about her proposal resurfaces and looms larger than the comfort of his acquiescence. The alternative that Criseyde is offering has a singularly unfateful quality about it. He had tried to make her promise more absolute by telling her how miserable he will be if she does not return (4. 1336ff.). Now he points out that her father may not fall in with her plans and may force her to stay (1450ff.). As a result of his doubt he twice proposes Pandarus' alternative: let us go to another city (1499, 1600ff.). But Criseyde clings as tenaciously to the decree and all it represents as he had earlier. Troilus fails to make the practical proposal that he and Pandarus will meet her on a specific night to bring her back across no-man's-land. In the end the decree still rules his life, but it has completely failed him as the fated way of order and peace. He is wretched in his freedom.

In book 5, the three stages of the pattern are the same and

correspond in certain specific ways to those in book 4. The opening scene, the exchange of prisoners and its aftermath, parallels the Parliament scene in book 4, but everything is more intense. Troilus watches an action proposed in book 4 actually taking place. The theoretical is now an immediate reality. In the end, as at the Parliament, he does nothing. He watches Criseyde go, and she is lost in the maze of another experience. He withdraws to his bed as he did after the Parliament, but his emotional anger here is profounder than in the earlier scene. He curses the universe, the gods, fate, nature, himself, everything but Criseyde. He compares himself now to Ixion, who was bound to the eternal punishment of Tartarus for his hybris in casting loving eyes on Juno. Troilus has not only given up all thought of action, but even the belief that any action is possible. The desperation of his loneliness comes out in nightmares where he is cut off both from the beauty of the earth and, in a moment of extreme danger, from his comrades (5. 246ff.). As in the first sequence in book 4, Pandarus comes along to release him with practical suggestions, the most useful of which is the proposed visit to Sarpedon's.

The second sequence begins on the tenth day on the wall. While the demarcation of this sequence is not as clear as the parallel scene in book 4—the soliloquy in the temple—it also climaxes on the issue of whether what is known at a given moment is fate. Criseyde breaks her promise to return on the tenth day; without reference to the time it took, we are given an account of her betrayal. Troilus endures the delay at first by finding excuses for her. When that fails he withdraws into a desire for death and into nagging jealousy, and dreams of the boar holding Criseyde in his arms (5. 1238–46). With Pandarus' interpretation—the boar is her dying father—he is still hopeful enough to write a letter to her. At last he gives up these semi-futile gestures and retires to his bed. He is released by his sister Cassandra's interpretation of his dream: Criseyde loves Diomede. Though this is precisely his own interpretation, he is so angry that he is cured. He is also free once more. As in the scene at the temple, he decides not to interpret given facts (decree, dream) as fate. Be it noted, however, that his returned awareness of freedom does not cause him to act positively, and in the vacuums of his lack of commitment, those "facts" slowly seep in to take over the position of "what happened."

The final stage begins on the day that Diomede's armor is brought into town. The brooch convinces Troilus that Criseyde's absence is final, that her promise is broken. Unable to give up his own love, Troilus withdraws from life as he had come to think of it and turns to war and the search for his death in battle. He is successful: Achilles kills him. In death he is released even further from the dictates of any fate as he looks down on the earth and laughs. The similarity between this final sequence and the sequence that concludes book 4 lies in the change Criseyde precipitates in his way of thinking. In their final night together her adherence to the decree causes Troilus to reject it and leads him to advocate a stand against it. What he takes as proof of her infidelity in book 5 leads to his rejection of her promise, the "fate" he has attempted to believe in throughout this book. In both cases, the decision amounts to a conscious rejection of fate for belief in the freedom of an alternative action.

Troilus holds to the idea that something outside him, not requiring his active support, governs his life: Fortune in the three years of Criseyde's love, the decree of Parliament in book 4, the promise of Criseyde to return in book 5. These representations of that "fate" he is determined to believe in are wildly dissimilar, and the scale descends in a pitiable way. Fortune belongs to the Boethian hierarchy and is universal. The decree has certain fateful qualities about it which enable us also to acknowledge its force. It represents the authority of an official body in human society; the business of state for the moment is war, and the exchange of prisoners is an important part of the rules. This exchange has neither knowledge of nor interest in the loves of Troilus and Criseyde. Its sublime indifference allies it at least temporarily to fate. Although it alters Troilus' world, it does provide some support for him in the way of laws and precedents.

In book 5, although the given is that the decree is fulfilled and Criseyde is gone, Troilus attempts to believe that it is her promise to return. The whole of the action of book 5 revolves around the illusion of his error. Her promise has the same effect upon him as Parliament's decree; it cancels any attempt at action. The truth of the new situation, as the exchange was the truth of the former, is that Criseyde is absent and helpless. This is the neutral fact against which he could act. Just as he saw in the final scene in book 4 that he could keep Criseyde from going to the Greeks by taking her to another city, so here he could steal across no-man's-land to get her, but Pandarus does not suggest this course of action, and Troilus thinks of it only in such a way as to reject it.

> And ofte tyme he was in purpos grete
> Hymselven lik a pilgrym to desgise,
> To seen hire; but he may nat contrefete
> To ben unknowen of folk that weren wise,
> Ne fynde excuse aright that may suffise,
> If he among the Grekis knowen were;
> For which he wep ful ofte and many a tere.
>   (5. 1576–82)

The inaccuracy of the belief that anything human can represent fate is, of course, inherent in Troilus' elevation of the decree. But his blind belief that fate is a fragile promise given to quiet his belated thoughts of action reaches tragic proportions. The promise is a human and individual makeshift created by Criseyde to mask her necessity, which is as deep as Troilus', to accept the decree. It has no authority; even in its inception, its strongest motives are peripheral to their love, for it is spoken by a fearful woman to a passive man about an unimaginable future to keep her word to her uncle not to cause Troilus any further unhappiness.

As it becomes apparent to Troilus in the course of books 4 and 5 that there will be no further help from divine agencies, he creates havoc in his relationship with Criseyde by his refusal to create his own independent pattern, to accept freedom, to ignore or reinterpret or transcend certain human relationships, codes, restrictions. Pandarus, at points, tries to teach him the advisability of acting in disregard of some of the protective duties he drags with him.

Freedom in *Troilus and Criseyde*

"Frend, thow maist, for me,
Don as the list; but hadde ich it so hoote,
And thyn estat, she sholde go with me,
Though al this town cride on this thyng by note.
I nolde sette at al that noys a grote!
For whan men han wel cryd, than wol they rowne;
Ek wonder last but nyne nyght nevere in towne."

(4. 581–88)

But Troilus consistently rejects practical advice that requires imaginative exertion. He wants everything to fit—his commitments to father, to country, to Criseyde, perhaps, above all, his commitments to an ethical code which will preserve the wholeness and goodness of things. Troilus is the example of man's determination to believe—from the point of view of Menippean satire, a hopeless effort—that there is an objective and comprehensible guiding reality, even when the images out of which his belief originates desert him. His failure lies in his inability to search with the necessary desperate imagination for a mode of action that will enable him to retain Criseyde in the face of these requirements. For action, he substitutes a belief in fate. But the fate he wants to believe in is not a compelling outside power dictating the totality of his future; it is simply "what has happened."

This is exactly the narrator's definition. Chaucer presents the narrator—the character representative of time in the Menippean dialogue, who struggles against the masterful "story" in the frame dialogue—in an experience parallel to Troilus'. On a much larger scale than Troilus, he attempts to make fate responsible for events so as to avoid the knowledge and consequences of having to deal with a story in which there is no explanation for the depths of human sadness. Desperately eager to find a culprit (other than his beloved characters) for the events he recounts, he alludes to Fortune over twice as many times as the other characters put together, and on occasion to the whole of the Boethian framework, eternal providence projecting destiny into time. We fall easy victims to the sense of doom that hovers over these passages, for we share the narra-

139

tor's level of knowledge. (Yet in this poem, as in any other which uses the device of the narrator, it is important that we come to our own level above him.) Even if, to begin with, we do not know the exact events of the story he is to tell us, we know that Troy fell and that the Calchas-Antenor episodes have a dramatic and tragic irony unfelt by the characters whose lives we witness. We know, too, after the first stanza of the poem, that what we are to hear is Troilus' double sorrow and the progression of his state "Fro wo to wele and after out of joie" (1. 4), and after line 56, that Criseyde betrays him. We wait for the announced, and hence for us as for him, dramatically fated final events. The narrator's references to fate, fortune, and destiny, in view of our bondage from the beginning, emphasize what we already accept.

But after these initial warnings, the remainder of the first three books contains no further hints, an indication that when the narrator has events that appeal to him to narrate, he does not concern himself with doom. But in the prologue to book 4, again he tells us that Fortune raised up Diomede and threw down Troilus.

> From Troilus she gan hire brighte face
> Awey to writhe, and tok of hym non heede,
> But caste hym clene out of his lady grace,
> And on hire whiel she sette up Diomede.
> (4. 8–11)

And book 5 opens with this analysis:

> Aprochen gan the fatal destyne
> That Joves hath in disposicioun,
> And to yow, angry Parcas, sustren thre,
> Committeth, to don execucioun;
> For which Criseyde moste out of the town,
> And Troilus shal dwellen forth in pyne
> Til Lachesis his thred no lenger twyne.
> (5. 1–7)

Finally, at the end the narrator associates the death of the city with the death of Troilus:

Fortune, which that permutacioun
Of thynges hath, as it is hire comitted
Thorugh purveyaunce and disposicioun
Of heighe Jove, as regnes shal be flitted
Fro folk in folk, or when they shal be smytted,
Gan pulle awey the fetheres brighte of Troie
Fro day to day, til they ben bare of joie.
(5. 1541–47)

We at first accept passages of this sort at face value as the conventions of epic, but when we think of the knowledge they are based on, in this narrator's case, we are forced to reconsider.

The narrator is sometimes thought of as being omniscient and therefore in a position to know whether fate and similar powers rule in the events of the world he presents to us. Since he says fate rules, it does not occur to us at first to suspect his motives for assuming the role of determinist. When the narrator declines to tell us of the city's destruction (1. 141ff.), we are nevertheless reminded of other accounts, and our regret for the destruction of things draws the stock responses from us. But if we place his omniscience against the definition of omniscience which we find in the *Consolation*, we see that he is only all-knowing about the past. This knowledge of past events does, it is true, dictate his present (his prayer to the gods for aid and his writing) and his future (his poem). But this present and this future have nothing to do with the time span of the story. About the events the characters live through, he is—to be precise—one-third as omniscient as the Boethian God. His knowledge is parallel to the view of God which Boethius rejects as absurd (bk. 5, pr. 3): a God whose providence is caused by things that happened long ago. The subject of the poem, its events, the lives of its people all fall into the category of what is already over. The narrator, knowing the story, can say the characters were doomed to do as they did. For him, as for Troilus, fate comes to be "what happened," a definition which reduces the concept to a nonsensical level. In a sense, the destinal passages, if we may call them that, are ornamental flurries, which, like a sudden outbreak of accompanying music, color and distract our reaction to the picture that is moving before us. These passages appear when events go wrong and warn us that the narrator's fatal structures are emotional rather than intellectual or factual necessities, which enable him to hide from what he feels and to endure the chaos that he contemplates.

It is evident in his method of narration that Chaucer intends the narrator's embrace of doom at certain points to represent an emotional necessity having little to do with the facts of the universe he portrays. The key events in the lives of the lovers, the epic devices which create a sense of fate in other poems, the characters' diverse reactions to sudden change, are handled in such a way as to remind us of the disconnected and inexplicable quality of events. He reminds us of a universe in which all explanations and chosen actions are only two levels of projection in an indifferent chaos. The two most important events in the lives of the lovers, the Festival of the Palladium and the decree that sends Criseyde out of town, are both treated as normal and customary and are set up without reference to the Boethian hierarchies. The festival, where Troilus by chance falls in love with Criseyde, is held every year, and it goes on in spite of the siege:

> Hire olde usage nolde they nat letten,
> As for to honoure hir goddes ful devoute.
> (1. 151–52)

The exchange of prisoners, where Criseyde is given for Antenor, belongs to the theme of chance by virtue of the kind of description the poet uses to explain its cause. Hector determines to fight "as he was wont to do" (5. 35). The Trojans have a bad day and lose many men; they arrange a truce to make some exchanges. The explanation is that "on a day" the "folk of Troie hemselven so mysledden / That with the worse at nyght homward they fledden" (4. 48–49). The narrator makes no references to either fate or fortune or any supernatural powers. The following truce is a normal event which grows out of the stresses, strains, and rules of war.

Similarly, the devices for indicating the presence of fate in an epic action, which Chaucer employs—the intervention of the

gods by oracle, act, or predictive dream—are handled in such a
way as to siphon off their normal fate-marking power in epic.
Chaucer undercuts Calchas' oracle from Apollo by having Calchas consult various other methods of predicting the future before he believes the oracle:[8]

> So whan this Calkas knew by *calkulynge*,
> And ek *by answer of this Appollo*,
> That Grekes sholden swich a peple brynge,
> Thorugh which that Troie moste ben fordo,
> He caste anon out of the town to go;
> For wel *wiste he by sort* that Troye sholde
> Destroyed ben, ye, wolde whoso nolde.
>
> (1. 71–77; my italics)

And later in book 4:

> "*Appollo* hath me told it feithfully;
> I have ek founde it be *astronomye*,
> By *sort*, and by *augurye* ek, trewely,
> And dar wel say, the tyme is faste by."
>
> (4. 114–17; my italics)

Chaucer also makes nothing of Calchas' general prophetic
powers. If in book 1 he had added a stanza for Calchas to be-
moan with helpless, tragic regret the danger in which he places
his daughter because of the god's compulsion, if in book 4 he
had added a stanza suggesting Calchas' prophetic, silent satisfaction that Antenor, for whom Criseyde is exchanged, will betray Troy and bring about the predicted event, if he had added
a stanza of at least minor regret (for a parent, the unhappiness
of a daughter in love is hardly on a par with the prospect of her
rape and murder in a burning city) at taking his daughter from
Troilus, Chaucer would have caused us to believe that there is a
fatal order dictating the action of the poem's present, which the
prophet, but no one else, perceives. Chaucer does not even
have Calchas tell Criseyde of the doom of Troy, that that is
why he left and why he has asked that she be given to him.[9] Because Chaucer makes nothing of Calchas' general prophetic insight, his foreknowledge has unfortunate affinities with the
natural instincts of rats who leave ships about to sink and mines

about to fill up with gas. His belated interest in Criseyde seems merely a resurgence of an equally primitive instinct: blood is thicker than water. The only strong sense of fatality his oracle sets off is that in our own minds; we know, as the narrator knows, that Calchas was right: Troy did fall.

This oracle, unlike the oracle in Sophocles' *Oedipus*, is also powerless to create an original and dramatic sense of fate because it is not linked to the direct cause of events at the beginning of the action. For instance, Troilus does not fall in love with Criseyde when he sees her kneeling before Hector, begging for mercy. Instead we get a new scene, a new story, and a new god. Hearing Troilus' contemptuous sneering at lovers, the God of Love hits him with an arrow.

> At which the God of Love gan loken rowe
> Right for despit, and shop for to ben wroken.
> He kidde anon his bowe nas naught broken;
> For sodeynly he hitte hym atte fulle;
> And yet as proud a pekok kan he pulle.
>   (1. 206–10)

But after this first bolt, Love tangles in the story no more. It would be perverse without Chaucer's outside help to read the story as the working out of the punishment for Troilus' initial contempt. The bolt has no fatal and tragic power like the love potion of Tristan and Isolde, who must love whether they will or not. There is no question of Troilus' taking a second "Criseyde" (Pandarus' suggestion), as Tristan takes a second Isolde, though with total lack of success at freeing himself. Troilus deliberately chooses to continue loving. The intervening gods of the poem begin events, but it is men's free choices that organize, interpret, and end them.

The epic dream, the boar kissing Criseyde (5. 1232–41)—a standard device that suggests the presence of a fateful foresight and doom dictating the course of the action—would be structurally predictive only if it preceded the action in question. Chaucer places it after the account of Criseyde's betrayal, and though the sequence of scenes at the end of the poem are not entirely chronological,[10] the dream, by being placed afterwards,

144

ceases to act dramatically as a prediction and seems for the reader at most an example of extrasensory perception, or possibly only of Troilus' repressed fears.[11]

Everything connected with the dream has a natural or simple psychological explanation. Troilus senses Diomede as a rival the minute he sees him; Cassandra's lengthy exposition can be read as a virtuoso teasing of a lovelorn brother. She smiles as she begins (5. 1457), a gesture that keeps us from feeling that she speaks *ex cathedra*. The only fact that she needed was that Diomede acted as escort for Criseyde; she doubtless saw that for herself on the day of the exchange. Lineages were no secret. Chaucer does not arouse the expectable ominousness by telling us that Cassandra was never wrong. We hear of her powers only in Troilus' furious rejection of them (1420ff.). Nor would this information have any point for trying to get us to believe in a fated action unless the dream and the interpretation both preceded the account of the betrayal. It is that ardent, but unsuccessful determinist Troilus who, after seeing the brooch, tells us long afterwards that the dream proves that the gods predict the future.

> "O Pandarus, that in dremes for to triste
> Me blamed hast, and wont art oft upbreyde,
> Now maistow se thiself, if that the liste,
> How trewe is now thi nece, bright Criseyde!
> In sondry formes, God it woot," he seyde,
> "The goddes shewen bothe joie and tene
> In slep, and by my drem it is now sene."
> (1709–15)

Had the narrator's determinism been of a philosophical sort, furthermore, he would not have left his characters with such varied reactions to the outside events that unexpectedly impinge upon their lives, events whose indifferent power is most fully apparent at the opening of book 4. On that day when the Trojans lose many men, forces interlock and profoundly affect the lives of the five main characters. They play variously with the opposing counters of fate and free will in this moment. For the characters of the Greek camp, Calchas and Diomede, the moment provides the opportunity to get something they want (in both cases, Criseyde), but their attitudes toward the oracle place them at different points on the scale of reactions to fate and freedom, the extremes of which are total belief in fate and total belief in freedom. Calchas believes firmly in the existence both of oracles that cannot be ignored and freedom to reorganize his own life as well as he can in the face of this given by first getting out of the city and then later retrieving his daughter before the city falls. His instinctive way of flinging himself out of the path of his city's doom is a successful exercise in the use of freedom. But that his human desire to avoid disaster makes him go over to the Greeks, the agents of this doom, to be on the right side at the kill, also makes us condemn his act, even if he tries to rectify matters a bit by retrieving Criseyde.

The opportunist Diomede believes only in freedom. By luck assigned to escort Criseyde to the Greeks, he has no awareness of fate, no awareness that there are ominous powers which will suddenly rise up and destroy the hopes of the great and small alike. The early death of his father, which deprived him of the kingship of Calydon and Argos, is a temporary setback which he intends to overcome (5. 932–35). He believes in his strength, in the Greeks' strength, and consequently in the doom of Troy. To Criseyde he says:

> "Swiche wreche on hem, for fecchynge of Eleyne,
> Ther shal ben take, er that we hennes wende,
> That Manes, which that goddes ben of peyne,
> Shal ben agast that Grekes wol hem shende.
> And men shul drede, unto the worldes ende,
> From hennesforth to ravysshen any queene,
> So cruel shal oure wreche on hem be seene.
>
> "And but if Calkas lede us with ambages,
> That is to seyn, with double wordes slye,
> Swiche as men clepen a word with two visages,
> Ye shal wel knowen that I naught ne lye."
>   (5. 890–900)

For him the chief function of Calchas' oracle is to frighten Criseyde into accepting his love:

Freedom in *Troilus and Criseyde*

"What! wene ye youre wise fader wolde
Han yeven Antenor for yow anon,
If he ne wiste that the cite shoulde
Destroied ben? Whi, nay, so mote I gon!
He knew ful wel ther shal nat scapen oon
That Troian is; and for the grete feere,
He dorste nat ye dwelte lenger there.

"What wol ye more, lufsom lady deere?
Lat Troie and Troian fro youre herte pace!"
(5. 904–12)

The attitudes of the three Trojan characters toward fate and
freedom are also diverse. Their lives are directly touched only
by the sequel to the oracle, the Trojan Parliament's agreement
to the Greek proposal. Criseyde, like Diomede, believes in freedom, but while his belief is occasion for opportunistic assertive-
ness, hers is occasion for terrified withdrawal. Her reaction to
the decree is sharply tempered by her original experience with
the results of her father's oracle. For an act in which she did not
participate, she finds that her fellow countrymen suddenly
turn as a mob against her. That Parliament's new interest in her
in book 4 is one carefully controlled by the laws of the truce is a
much lesser threat to her. The catastrophic nature of this event
which breaks up her love affair is therefore sharply repressed,
and with Pandarus' persuasion she attempts to sink it to the
level of a normal phase of expectation. She has only to do what
they say, and she will be safe; she will not have to be terrified of
being in that wall-less place where only freedom operates.

Her inability to bear terror makes her turn great things into
trivial ones. The lament Chaucer gives her in book 4 after the
departure of the women, who concretize the rumor through
which she has first heard of Parliament's decision, is almost a
rhetorical exercise in the method of diminishing a lament. She
rends her curly blond hair and wrings her small, long fingers.
The tears fall like April showers. She compares herself without
Troilus to a fish without water, a plant without proper soil. She
promises to starve herself to death for fear of touching cruel
pointed instruments, promises to wear black in token of death,

147

and wishfully thinks of the two of them after death as an Orpheus and Eurydice. The narrator's sympathy only diminishes the effect further.

> How myghte it evere yred ben or ysonge,
> The pleynte that she made in hire destresse?
> I not; but, as for me, my litel tonge,
> If I discryven wolde hire hevynesse,
> It sholde make hire sorwe seme lesse
> Than that it was, and childisshly deface
> Hire heigh compleynte, and therfore ich it pace.
>
> (4. 799–805)

Criseyde, unlike her lover and her father, has no contact with the gods and no belief in them, either in her father's one-dimensional oracle god, or in Troilus' all-embracing God of beauty, harmony, and order, whom he has discovered in the ineffable splendor of his love for her. The size of her universe is determined only by her own projections, which Pandarus has done much to augment. The size of her world shrinks immediately upon being threatened. Criseyde has a sense keener than any character but the narrator of what it is that makes men want to believe in the gods and fate: the great abyss of chance and a universe without walls. She craves security as much as Troilus, but the security she wants is the security that only human beings can give to one another. Her necessity to allow diminution of thought, feeling, possibility, to protect herself from freedom, destroys their love quite as effectively as Troilus' necessity to believe in fate.

Pandarus' reaction to the unalterable event is similar to Calchas'. At the Parliament he has no doubts that the exchange affects their lives deeply:

> Pandare, which that in the parlement
> Hadde herd what every lord and burgeys seyde,
> .   .   .   .
> Gan wel neigh wood out of his wit to breyde.
>
> (4. 344–48)

Like Calchas', his reaction is to find alternatives, to deal with the situation as creatively as possible, and with a similar dismissal of moral obligations. While he retains his allegiance to Troilus, he writes Criseyde off—there are at least twelve women in Troy as fair as she (4. 400–406). But when Troilus will not listen, he tries to goad him into action by writing off any commitments Troilus has to duties outside Criseyde. Pandarus, like Calchas, accepts the idea that the looming up of insurmountable obstacles calls for changes in action. Both men recognize that human beings are free to choose acts of their own in the face of compulsion. Success, for both men, is the act of analyzing whatever alternatives are available and committing oneself with energy and, if need be, amorality to the new course one carves out.

The decisions of the characters about fate and its lieutenants indicate their character quirks, not the reality of the universe upon which they exercise their minds. The poem juxtaposes a linear flow of events whose causes are unknown against the projections of the various characters. Their projections vary in beauty and scope and goodness. The characters vary most, however, in the strength they possess to survive the dawning recognition that the courses of their lives are subject to alteration. The readjustments in the story are Calchas' willingness to take on a new nationality, Pandarus' willingness to create a new affair for Troilus, Criseyde's willingness to try to love Diomede forever, all of which are contrasted with Troilus, who holds to his love for Criseyde till the end.

> "I ne kan nor may,
> For al this world, withinne myn herte fynde
> To unloven yow a quarter of a day!
> In corsed tyme I born was, weilaway,
> That yow, that doon me al this wo endure,
> Yet love I best of any creature!"
> (5. 1696–1701)

Without Troilus and the narrator, who both embody the Menippean temporal spokesman's desire to find a single theoretical order (and in the *Consolation* "ordo" is a synonym for "fatum") in the chaos and indeterminancy of life's contingencies, the sense of fate in the poem would be negligible.

Chaucer's very moderate use of the stage devices for producing the effect of fate and his use of characters who stand in varied relationships to their own freedom hammer to death the notion that fate rules. The free universe being proposed by Chaucer is not completely without restrictions, of course—as Patch points out,[12] everyone admits a degree of compulsion in human affairs—but it is not as restricted as Troilus and the narrator would have it be. The "fate" we feel in the poem is not an overwhelming power emanating from some titanic force which manipulates the universe and its men. Fate comes to the fore as freedom is refused. It is associated with the weight of patterns, conventions, rules—traditional obstacles which men drag around with them and accede to without thinking, in preference to operating in the void of freedom before them. These are the norms Menippean satire uses as its obstacles for attack. These are the weights that Menippus and Philosophy triumph over, the weights that Pandarus, who plays the role similar to theirs, unsuccessfully seeks to countermand for Troilus. But the concept of fate that is talked about in the poem is only the name of an organizing concept for the characters which removes some of the responsibility for freedom, which, if they are perceptive, as the narrator and Troilus are, they can hardly bear. The narrator's struggle to create a sense of doom parallels Troilus' effort in the temple to prove that all is determined. It is his way of resisting the omnipresent existence of freedom, the uneasy fact that nothing seems to have a purpose, and the intolerable idea that the reason Troilus and Criseyde act as they do is that they choose to, that the world's terrible sorrow is caused by the weakness of the human imagination.

What obsesses the narrator—for his imagination, too, betrays its human faults—is not an external inevitability that haunts the present moment of human life, but the abysmal emptiness he senses, an emptiness that offers neither guidance nor interference. He hangs onto fate much the same way he hangs onto the belief that his story is true and cannot be changed. Though he acts the part of historian, as Bloomfield points out,[13] he is continually reminding us of what any historian would simply assume, namely that he had no part in and cannot control the events he narrates. His protestations are excessive and make us uneasy, not to say suspicious, about his motives. For instance, we may wonder why he should elect to retell a story that makes him so sad. He takes as his subject the "double sorwe" of Troilus with himself as the "sorwful instrument" of the story. Even the third book, where he puts aside his woe for a while, ends on a note of weariness at keeping it up ("I kan namore"), of enduring the inspiration of the deities who have permitted him to sing of such joy. The last two books are full of his desperate sadness, a sadness which overtly, at least, reaches its climax when he must speak of Criseyde's infidelity. We are probably taken in by all this protesting until we see that the sadness topos represents a kind of backhanded atonement for his refusal to exercise his authorial freedom.

For example, in the midst of the account of Criseyde's betrayal he suddenly has her utter a lament. At this point and, indeed, through the end of the poem, the love affair is known only to the lovers and Pandarus, is suspected only by Diomede and Cassandra. Criseyde says:

> "Allas! of me, unto the worldes ende,
> Shal neyther ben ywriten nor ysonge
> No good word, for thise bokes wol me shende.
> O, rolled shal I ben on many a tonge!
> Thorughout the world my belle shal be ronge!
> And wommen moost wol haten me of alle.
> Allas, that swich a cas me sholde falle!"
>
> (5. 1058–64)

In this speech, which is a part of the narrator's attempt to excuse Criseyde, he completely violates what he has presented as her normal reaction under pressure: to diminish the event. Here there is only gross exaggeration. It might be argued that her infidelity is the most violent of the situations in which she finds herself in the poem and would therefore call forth a different reaction. But the nature of the narrator's exaggeration is such that he raises Criseyde into his own level of awareness; he gives her a vision of the future out of his knowledge of the past. Criseyde laments as if she knew she were to be a character in a

151

story known to later generations. This is the narrator's most frantic effort to avoid the freedom to interpret, to penetrate, a freedom he does not wish to accept. He supports his bondage from the most unlikely source possible, the vision of his character, who is necessarily blind to the future. Like Troilus, he wants to find the higher happiness and order, different from the cruel freedom of the natural world. He is even less successful than Troilus.

His attitude to his story is like his attitude to fate, an illustration of his attempt to find an authority that will hold and free him from having to take on any responsibility. It might seem, of course, that the narrator was barred from changing the events so that they would have pleased him better. But such changes are hardly an unheard-of liberty for authors. In the original story of King Lear, both Lear and Cordelia survive the events of Shakespeare's play. Shakespeare kills them. Shakespeare himself in telling the story of Cressida and Troilus told it in a quite different manner from Chaucer. And Chaucer is certainly not adverse to making changes in his sources. His Palamon, not Arcite, sees Emily first. His Pertelote, not Chauntecleer, mocks the significance of dreams. Pandarus the friend becomes Pandarus the uncle. Criseyde the whore becomes Criseyde the enigmatic. Certainly without changing any major event of the story, the narrator was free to explain Criseyde's failure to return in any number of ways, free to react against a set pattern of events by interpreting them so as to leave Criseyde blameless, at least for a reader who could see the situation in its completeness. For instance—various possibilities spring to mind —she could have been physically imprisoned and so closely watched that escape was impossible; her mind remaining free, she could have been made to stay with the threat from Diomede that if she is not friendly, he and his friends will do nothing else all day long but try to kill Troilus. There are obviously many ways of explaining her staying, but the narrator does not avail himself of any of these. Instead, he weeps, he loves her, and he protects her from the charges against her by relentless apology (which often, be it noted, deepens our sense of her guilt).

But more profound than his regret about Criseyde is his love of Troilus. Graydon makes an excellent case to show that Chaucer adopts Benoit's time scheme for the events of book 5, rather than Boccaccio's, where we are certainly to assume that Criseyde accepts Diomede in sixteen days or so.[14] The adopting of Benoit's time scheme means that two years elapse before she accepts Diomede, not, in fact, until the night he returns from the battle where he lost his armor with the brooch on it. The narrator carefully gives the betrayal no date in the time-warp passage (5. 1032–85), but because we have read of her defection, Troilus' doubts about her fidelity in the remainder of the book seem legitimate as we read them, and not the manifestations of a shameful distrust in a man who cannot will an act to help her. The narrator's tactics obscure the impact on events of Troilus' tendency to inactivity, which begins after his first encounter with Criseyde and continues in the Parliament, in the temple, and in their last night together, when he tells her over and over that she will not come back again. When his jealousy causes him to reveal their secret love to Cassandra and when he adds insult to injury by accusing Criseyde of betrayal in his letters, we casually assume that he has grounds for complaint. The narrator's withholding of information helps cover Troilus' hopeless passivity and fatalism, whose awful effect is to destroy the possibility for renewal and continuance of his relation with Criseyde. If the narrator attempts to protect Criseyde, so does he rather more successfully protect Troilus. The confusion of time scheme allows him to avoid stating one of the terrible rules in Menippean satire about the power of the human mind—that Troilus found at last what he imagined and Criseyde at last what was imagined for her.

This narrator—a man obsessively trying to protect his two main characters from the results of their story, yet at the same time exhibiting those unalterably human traits he desperately wishes absent in them, fatalism and hesitancy—is Chaucer's masterly device for focusing, underlining, and universalizing the Menippean view of the human condition dramatized in the poem.

In the end, the surfacing of the brooch having drained the possibilities for hope or concealment out of the "old story," and its authority having failed him, the narrator is forced to go on by himself. In the epilogue, he is no better at "telling his own tale" than he is as the narrator of the *Canterbury Tales*.[15] He intersperses the final events of the story with an explanation about his choice of subject matter (Troilus' deeds of love rather than his deeds of arms), an apology to ladies for telling of Criseyde's betrayal, a warning against the wiles of men, and an address to his book. With the words "But yet to purpos of my rather speche" (5. 1799), he comes back to recount the death of Troilus and his laughter from the eighth sphere. At this point, the story having failed him absolutely, he frantically switches to another vision of happiness: an address to "yonge, fresshe folkes" (1835) telling them to love Christ, a condemnation of his old pagan story, and finally a dedication to Gower and Strode, which ends with an address to the Trinity. The style Chaucer has chosen for this conclusion—that of random outbursts on a variety of inconsistent subjects—belies any attempt to believe that he here represents for the narrator a definite alternative. All the characters have struggled with varying degrees of energy to project into the meaningless nothingness of habits, conventions, and uninterpretable events, a pattern of coherence through which they can achieve happiness. Troilus, Criseyde, and the narrator are unable to will new forms of projected thought and action. Willy-nilly, they defeat themselves.

Chaucer calls *Troilus* a tragedy: "Go, litel bok, go, litel myn tragedye" (5. 1786). Like *Hamlet*, however, it is not a classical tragedy, nor is it, as it is sometimes said to be, an illustration of Fortune's definition of tragedy in the *Consolation* (bk. 2, pr. 2), not, in other words, a so-called medieval tragedy.[16] In terms of the classical definitions—these are the terms in which most of us first try to read it—the poem is nearly too depressing to bear, so depressing, as Lewis says, that no one would willingly read it a second time.[17] There is no Aristotelian catharsis, no purging of the illusions in the three characters' and the narrator's visions of the events in which they take part. We have no sense that whatever the ravages wreaked by an inexorable fate, there is a spiritual triumph which illuminates and makes infinitely worthwhile men's efforts to find the limits of their humanity.

Criseyde drifts into another love story. Pandarus, the controlling figure in the poem whose delineation provides whatever sense of intellectual stability is left at the end, knows only what he knows at the beginning: change is the only certainty. The outright rejections of earth which we encounter in the epilogue destroy even further the possibility for classical catharsis. Troilus, from the eighth sphere, by laughing at those mourning his death, dismisses the effort of men to celebrate each other's significance. The narrator turns from human love to divine love, a shift of perspective even more startling than that of Troilus.

Nor can the tragic sense that the poem establishes be well contained by Fortune's shallow echo of Aristotle in the *Consolation*, a definition which Chaucer satirizes so relentlessly in the *Monk's Tale*: "What other thyng bywaylen the cryinges of tragedyes but oonly the dedes of Fortune, that with unwar strook overturneth the realmes of greet nobleye? (*Glose. Tragedye is to seyn a dite of a prosperite for a tyme, that endeth in wrecchidnesse*)" (bk. 2, pr. 2; p. 331).[18] Troilus' reactions to the events of his life represent a spiral rather than a simple fall. He moves from scoffing laughter at love to unhappiness in love, to joy, to despair, and up and around again to scoffing laughter at all human emotion. Negating further the sensation of his "fall" are the occasional references to his public life. Troilus' status moves from that of good warrior to that of superlative warrior infinitely ennobled by his love (1. 1972–85; 3. 1772–1806), to that of great hero who dies like Hector fighting Achilles. The narrator, though he occasionally elects to forget about it, knows from the beginning that he recounts a "double sorrow," and thus can hardly be thought to "fall." Criseyde's bursts of commitment to the various actions that she takes are too controlled and doubting for us to view the end as a plunge. In fact, only Pandarus' relation to events can be understood in relation to a pattern of "fall from high degree." He begins as unchallenged controller of the action and descends into the position of a total incompetent, who has succeeded in giving his friend only a knowledge of love's frustrations very much like his own.

The tragedy of *Troilus*, like the tragedy of *Hamlet*, finds its axis in the cosmic state of uncertainty.[19] Neither protagonist will accept the *status quo* after the encounter with the supernatural figure (ghost, God of Love); each must go on hoping there is some better way of understanding and acting in the universe. Both characters share a preoccupation with the problem of how the complexity of human thought can be translated into matching action. Neither learns, but in the end, each has done as directed. Hamlet has killed Claudius. Troilus has loved Criseyde. The uneasy sense of incompleteness we have at the end of both works is caused by the absence of an outside force, plan, or law manipulating events, the absence of what T. S. Eliot called the objective correlative. There is no sense of fate, *dike*, balance, or *Wyrd*, such as we feel in Aeschylus and Sophocles, or in *King Lear, Macbeth*, and *Beowulf*. As we watch and experience the failures of characters caught in the attempt to find a way of validating the projections they wish to cast upon the universe, we are saved from the abysmal sense of emptiness only by the profundity of our conviction that they deserved indeed to experience the metamorphosis that would transmute the beauty of their imaginings into some tangible reality.

Classical tragedy's catharsis depends on the principle of compensation (loss and gain) or balance (the equality between two things) and climaxes in the protagonist's and audience's recognition that one set of forces is identical with another, that one chain of events is equal to the other. This moment, when we sense that things suddenly manifest themselves as they truly are, is a coming into light after darkness. The catharsis of Menippean tragedy depends on a shift from rigid obsession to a state of fluid indifference where searching is again possible. The release occurs when the fixation on one formulation (fate and human love, in the case of *Troilus*) ends. We come back—reluctantly, it is true—into the milling complexities of our alien, but usually undemanding, universe. Bakhtin describes the non-Aristotelian catharsis of Menippean satire thus: it is the realization that "nothing definitive has yet taken place in the world, the final word of the world and about the world has not yet been said, the world is open and free, everything is still in the future and will always be in the future."[20] It is this effect that Chaucer strives for in the epilogue, and, I believe, achieves. The future has no form, but it is there ahead of them, laughter for one failed determinist, an alternate love system for the other. Released from their fatalistic obsession with the past, Troilus' and the narrator's new views restore freedom and its dislocating peremptoriness to the provenance of this world. We discover the feeling that we have as little inherent right to our despair as we have to our laughter. The release encourages us to ignore what we cannot encompass and go forward to look for what we can.

In conclusion, then, what Chaucer took from Boethius was primarily his Menippean vision: freedom is the most profoundly elating, if also the most intolerable, condition of human existence. Secondarily, for purposes of parody, he made use of Boethius' framing of certain of the topoi by which men defend themselves from the consequences of this thought. The center of this tragedy lies not in the explosive conjunction of event and character, as in classical tragedy, but in their whimpering disjunction, in that cacophony where event, character, theory, and undertaking exist without the validation of some distant, mysterious universal force. The poem does not portray the titanic energies of men expended to find a meaning in life in spite of a conflict with fate, with diametric "other," with an outside force that thwarts their desires. It portrays instead their failure to find a distinctive opposite against which they can measure themselves. As they use their energies in the attempt to formulate a fateful authority, the defeats they encounter are self-referential. No fate defeats them; their own prior and counter desires defeat them. The universe and its events wander before them in a place beyond comprehension, taking note of them in no constructive or destructive way. Everything is only a part of an interesting, sometimes moving, but totally incomprehensible panorama. The most beautiful lines in *Troilus*—as many have felt, the point of final clarity—embody this recognition:

> and thynketh al nys but a faire
> This world, that passeth soone as floures faire.
> (5. 1840–41)

The gorgeous display of goods at this fair provides the illusions which all the characters attempt futilely to mold into solid constructions that will contain and order their desire. Because the narrator in his conclusion can do no better than fling indigestible fragments of thought at us, we are, in effect, asked by Chaucer to experience the confines of a mind which views the universe described by Menippean satire as intolerable and tragic beyond bearing. We are forced to move into the realm of Menippean release by ourselves; the final dimension of the poem's profundity is to experience what is here presented as the loneliness of this vision.

6

Foreknowledge and Free Will: Three Theories in *The Nun's Priest's Tale*

The gleeful attack on theoretical explanations, one of the dominant characteristics of Menippean satire, finds its most startling representation in the attitude of the narrator in the *Nun's Priest's Tale*. He is particularly interested in the possibilities for satire set up by medieval writings on the question of the relation of foreknowledge and free will, the subject Boethius deals with in his final book of the *Consolation*. While the Nun's Priest alludes to and satirizes the views of Augustine and Bishop Bradwardine, it is the Boethian theory that engages the largest share of his mockery. His gleeful and often very funny attacks implicity accuse the theorists of abstracting and thereby misrepresenting the realistic facts of life and freedom, death and fate, which are the true lot of mortals and roosters struggling on this earth.

The problem of the relation between foreknowledge and free will was proposed by Augustine, who, as Sir William Hamilton notes, concluded that it was of such difficulty that it was "intelligible only to a few." Sir William continues: "Had he denounced it as a fruitless question, and (to understanding) soluble by none, the world might have been spared a large library of acrimonious and resultless disputation."[1] But Augustine had written what he had written, and the debate went on for centuries. Anyone who studied philosophy and theology encountered the problem; and anyone who made the slightest progress in advanced studies fought his way through its assumptions, obstacles, and propositions. The Nun's Priest apostrophizes Chauntecleer with mock concern about his predestined meeting with the fox for an audience thoroughly familiar with, if not the ins and outs of the problem, at least the knowledge that the problem contains staggering complexities.

> O Chauntecleer, acursed be that morwe
> That thou into that yerd flaugh fro the bemes!
> Thou were ful wel ywarned by thy dremes
> That thilke day was perilous to thee;
> But what that God forwoot moot nedes bee,
> After the opinioun of certein clerkis.
> Witnesse on hym that any parfit clerk is,
> That in scole is greet altercacioun
> In this mateere, and greet disputisoun,
> And hath been of an hundred thousand men.
> But I ne kan nat bulte it to the bren
> As kan the hooly doctour Augustyn,
> Or Boece, or the Bisshop Bradwardyn.
>
> (3230–42)

After this insistence on the problem's great unintelligibility, the narrator goes on to mention the views of the relation between foreknowledge and free will held by the scholars he has named. While both Bradwardine and Boethius, in the final analysis, support the orthodox position established by Augustine that man has free will and God absolute foreknowledge, their emphases are different. The narrator's summations take note of the aspect of the controversy that dominated the interest of each one.

The first theory the Nun's Priest questions supposes that simple necessity governs all.

> Wheither that Goddes worthy forwityng
> Streyneth me nedely for to doon a thyng,—
> "Nedely" clepe I symple necessitee.
>
> (3243–45)

If this is true, then the mind and the body are under the compulsion of God's providence. Freedom is an illusion. Thought and action are as inevitably laid out as that simple necessity, death. Such a view corresponds with Bishop Bradwardine's extreme position as determinist. His effort in *De Causa Dei* to combat Pelagianism and its denial of original sin leads him almost to deny any freedom. Gordon Leff describes his views in this way:

> [Bradwardine's] intention was to win back for God all power which he considered to have been usurped by men. His whole system was designed to establish God as the senior partner in all that concerned His creatures. This allowed no independent area of freedom to them at all; and it is the essence of his system. The importance of this divine control, which I have called the 'principle of divine participation,' cannot be overrated: by making God the most immediate cause of all that they do, men were left with no autonomy; they became dependent upon Him for their being, movement and worth; they had no positive qualities or powers to call their own. In this way the whole world became, in effect, nothing more than the extension of God's will, with no part of it capable of acting but by His immutable decree.[2]

The second theory which the Nun's Priest questions supposes that human freedom exists independently of any compulsion in God's foreknowledge.

> Or elles, if free choys be graunted me
> To do that same thyng, or do it noght,
> Though God forwoot it er that was wroght.
> (3246–48)

This view corresponds with Augustine's theory, which is most extensively stated in an early work, *De libero arbitrio*:

> Accordingly, we do not deny God's foreknowledge of all things future, and yet we do will what we will. Since God has foreknowledge of our will, its future will be such as He foreknows it. It will be a will precisely because He foreknows it as a will, and it could not be a will if it were not in our power. Hence God also has foreknowledge of our power over it. The power, then, is not taken from me because of His foreknowledge, since this power will be mine all the more certainly because of the infallible foreknowledge of Him who foreknew that I would have it.[3]

In terms of this theory, men do freely whatever they do; God foreknows the action they will take. This theory involves the postulation of a hiatus which separates the understanding of philosophers and the mind of God and suspends the logical absurdity of supposing that human freedom exists in the face of God's foreknowledge. The simultaneous existence of free will and foreknowledge is a paradox that must be accepted by faith.

The third theory the Nun's Priest questions supposes that there is no compulsion in God's foreknowledge except in terms of conditional necessity.

> Or if his wityng streyneth never a deel
> But by necessitee condicioneel.
>
> (3249–50)

Boethius spends the greater part of book 5 of the *Consolation* on the problem; the passage relevant to Chaucer's lines is found in his translation of the last prose:

> For certes ther ben two maneris of necessities: that oon necessite is symple, as thus: that it byhovith by necessite that alle men ben mortal or dedly; anothir necessite is condicionel, as thus: yif thou wost that a man walketh, it byhovith by necessite that he walke. Thilke thing, thanne, that any wight hath iknowe to be, it ne mai ben noon oothir weys thanne he knowith it to be. But this condicion draweth nat with hir thilke necessite simple; for certes this necessite condicionel—the propre nature of it ne makith it nat, but the adjeccioun of the condicioun makith it. For no necessite ne constreyneth a man to gon that goth by his propre wil, al be it so that whan he goth that it is necessarie that he goth. Ryght on this same manere thanne, yif that the purveaunce of God seeth any thyng present, than moot thilke thing ben by necessite, althogh that it ne have no necessite of his owne nature. (Bk. 5, pr. 6; p. 383)

The first theory is the simplest; it offers no room for thoughtful consideration, since all is fated. The second offers no terms by which to consider the possibilities it does allow; the relationship is incomprehensible. The third theory, the theory of conditional necessity, is the most complex and interesting, because it offers infinite understandable possibilities for the investigation of the relation of event and character and how they are created out of the forces of freedom and compulsion. In passing, it is worth noting that all three theorists take far more delight in elucidating the terms of God's foreknowledge than they do in elucidating the terms of man's freedom.

In spite of the Nun's Priest's disclaimer—"I ne kan nat bulte it to the bren" (3240)—he satirizes the three theories in the tale with every mark of accurate understanding. He presents the position of the thoroughgoing determinist in Chauntecleer's argument with Pertelote. The substance of Chauntecleer's proof is indeed ominous, for it precludes the possibility that the will can alter the fated fact. It, too, is a fated fact. In the examples he cites, the event forecast in the dream occurs; the dreamer's foreknowledge allows his will to influence his waking action only if he is not personally involved in the event. Thus, the second dreamer avoids drowning because the ship is fated and not he. Applied to the tale, Chauntecleer's argument indicates clearly that his will is fated to take him to the meeting with the fox.

The theory of the determinist is satirized in the first place merely by its being given to a rooster, but it is further undermined by its being given to a rooster whose motives in uttering it are anything but philosophical. What drives Chauntecleer to explain and explain and explain is Pertelote's suggestion that his awesome dream is caused only by the need of a laxative. Out of chagrin, he avoids the prime subject of irritation and sets about reprimanding her in the most elaborate terms possible. Without effort, he forgets his fear and even the implications of his argument to destroy her presumptuous interpretation of his dream. In failing to analyze the primary experience and the implications of his own theory, in using all his books to crush her one little book because she has insulted him, he departs in the opposite direction from the goal of philosophical endeavor. He uses his precedents only to prove the contrary of what someone else has argued, rather than to master his primary experience in order to interpret it. He is, of course, not the only philosopher who has been guilty of this error.

His disbelief in his own words is indicated not only by his momentary concession after an overwhelming number of examples which prove the contrary ("dremes be somtyme—I sey not

alle— / Warnynge of thynges that shul after falle" [3131–32]),
but also in his final rejection of the whole issue:

"I am so ful of joye and of solas,
That I diffye bothe sweven and dreem."
(3170-1)

His indifference to his proof is confirmed by his subsequent actions, in which he goes about the business of the rooster as
usual. Roosters are never so sure of their freedom as when they
have irrefutably proved that everything is determined.

The satire on the second theory, the Augustinian, depends on
the Nun's Priest's dramatization of its tenets in the fable. This
second theory holds that man, because of his limited mind,
must believe in the paradox of the simultaneous existence of
both free will and divine foreknowledge. For all practical purposes this means that men go along living their lives, making
choices, willing things, avoiding things, as if there were no divine foreknowledge. God foreknows whatever they will do, but
they know nothing about his knowledge and cannot therefore
concern themselves with it. The satirical attack on this theory is
more subtle than that on the first, since it depends on the perception of the similarity between a mind writing a theological
tract on God's foreknowledge and one writing an animal fable
where "God's foreknowledge" is portrayed.

According to the rules of hierarchy in fable, animals move up
into the role of men, and men move up into the role of gods. In
the tale, the widow and her farmhands are the gods; Chauntecleer and his sisters are the human beings. The knowledge the
two groups possess is radically different, as we may see by focusing on Chauntecleer's dream:

"Me mette how that I romed up and doun
Withinne our yeerd, wheer as I saugh a beest
Was lyk an hound, and wolde han maad areest
Upon my body, and wolde han had me deed.
His colour was bitwixe yelow and reed,
And tipped was his tayl and bothe his eeris
With blak, unlyk the remenant of his heeris;

His snowte smal, with glowynge eyen tweye.
Yet of his look for feer almoost I deye."
(2898–2906)

Chauntecleer does not know the name of the animal nor what
the facts of the dream mean (though certainly he soon has a
most impressively presented theory). The dream contains information outside his conscious experience; he does not have the
necessary associations to draw on to understand what threatens
him. He is an orphan who has had no ancestors to hand down
the traditional lore of the chicken race. Without insight into
the divine worlds above him, he freely wills to go out into
the barnyard. In contrast, the widow holds the key to the information that is revealed in the dream: she knows that a fox
will pounce on a chicken if he can; she knows that the chicken
will be terrified. She knows the name of the animal in the
dream. We know she knows these things because we know them
too.

The projection of the Augustinian theory is comically exact.
The widow's knowledge exceeds Chauntecleer's by a godlike
degree. Her knowledge does not influence Chauntecleer's actions in any way. She can be said to foreknow that he will go
into the barnyard because that is what roosters do every morning. But, as in the tract of the theologian, what this particular
"divine" mind knows is the state of affairs in the present, in the
past, of course, but not in the exact future. Such foreknowledge
as she has is general and distant. The narrator makes no effort
to elevate her position. He does not include an account of prior
human attempts to protect the rooster and chickens against the
fox, an account which appears, for instance, at the beginning
of one of the tale's analogues, "Reinhart Fuchs."[4] Nor does he
take advantage of the opportunity to give the widow a little divine mystery by using similes to compare her and her fellow human beings to the Greek gods, as the chickens during the chase
at the end of the tale are compared to epic heroines.

In the truncated deity that the widow comes to represent,
what is satirized is man's habit of projecting states concocted

out of his finite imaginings into the province of the divine. Satirical light is thrown on the constructs of theologians and philosophers merely by putting their problems in an animal fable, for in the theological tract, men thinking elevate themselves to the stature of God. The thinker with his instincts and with his knowledge of the patterns of the past actions of things adjusts the tenses of his verbs and transfers them to the frightful silence which he calls the future, saying that they are constructed by God. This act pacifies him; it undoubtedly gives him a sense of freedom because he thinks he has mastered what the universe is up to behind his back. But it does not reveal the nature of God nor does it even explain the concerns of his rooster-self, who must go, and wants to go, to the encounters that make up his existence whether he knows what sequence of events compels him to go or whether he knows what will face him when he gets there. With this theory, like the first, the major intent of the satire is to dismiss it as a comic irrelevance, mere "chaff" in the total assessment of the relation between man's real experience of the struggle between freedom and compulsion and his verbal attempts to resolve the struggle.

The third theory, however, the Boethian, the narrator attends to more energetically; he plays about with its tenets on every possible occasion and in every conceivable way. According to this theory, God's foreknowledge restrains man only by conditional necessity. While God' knowledge of acts in time is absolute—for he sits outside it and views past, present, and future as an eternal present[5]—his knowledge places no more necessity upon human acts than men's seeing a man walking constrains that man to walk. The man's walking, however, constrains him to abide by that action. There are, in other words, many courses in the universe which, depending on choice or inadvertence, man may or may not enter upon, but if he enters one, then he must abide by its rules. Between birth and death, there is absolute necessity imposed on action only after the entry to the course is made; but neither God's foreknowledge nor fate dictates which course a man shall choose. If this theory, which focuses ultimately on verbal formulations of experience, both syllogistic and narrative, is as clearly rejected in the end as the first two, it provides, nevertheless, the most complex level of the satire.

What attracts the narrator's satirical interest in this theory are (1) the assumption that if a man enters a course, he is compelled to abide by its rules; (2) the absurd proposition that describes it (If I see a man walking, then he walks); and (3) the projection of a vision of the world in which only one thing will happen at a time. Considerations of this sort vigorously undermine the decorum of logic's world. At the level of narrative, language, and action, the Nun's Priest prods the assumptions of the theory of conditional necessity with satiric, comic, and ultimately philosophical effect.

For instance, the genre which the narrator is employing is a "course" which has its own rules of procedure. The conditional necessity which attends the writings of animal fable is that the writer shall not violate the major tenet of the form, which is that animals play the parts and have the abilities of men to think, speak, and, if need be, sing. If a writer writes a fable, he writes a fable. But this particular writer is already violating the form by writing simultaneously with the fable a romance, a mock-epic, and several other things which lend themselves less easily to being named. Even within the fable itself there are violations. On the one hand, the narrator seems to feel that to ask his listeners to swallow the tenets of the form is to make excessive demands on their gullibility. The song and speech of the chickens disturbs him into throwing his setting back to the golden age: "For thilke tyme, as I have understonde, / Beestes and briddes koude speke and synge" (2880–81). Later he appeals to the authority of the bestiary: "For Phisiologus seith sikerly / How that they syngen wel and myrily" (3271–72).

On the other hand, he fails to regard the animals' right to a human role consistently and turns them back into animals. "Ye been so scarlet reed aboute youre yen" (3161) might be accepted as an appropriate satire on "Beauty is in the eye of the beholder." But Pertelote's "Pekke hem up right as they growe and ete hem yn" (2967) is not acceptable fable talk, nor is the narrator's description of Chauntecleer after he flies down from his perch:

And with a chuk he gan hem for to calle,
For he hadde founde a corn, lay in the yerd.
Real he was, he was namoore aferd.
He fethered Pertelote twenty tyme,
And trad hire eke as ofte, er it was pryme.

(3174–78)

This charming portrayal of chickens is a part of the technique of intentional violation of the conditional necessity governing literary genre. We have no compelling sense of shock that the genre is being violated. We laugh. Our lack of indignation suggests that we, like the narrator, are more wrapped up in the truth of chickens than we are in the demands placed upon genre by the fate inherent in definition.

Inconsistencies equally unnoticeable, but in the long run far more startling, are the inconsistencies in the narrator's own commentary. He violates the logical axiom "If a man takes one position, he cannot take another." One of his most flagrant violations is in his account of Chauntecleer's meeting with the fox. First of all, he introduces the meeting with two equivocations; we have merely to check what he has told us before. His statement "Thou were ful wel ywarned by thy dremes" (3232) is inaccurate. The dream does not warn Chauntecleer that the coming day is perilous to him; it warns him that the animal only we and the widow know to be a fox is perilous to him. It is the narrator who is suddenly taking the liberty of saying that the dream is a fateful warning about this day's events. The second comment of the narrator is also inaccurate. He cites Pertelote's counsel as the reason for Chauntecleer's walking in the yard. But Chauntecleer does not go down to the barnyard because of her advice: he goes because her beauty and sexual attractiveness fill him with such joy (that and several other delights philosophic and heroic) that he renounces and defies her laxatives, his interpretations of dreams, and even his fear. The narrator sweetly confuses in this comment Pertelote's solicitous advice and sex appeal and ignores any of the complexity behind the causes of Chauntecleer's final entry into the yard.

There is more equivocation. When Chauntecleer first sees the fox, he fails to recognize him as the beast in the dream. The absoluteness of the failure is seen in the contrast of Chaunte-cleer's two reactions. He is afraid in both the dream and the meeting, but the fear in the dream is the primitive, gripping, conscious fear of the negation of being and the loss of freedom. The fear at the meeting is only the startled, unconscious fright of a man who sees a fox instead of a butterfly. We all gasp our equivalent of "Cok, cok," at similar discrepancies. We accept this difference, in heroic terms, as the ironic commonplace of the tragic event. When the hero faces the actual crossroad which his oracle, prophecy, or dream has warned him about, he fails to recognize it. Since the narrator has said that the dream is such a warning, we expect him to lament about the failure of perception in men and roosters. But, on the contrary, he now ignores the dream altogether and explains instead:

> For natureelly a beest desireth flee
> Fro his contrarie, if he may it see,
> Though he never erst hadde seyn it with his ye.
> (3279-81)

The narrator ignores fate and satirizable conventional response to the fateful confrontation and talks about Nature. He does this (conveniently) in the face of the only remarkable fact in the dream, the only one which might connect it with fate, the appearance of an image of a fox, complete down to the color of his ear and tail tips. Are we then to think that the narrator abandons fate as a useless force and is seeking naturalistic interpretations? Not at all; his next comment a few lines later mutters of destiny once more:

> O destinee, that mayst nat been eschewed!
> Allas, that Chauntecleer fleigh fro the bemes!
> Allas, his wyf ne roghte nat of dremes!
> And on a Friday fil al this meschaunce.
> (3338-41)

Nature is now abandoned in its turn and what we find is not one but three different conceptions of freedom, the three in fact which he mentions in the foreknowledge apostrophe. If destiny may not be eschewed, then Chauntecleer had no freedom to do other than what he did (theory 1). If the choice made can cause the lament, "alas," then there were other (hidden, to be sure) alternatives, and fate is not the dominating factor in the action (theory 2). If he had not gone out on a Friday, then he would not have met a fox (theory 3). The Nun's Priest's interpretations and morality are not of the fixed sort requiring consistency. There is perhaps nothing in the tale so damaging to the sanctity of theoretical explanations as the air of unrepentant and enthusiastic interest that surrounds the wildest of the narrator's interpretations of his observed events.

Allusions to the Garden of Eden myth show a similar lack of consistency. Conditional necessity demands that if a writer is going to draw on a myth in a serious way (the narrator can be thought to do so),[6] his allusions must be serious and consistent. (Consistency is very important for critics.) The chief allusion is contained in these lines:

> My tale is of a cok, as ye may heere,
> That tok his conseil of his wyf, with sorwe,
> To walken in the yerd upon that morwe
> That he hadde met that dreem that I yow tolde.
> Wommennes conseils been ful ofte colde;
> Wommannes conseil broghte us first to wo,
> And made Adam fro Paradys to go,
> Ther as he was ful myrie and wel at ese.
> (3252–59)

It is useless to beat around the bush with polite mutterings about inconsistency; the whole statement is a lie. Eve did not give Adam any counsel; she gave him an apple (at any rate, all commentators are agreed, a piece of fruit), which is a long way from "counsel." Pertelote gave Chauntecleer advice all right, but to prove that what she said lured Chauntecleer out of the hen house would take the combined ingenuity of the hundred thousand clerks and the three masters.

Let us ignore the surface lie and assume that it contains some hidden truth. (If we dismiss the passage we run the danger of throwing out the only concrete allusion to the Adam and Eve story.) We find that according to the analogy of the passage, the Fall of Man is the descent from the hen house. This is a surprise; we would have thought that the narrator would save the meeting with the fox for this purpose. We are also a little surprised by what Paradise turns out to be. We are prepared to believe that a rooster thinks his barnyard a paradise; we are not prepared to believe that he thinks his chicken house is. Even on the basis of this tale, Chauntecleer has a much better time outside; on the roost he can only talk. We struggle on, clutching to our hearts the Paradox of the Fortunate Fall.

Accepting the Fall of Man as the descent from the chicken house, we are provided with a difficulty. What is the meeting between Chauntecleer and the fox? Brief consideration provides the answer. The meeting is, of course, the meeting of Cain and Abel, in the guise now of grain-eating rooster and meat-eating fox. Fox-Abel at this meeting also obviously "did not well," and Chauntecleer-Cain "rules over him." The thought that Chauntecleer and the fox represent Cain and Abel is, at least on the surface, a useful comparison because we are otherwise quite taxed to understand why the fox is compared not only to murderers, but also to traitors (3227–28). Strictly speaking, a fox cannot betray a rooster; but, of course, if he is really his brother, he can. But we raise more problems than we solve. There is an antibiblical thrust in this analogy. Abel wishes to kill Cain. The widow-god prefers the Cain figure; the God of Genesis, Abel. There may be nothing more ominous in that than the fact that she prefers chicken meat; we are not sure.

We struggle against the temptation of overliteralness—overliteralness being the attempt to interpret everything by anything that is immediately under our noses. With the narrator's example before us, the temptation is all but insurmountable. Let us suppose (ignoring the *precise* dictates of the Paradise passage) that the meeting between Chauntecleer and the fox is Adam-Eve's meeting with the serpent. We are instantly more comfortable: the fox is an acceptable allegorical figure for the devil.[7] But the exasperation of this parallel exceeds all previous exasperations. At the Fall, man acquired the knowledge of good and evil and a sense of his own nakedness; he experienced divine wrath, and he was forbidden to live in Paradise (among other things). There are no parallels to these events, for nothing changes as a result of the encounter in the barnyard. Chauntecleer's feathers do not fall off to embarrass him. He does not lose the right to either the barnyard or the chicken house. Worst of all, he has triumphed over the fiend in spite of his innocence. He is Adam Unfallen (or perhaps more realistically, Adam-Still-to-Fall). That may accord rather well with what he has acquired in the way of knowledge, which we may suppose to be very little. He still does not know that the name of the animal is "fox." Nor is he any better prepared to defend himself than he was if at their next meeting the fox banks on speed rather than talk to approach him. We could struggle on with the implications of the allusion to the Garden of Eden, but the truth of the matter is that every important relationship, fact, or result of that myth either is not there or has suffered comic transformations.

The Nun's Priest's enthusiastic satire on the rules of conditional necessity carries over into the rhetoric of the tale. The linguistic formulation of conditional necessity, it will doubtless have been observed, has a certain tautological air about it. The basic formula can be varied a little, but nothing helps very much. For example, fire is hot (simple necessity). The existence of fire depends on whether the relevant substances have been brought into conjunction (conditional necessity). To avoid the formulation, "If a fire is kindled, then there will be a fire," we can say, "If a fire is kindled, then it will be hot," or "If a fire is kindled, then the natural result is heat." In a similar way we can avoid the formulation of Boethius' example, "If I see a man walk, then he walks," by saying, "If I see a man walk, then he must place one leg after the other on the ground ahead, behind, or to the side of him," or "If I see a man walk, then the natural result is movement away from his original position." All these statements, though progressively less efficient, are logically true statements. But we hardly care whether they are or not. We long for the release in the statements, "If a man builds a fire, then the ice cap at the Arctic melts," or "If I see a man walk, then I know the car industry is folding up." We long for the second clause not to repeat the first, for what we do and know to have a consequence beyond itself.

The Nun's Priest evidently has similar longings. In the final episode of the tale, the formulations of the three morals, which parody the "if-then" formula, provide outrageous substitutions. The narrator explains the capture of Chauntecleer with what boils down to the statement, "If a man is susceptible to flattery, then he is a lord" (a parody of "then he will be flattered"):

> This Chauntecleer his wynges gan to bete,
> As man that koude his traysoun nat espie,
> So was he ravysshed with his flaterie.
> Allas! ye lordes, many a fals flatour
> Is in youre courtes, and many a losengeour,
> That plesen yow wel moore, by my feith,
> Than he that soothfastnesse unto yow seith.
> Redeth Ecclesiaste of flaterye;
> Beth war, ye lordes, of hir trecherye.
> (3322–30)

Chauntecleer's own explanation for his capture boils down to "If a man closes his eyes when he should see, then he will be carried off by a fox" (a parody of "then he will be blind"):

> "Thou shalt namoore, thurgh thy flaterye,
> Do me to synge and wynke with myn ye;
> For he that wynketh, whan he sholde see,
> Al wilfully, God lat him nevere thee!"
> (3429–32)

The fox's explanation for the loss of Chauntecleer boils down to "If a man jangles when he should hold his peace, the rooster in his mouth will fly into a tree" (a parody of "then he will jangle"):

> "Nay," quod the fox, "but God yeve hym meschaunce,
> That is so undiscreet of governaunce
> That jangleth whan he sholde holde his pees."
> (3433–35)

We do not immediately notice the parody because the narrator distracts us by hiding the main clause of the first under an apostrophe to lords and the main clauses of the second and third, under Chauntecleer's and the fox's malediction on those who are guilty of their errors. Other points of the action resolve themselves into similar antilogical formulas. "If a rooster has a dream, he has a dream" becomes, for Pertelote, "then his humors are out of balance"; for Chauntecleer, "then he has been given a divine premonition." "If a fox is in the barnyard, he is in the barnyard" becomes, for the narrator, "then the archetype of the great traitors of history is present and empires are about to fall."

Even the proverbs scattered throughout the tale are inadequate statements of logical relationships. "If a man listens to the counsels of women, then he will get a woman's point of view" becomes "then he will get bad counsel" ("Wommennes conseils been ful ofte colde; / Wommannes conseil broghte us first to wo" [3256–57]). "If an action is undertaken on Friday, then it will be a Friday's action" becomes "then it will be an unlucky action" (3341ff.). "If a man commits murder, then he will kill somebody" becomes "then it will out" ("Mordre wol out, this my conclusioun" [3057]). None of the proverbial utterances are logically true, but they are offered as truth for the case to which they are attached, and offer man the hope of a freedom which bypasses the tautology of logic: the hope that murder is punished, that the ills of life can be blamed on the counsels of half the human race (the half of which the author is himself fortunately not a member), that bad luck is the result of actions undertaken on Fridays. The hope is short-lived. I have already commented on the doubt the tale casts on the proverb of women's counsel. This particular Friday is, in fact, a lucky day for Chauntecleer, as it ends by his going triumphantly free from the clutches of a much stronger and cleverer opponent. Another proverb, "For evere the latter ende of joye is wo" (3205), is refuted by the same evidence. As to murder, Chauntecleer does not suggest that the assassination of Kenelm, a later exemplum in his diatribe, met with retribution (3110–21).

The proverbial and the logical formulations which the Nun's Priest satirizes are aspects of the useless human effort to predict and codify the outcome that can be consistently expected from particular human choices. The proverb struggles, albeit unsuccessfully, to turn the results of vivid single experiences into generalizations. The logical proposition struggles to abstract a truth beforehand from the whole of a potential experience, but, perforce, robs incidents of their complexity and unfortunately, in a sense, of meaning. Proverbs, based on known results of types of incidents, become feeble half-truths when they are taken as unambiguous examples of human foresight about life. These inarticulate half-truths are the original and private attempts man has made to evade the implications of his primary experience, which is that he cannot find the consistent outcome of any human action (his real simple necessity). The logical proposition, the attempt to foresee what must be true in every instance, is a colorless description of an aspect of an event in human life. It is man's corporate method of trying to capitalize on his intellectual tradition by isolating a method whereby he may balance in the light above the morass of his ignorance and make a truthful statement. "If that is true, then this must follow." The logical formulation reasons on a controlled abstraction from an event but, with this abstraction, is forced to exclude the richness, complexity, and unexpectedness of experience. The proverb, drawing its conclusions from hindsight, leaves the implicit richness, complexity, and unexpectedness of an incident intact but, in having insufficient evidence, utters a conclusion too limited in application. As an "explanation," one tends toward the precise and tautological, the other toward the imprecise and wishful. The Nun's Priest's satirical contempt for both methods is amusing.

When we move from the rhetoric of the tale into an investigation of the tale's central action, the Boethian conditional necessity fares no better. The trouble, which becomes clear in any effort to reduce even a relatively simple action to logical terms, is that logic treats man as if he were most of the time an immobile automaton who intermittently performs an act of his choice under the terms of the given necessity and then returns to immobility to await the moment when he next shall choose. Boethius' example of the sun rising and the man walking (bk. 5, pr. 6) suggests a film stopped on a single frame: "Ryght so as whan ye seen togidre a man walke on the erthe and the sonne arisen in the hevene, albeit so that ye seen and byholden the ton and the tothir togidre, yit natheles ye demen and discerne that the toon is voluntarie and the tother is necessarie" (p. 383). When the logician flips the lever up, then the sun slowly rises and the man walks. When he flips the lever down, both stand still. For the impatient, the wildly creative, or the quieter soul simply disturbed by the confining oppressiveness of this conception of linguistic truth, the activity is unsatisfactory. It unrealistically imagines the mind as capable of stopping the things it observes, and worse yet, of stopping its own observations at its leisure. It is unsatisfactory because it turns an oak tree into a toothpick. We do not object when we are concerned with a toothpick, but otherwise we are compelled to wonder what happened to the rest of the wood. To be somewhat more literal, it projects single acts (although human acts are never single) as if they were surrounded by great vacuums of inactivity and rest (which they never are). This vacuum may, in fact, be said to be psychological, as well as the linguistic condition of logic.

The "extra wood," of which the Nun's Priest makes us acutely conscious, interferes as we try to reduce the action to fit the formula. The tale's central assumption seems to bear some tantalizing relationship to the formula, "If a man walks, then he walks." This is "If a fox meets a rooster, he will try to eat him." Of course the slight discrepancies in the pattern make us aware immediately of the difficulty of making a logical formulation out of the relationship. For instance, there is no natural condition under which a walking man is not walking. There are at least two unlikely but entirely natural conditions under which a fox would not eat a rooster. One is a momentary surfeit of roosters; the other is a decrepitude which fears the rooster's spurs. Furthermore, if we were formulating the statement about the relation of foxes and roosters without the evidence of the tale before us, we would undoubtedly say, "If a fox catches a rooster, then he will eat him," not "try to eat him," since many more roosters caught by foxes are eaten than escape, and logic searches for what is generally true. The denouement of the tale, recounting Chauntecleer's successful flight into the tree, forbids this exactness. It soon becomes apparent that the formula for conditional necessity will help us only if we break the event down into a series of fragments. If a fox meets a rooster, he meets a rooster. If he catches a rooster, he catches a rooster. If he loses a rooster, he loses a rooster. We learn little about Chauntecleer's free will from this discovery.

To avoid this thudding dead end of the formulaic expression of conditional necessity, we can attempt to see the theory in more general terms as an operative force in the interplay between will and event. In the story as a whole, conditional necessity would seem to provide a reasonably straightforward explanation for the meeting of fox and rooster. Thus, foxes are the enemies of roosters, a simple necessity established by nature. If their chosen, inadvertent, or habitual acts lead to a confrontation with one another, then the fox will carry off the chicken. This is conditional necessity. The fox, according to his own testimony, is aware of simple necessity on the basis of past experience— what brought about his initial awareness is not revealed directly —and elects to go into the barnyard to bring about the confrontation, which, if managed successfully, will, by the terms of conditional necessity, result in a meal for him. The fox, his hunger aside, acts both freely and knowingly in bringing about the meeting.

Chauntecleer, too, elects to go into the barnyard; however, he has no knowledge that a confrontation is possible. He has had a dream which frightened him; he has been through a long argument about dreams which should have frightened him more, but which has had the opposite effect of canceling the memory of the dream and making him yet more vulnerable. He freely—that is to say, naturally—enters the course of conditional necessity in a state of blithe unknowing. In this state of exaltation over the beauty of the day, the beauty of his wife, and later over the fox's words about the beauty of his mind and voice, he does not know that any evil can threaten his little circle of light.

Thus we see the dichotomy set up between foreknowledge and free will in this relationship of fox and rooster. In terms of the theory, the fox has more freedom than Chauntecleer because he arranges the possibility for the meeting into which Chauntecleer inadvertently wanders. We are tempted to quote

Boethius: those with the most knowledge have the greatest freedom (bk. 5, pr. 2). Unfortunately, the tale contradicts this
idea, since the fox's success is only momentary. Our sense of decorum, though not necessarily our dim suspicion, forbids us to
reverse the statement: those with the most ignorance have the
greatest freedom. Nevertheless, Chauntecleer's act of freeing
himself from the fox, of triumphing over the perpetual enemy,
is the key act upon which all theories must stand or fall.

We can only conclude that the denouement provides the justification for the narrator's enthusiastic satire on conditional
necessity, which is reflected in his use of genre, myth, editorial
commentary, and rhetoric. Chauntecleer, having entered the
course of conditional necessity, is not compelled to abide by the
rules; the action involving him cannot be accurately formulated by the linguistic rules of conditional necessity; he does not
inhabit a world where one thing can happen at a time. The theory of conditional necessity is as unilluminating an account of
Chauntecleer's freedom as are the theories of the determinist
and the theologian.

The narrator values the three theories for purposes of satire
in proportion to the closeness of their approach to an explanation which has something to do with man's actual sensation of
freedom. The theory of the determinist treats the feeling as an
illusion. This explanation is humiliating. It is useful only as
men exercise their freedom by trouncing an opponent whose
medical determinism is even more humiliating. The theory of
the theologian says that the feeling is truthful to man, but en-
compassed by God in his infinite visions. This explanation is
frustrating. To say that God foreknows everything but man is
unable to see how merely shifts all emergencies into God's
hands and leaves man in ignorance, playing out a scheme
which, if it is not said to be ruled by fate, might as well be for
all the responsibility it allows man in manufacturing his world.
It is a paternalistic theory, largely useful when men wish to
portray what God knows. Its underlying truth is that what God
can be said specifically to know about men's lives, men know
too, and what he can be said to know in general that they do
not, is also defined by men's own speculation. The third theory,
conditional necessity, says that the feeling is truthful for both

Foreknowledge and Free Will in *The Nun's Priest's Tale*

God and man, that only the feeling put into action causes it to encounter necessities that it must abide by. The satire against this theory hinges on the definition of these necessities and on the unsuccessful efforts logicians make to stop life and thought so that they can categorize and formulate them in language.

Because of the Nun's Priest's enthusiastic acceptance of the chaotic nature of experience, we are distracted from the satiric implication in the tale that these theories in all their minimal glory exhaust the possibilities in man's capacity for rational thought. Underneath the satire there is an insistence on life's cacophony, on the independent existence of events and matter which simply elude all consistent theoretical explanations. The narrator implicitly proposes that as we face our moments in the universal chaos of things, we will find our freedom only through illogical and deceptive inventiveness. In the final tableau of the tale the delightful confusions and energies, heretofore the province of the mind and its formulations, find their literal representation in the cacophony of the barnyard chase. The hens are shrieking epic laments. The widow and her daughters are yelling. The dogs are barking, the cow and calf are running, and so are the hogs. The ducks are crying, the geese are flying, the bees take this moment to swarm. The trumpets of brass, boxwood, horn, and bone are blowing and touting amid the yells of the farmhands. We might even imagine that the narrator here tells the truth: "It semed as that hevene sholde falle" (3401). In the midst of this confusion, Chauntecleer, frightened but calm, says to the fox:

> "Sire, if that I were as ye,
> Yet sholde I seyn, as wys God helpe me,
> 'Turneth agayn, ye proude cherles alle!
> A verray pestilence upon yow falle!
> Now am I come unto the wodes syde;
> Maugree youre heed, the cok shal heere abyde.
> I wol hym ete, in feith, and that anon!'"
> (3407–13)

This is, of course, a lie, for what he means is, "If I were me, I would open your mouth," or more remotely, "If I were you, I would not open my mouth." The fox, however, too confused by

179

the noise to hear the deception, listens to the directions under his nose. He opens his mouth and Chauntecleer flies free.

The Nun's Priest hints that what human beings live with on the one hand is a continual stream of chaotic facts and incidents, and on the other, that impulse which so delights the heart, the impulse to organize and explain. With his satire, he tells us further that the chaos provides delightful opportunities for freedom totally lacking in the pedantry of the theories. It is true that Chauntecleer does not meet his fate on this day, and the reasons for that seem a long world away from the explanations of Bishop Bradwardine, Saint Augustine, and the rules of the Boethian conditional necessity, in spite of the delightful possibilities for satire which its bright tautological formulations offer. But before we become too entranced with the Nun's Priest's directions for dismissing the efforts of some of the world's great thinkers to make chaos intelligible, we might do well to sense that there is something odd going on beneath this satire. It wants something more precise than the freeing up of the rigidities of the intellect, Menippean satire's usual purpose in its attacks on theory. Just what the Nun's Priest wants, we shall examine in the next chapter.

7

The Eaters and the Eaten in
The Nun's Priest's Tale

It is not surprising that in the *Nun's Priest's Tale*—which we
sometimes feel can be taken as a satire on practically everything
—we find Chaucer experimenting with the extreme limits and
implications of the symbolic attitudes embodied in the two Menippean dialogue figures. In Chauntecleer, we have the most
ridiculous possible presentation of the buffoon in love with
time (an animal in a combination of a fable without a stated
moral and a mock-epic without an obvious issue) In the Nun's
Priest, we have the most destructive possible presentation of the
omniscient catechist, the attacker of all presumptuous theorizing, whose conclusions about men's failures do not halt at cynicism, or stoicism, or, where Chaucer's persona halts, at wistful
sadness, but fall over the edge altogether into the cheerful, negative glee of the arch-scoffer. The reader is the potential victim
of the Nun's Priest (a position he will do well to avoid if he can)
in the outer dialogue; and in the inner dialogue Chauntecleer
is, of course, the potential victim of the fox. Chauntecleer's escape provides the one note of hope in an otherwise appalling vision of the life of man, and it is this rooster, like it or not, we do
well to emulate if we would engage with the Nun's Priest and
yet go free.

/ The subject on which the tale focuses is death—literal death,
the mind's death, the death of all human ideals / The Nun's
Priest indulgently and satirically explores men's rooster-like efforts to act and think freely in the face of these inevitable ends.
He puts us completely off guard as to the grimness of his subject
by raising mountains of rhetoric over a funny and seemingly
trivial fact in the sum total of things: chickens ought to be
afraid of foxes. His energetic exploration of the ramifications of

this extraordinarily irrelevant observation seems too harmless to arouse anything but our laughter. But we should not be taken in so easily. No matter how agreeable the opposing members of the Menippean dialogue may at points be to one another, the real issue at stake between them in this fable, with its allegorical overtones, is that uncomic fact death, by general consent the most chaotic, the most terrible of facts, the one we are least able to endure, yet at the same time the most common, the most insignificant of facts. The basic goal of the Nun's Priest and the fox is to kill the "rooster" and feed on him. It happens that the fox is temporarily unsuccessful, and the respite that Chauntecleer achieves must give us hope that a similar respite from the Nun's Priest is also available to us.

The symbols of the implicit violence in this extreme version of the Menippean dialogue, in which the controlling characters are the "eaters" and their victims are the "eaten," is established by the dream. It is the tale's chief symbol, and all the action and ultimately all the rhetoric are related to it. Chauntecleer takes up half the story clarifying his conviction that dreams have an important relation to the future. The narrator, with an adopted blindness equal to Chauntecleer's, three times insists on its fateful prediction for that day: he mentions it in the opening of the apostrophe to Chauntecleer (3232) and again at the end (3255); he mentions it a third time as the fox flees with Chauntecleer (3340). The dream has further importance in defining the structure of the narrative, which opens with Chauntecleer's groaning over the potential threat of the fox and climaxes with Chauntecleer's actually experiencing the intention of the fox 'to have him dead.'

> This Chauntecleer gan gronen in his throte,
> As man that in his dreem is drecched soore.
> And whan that Pertelote thus herde hym roore,
> She was agast, and seyde, "Herte deere,
> What eyleth yow, to grone in this manere?
> Ye been a verray sleper; fy, for shame!"
>   And he answerde, and seyde thus: "Madame,
> I pray yow that ye take it nat agrief.

The Eaters and the Eaten in *The Nun's Priest's Tale*

By God, me mette I was in swich meschief
Right now, that yet myn herte is soore afright.
Now God," quod he, "my swevene recche aright,
And kepe my body out of foul prisoun!
Me mette how that I romed up and doun
Withinne our yeerd, wheer as I saugh a beest
Was lyk an hound, and wolde han maad areest
Upon my body, and wolde han had me deed.
His colour was bitwixe yelow and reed,
And tipped was his tayl and bothe his eeris
With blak, unlyk the remenant of his heeris;
His snowte smal, with glowynge eyen tweye.
Yet of his look for feere almoost I deye;
This caused me my gronyng, doutelees."

                                                 (2886–2907)

Because of the narrator's misdirections we tend at first to take the dream as a satiric epic dream, or in medieval dream terminology as a satiric *visio*, which, according to Macrobius, is a dream in which "events come to pass precisely as they appear to the dreamer."[1] From this angle, the dream is satiric, because, though it raises epic consternation, it in fact predicts no action. Instead, it presents us with a tableau containing three pieces of information: there was an animal; the animal wanted to kill Chauntecleer; Chauntecleer was afraid. We know that the animal, like a hound, with a color between yellow and red, black-tipped tail and ears, a small muzzle, and two glowing eyes, is a fox. We share this knowledge with the widow and the narrator. And it is true that later that morning a fox is discovered to be in the barnyard. But to explain these facts, we need hardly drag in fate. What the epic dream or *visio* predicts must be unknown, out of the ordinary, not foreseeable in terms of normal expectation. Our knowledge of the simple force of nature is enough to account for everything in the dream. Nature gives all foxes the intent to capture and eat chickens, and all chickens the fear of being supped upon by foxes. There is no supernatural information contained in the dream. That a fox does appear on the same day as the dream is, as far as the evidence of the dream is concerned, a coincidence. The fox has been there before to eat Chauntecleer's parents and can be expected to return to try for Chauntecleer again.

If we ignore the narrator's directions, which treat the dream as a *visio*—and there are very good reasons for doing so, since he is the proverbial father of lies—the dream is actually a *somnium*. The *somnium*, too, according to Macrobius, reveals the future, but it "conceals with figures and veils with ambiguity the significance of a thing not capable of being understood except by interpretation; though we cannot explain it as it is, still a man with experience in such matters may reveal to us its hidden meaning."[2] When we consider the dream as the representation of a man's (or a rooster's) reality, rather than as the projection of a single future event, it provides for us the Nun's Priest's ideas of fate and freedom, those absolute ideas on which the theorists have erected their dubious, if delightful structures. Or, to put the matter in terms of the Boethian metaphor, it provides the garment from which the theorists have torn their pieces and conceitedly thought they had all of it.

Death—which is the fate, the foreknowledge of the tale—is at once more primitive and more complex than the formulations the theorists deal with and more primitive and more complex than the elegant forecasts of a traditional epic dream or oracle. In its primitive phase, the fate this action and this rhetoric struggles around is the death caused by hunger. The fox, whose presence provides whatever small action exists in the tale, is at the most literal level the fell Sergeant, whose arrest will destroy the body. The "foul prisoun" that Chauntecleer fears is the grave, this particular grave being a stomach where the body, already ground to pieces, will be divided into blood and waste. Violent physical death, which the fox threatens to bring about, is an obvious constant theme of the stories in the barnyard. Chauntecleer's mother and father died by the violence of the fox; Chauntecleer is threatened by the same violence. In Chauntecleer's *exempla* the deaths alluded to are all violent. We have a murdered man under a pile of dung, a drowned man and his companions in a sunken ship, an assassinated boy king of England (Kenelm), two hanged men (the Pharaoh's baker and Croesus), and Hector's death and (as we remember) attempted mutilation at the hands of Achilles. We have allusions later on to the death in combat of another English king (Richard I), to the slayings of Priam and Hasdrubal in their fallen cities, and to Nero's murder of the Roman senators. Two of the three traitors of literary history whom the narrator mentions died by memorable violence; Judas hanged himself, and Genelon was torn apart by four stallions galloping for a mare. The carnage hinted at is at points considerable. There are the hosts of dead in the Jack Straw rebellion in London, in the burning cities of Troy, Rome, and Carthage, and in the collapses of empires and finally the earth in the apocalyptic dreams of Daniel. The agents of these killings, whether God, man, or fox, have various motives, which boil down to hunger for food, money, power, or vengeance, for maintaining and shaping an ideal world. But ideal worlds take a deadly toll. The fate of all but God is to be eaten eventually. Power, which ultimately only God has, is the ability to eat, by destroying or consuming or manipulating offending bodies which are obstructive or uncooperative and which, in some way, provide food for the eater's desires.

The violence of death in the barnyard stands in contrast to death in the frame story, which presents us with the human beings, the gods of the middle ground, where all is peaceful, temperate. The death of the widow's husband is alluded to without any hints of surrounding violence. The only visible threats in the widow's world are hunger and the fox. Hunger is not a violent death, nor can the husband have died of it, judging by the animals the widow still has. Foxes do not kill men. The peace of death in the widow-god's world, which stands in contrast to violence of death of the rooster-man's world, sets up a goal for men. To attain the peace of the death of the gods, to die in his own bed ("tree" is probably the better word in view of the tale's metaphors), may be said to be the aim of man's attempts to contain the violence of his end, to avert the knowledge of the universal hunger which will finally annihilate him. An essential ingredient for the happiness of this position is for men to separate themselves from the awful and unendurable comprehension of death's violence to human sensibilities. A great part of the tale's rhetoric is at least superficially concerned with this effort. In the explanations man uses to adjust himself to or to ignore what finally faces him, he attempts, often successfully, to attain this goal.

In the major scenes of the tale, the Nun's Priest alludes, albeit satirically, to the significant ways in which man neutralizes death's terror to find this peace. In Pertelote's speech we find the explanation of medicine, which faces death by keeping the body healthy as long as possible. In this view the body is a machine which can be repaired for a while but whose functions, mental and physical, will inevitably cease. It concerns itself with that limited freedom man has to protect himself (or kill himself, as the case may be) by temperance and potions. This neutralization can be seen in the way that Pertelote treats the figure of death-the-fox. She takes account of him only so far as to resolve his red and black hair into excesses of Chauntecleer's red and black bile, which need to be balanced by laxatives. In this simplification, she makes the mind an appendage to the body and merges the figures of rooster and fox. For her, the predator is within; herbs will silence him. In her terms, she quite rightly ignores the fox as a significant figure in her interpretations. Man has no freedom to prepare for the ultimate predator, either for the fox or for the widow, who is a much greater threat. In fact, when the widow elects to eat this bird, there will be no recourse either to cleverness or outside aid. While there is no deception in Pertelote's counsel of "Eat your herbs and dream no dreams," there is also no room for pride, imagination, or joy. Hers is a low-key solution, for life is brought down to death. Death and life are both denuded of meaning, for as life excites no joy, so death excites no terror.

Chauntecleer's words on dreams allude to the determinist's way of handling death. This theory protects itself against the recognition of death as a cataclysm by placing every event in human life on the same continuum of inevitability. If it denies man any room for personal action or thought, it also provides security against having to conceive of the unimaginable breakup of the body by insisting that life and death are actually alike. As man is fated to die, so too is he fated to live. It offers the freedom of sameness, for the unknown is like the known, and death is elevated and joined to the most complex thoughts of which the mind is capable. In Chauntecleer's speech, the fox as the bringer of death explodes into manifold agents: an innkeeper, mischance, a political party, a pharaoh, a conquering king, a Greek hero. As none of these hold any immediate threat for Chauntecleer, he loses his fear of the fox.

In the conclusion to Chauntecleer's speech, we have another of the traditional distractions which avert the thought of death, the perception of the beauty of woman, or simply of beauty. The freedom that beauty allows from the ghastly confrontation with death is an intense joy in the moment. This moment becomes transcendental because it allows a vision of divine harmony and wholeness and gives an illusion that joy is immortal. The triumph for Chauntecleer is not only that by the elaborateness of his explanation, he has managed to neutralize the threat of death; it is also that the sudden recognition of Pertelote's beauty gives him an even higher sense of transcendent freedom. With his words "In principio / Mulier est hominis confusio" (3163–64), he includes her in a new synthesis which pays the highest possible compliment to her. It is not a mistranslation that he lyingly offers her: if she can read Cato and the medical authorities whom she cites, she can certainly understand his statement and the word *confusio* with its double meaning, "confusion" and "union." His translation is rather, as he says, an interpretation of his "sentence": "Womman is mannes joye and al his blis" (3166). That there must be a next moment, the moment when the fox comes, is something that Chauntecleer is able in his freedom to forget altogether.

In the fox's speech, the narrator alludes to the ideals of heroism, which adjust to death by making it the occasion for the belief in the intense meaning of existence. For its celebration of life, we have merely to remember Achilles' words from the Elysian fields: "Better to be the meanest slave on earth than king of all these dead men." Unlike the appeal of beauty, which concerns itself with the moment, the heroic code contemplates the past, the present, and the future. Its memory is glorious aristocratic tradition and ancestry, which commit the individual to its ideals. Its present, in peace, is the celebration of its concerns by courtly rituals in domestic and foreign countries, and its present in war, by glorious deeds. Its future is fame, which gives it earthly immortality for its acts performed in the present. The fox as the agent of death celebrates the heroic worth of the king to whom he speaks. He tells the orphan Chauntecleer of the courtliness of his parents, who once visited the fox's country. He speaks to him of the distinction of his father, of his lineage in a race able to defeat priests. He speaks to him of his success in his vocation of music, where he carries on the tradition of his father. He challenges him to prove that he is worthy of his position. Chauntecleer, like the average hero, closes his eyes in the direct confrontation with death-the-fox in order to rejoice in the glory of his beliefs a little longer.

This series of explanations, through which man attempts to find some peace from the thought of death, alludes to progressively more complex and conventionalized literary forms and language. Thus medicine, science, would deal only with the bare facts and a language denuded insofar as possible of metaphor or stylized expressions of any kind. Philosophy, accepting metaphor and example as a necessary evil, would nevertheless maintain that it describes facts also, not only natural laws but the facts of the mind's laws and perceptions. Love poetry intends only to describe a feeling. While all would call sex a fact, few have been content to describe love in that fashion. The literary conventions are readily acceptable as necessary stylizations which help to capture the illusive and unnameable. Heroic poetry, the most elaborate of all poetic forms and the great summit which poetic language is capable of attaining, abounds in conventions and stylizations. If its central perception is death and hell, it nevertheless celebrates the rituals of life that enable man to tolerate his end and believe in the ecstasy of his joy.

The success of these explanations in averting the despairing recognition of our fate (which is to be eaten in the end) may be seen in Chauntecleer's reactions to them. Each explanation becomes a little more effective than the last at blinding him to the realities of the physical death hinted at by the dream. As he listens to Pertelote, he should be reminded that his body will disintegrate; as he listens to his own philosophy, he should be reminded that man is fated to die. As he perceives the beauty of his wife, he should be reminded of the imminent decay of all things warmly beautiful. As he listens to the fox, he should be reminded of the vision of life whose gut-level assumption is the hell of death. But, of course, he is not reminded at all. His joy increases, not his despair. His delight with himself and his earth expands with each successive explanation.

This little fable points a moral; the force of language's ambiguous power suddenly makes itself felt. While it is true that language may defend us from the knowledge of death's crude demands, it also has the power to destroy our natural awareness of its own threat. In the face of each explanation Chauntecleer becomes a little more vulnerable. Pertelote's clearheaded but unimaginative interpretation of his dream—go out and eat herbs—makes him angry. His anger leads him into the intellectual hybris which can be fed only by trouncing an opponent. He proves neither that he ought to stay in or go out but that wherever he is, he is an important recipient of an awesome message. The balance toward the choice of going out is tipped by the beauty of his silent opponent, which reminds him of the inadequacies of his perch to the actions demanded of a superior being. He goes outside to make love and encounter death. The words of the fox, his killer, send him into that euphoric state that removes all obstacles and irritations from his comprehension. At the last, in the consummate experience of having for the first time in his life a connoisseur to celebrate that great excellence he imagines himself to possess, he is caught by the neck with the teeth of the fox. The fox's words have put him in that foul prison which so terrified him in the dream. The end of his dialogue is imminent.

The totally disconcerting use to which the Nun's Priest puts man's very serious verbal efforts to defend himself against the insignificance of his mortality is sufficient to warn us that the emphasis on physical death fulfills only the peripheral function of providing a point of reference: it concretizes the tale's morality (to use the Nun's Priest's word). In the first place, none of the speakers uses the verbal appeal in the belief that death is the immediate inevitability that man (or chickens, as the case may be) must struggle to face and master. There is a comic discrepancy, therefore, between the words of the speakers and their real intents. Pertelote, in spite of her role as physician, is not so much interested in a healthy husband as a brave one who will not groan over dreams in his sleep. Medicine has at best a dubious relation to bravery, especially if the hero is not sick to begin with. Chauntecleer in his role as determinist is not so much interested in luxuriating in the mental triumph of his ability to prove that death is inevitable as in drowning his wife in authorities. As connoisseur of beauty, he is not so much interested in the exquisite joy it allows to mortal man as he is in these soothing words which insure that Pertelote for all his mental squashing is still receptive to the rather milder form of squashing in his treading. The fox in the role of epic bard is not so much interested in the celebration of action in the face of death's inevitable negation of action as in eating Chauntecleer, or as we might say, of taking him in.

In fact, from our point of view, each of the explanations is used on an inappropriate subject. Chauntecleer is not sick, Pertelote is not interested in dreams, nor is she beautiful. Chauntecleer is not a hero; he is a crower, and not even a crower of tales. All the characters are interested, not in their theoretical explanations, which pacify man for a moment, but only in the body of Chauntecleer. Pertelote is interested in healing it, Chauntecleer in using it to enjoy Pertelote's, the fox in eating it. The specialized knowledge each of them exhibits is called forth by an interest which is manifestly less and less related, as the tale goes on, to the form of advice employed.

The Nun's Priest's really devastating satire against these explanations, however, lies in the implication that the deviousness of the characters who use them is not peculiar to them. On the contrary, there is a strong suggestion that their real intents are only too often the intents of all who use this language. The elementary and confused remedy against death suggested by Pertelote, a remedy that ignores pride and is incapable of recognizing the spiritual implications of death's terror, is a quite accurate portrayal of the medical profession and its advice. The intent of the determinist is traditionally associated with the psychotic need to put down an opponent. Love poetry is notoriously interested, for all its idealism, in the treading process. While I suppose that few would maintain that Homer and Virgil are trying to kill us, the same cannot be said for the Nun's Priest (with whom I shall deal a little later), who mocks epic values quite as deviously as the fox.

What this tale is primarily concerned with is not the primitive potentiality of the body's imminent death, but the complex and sophisticated potentiality of the mind's death in the face of authority, particularly as that authority confronts us in language. This threat, too, is contained in the dream and is also represented in the fox. His presence brings silence, for he is the killer of the ability to retort. The voluble Chauntecleer has nothing to say in the dream and can only groan in his sleep. This numb terror, the dream perception of this devouring reality, is in this context a comic representation of a power profound enough to destroy the mind utterly, even before the body has been touched. The terror is the observer's terror of the moment when the dialogue ends, when he may no longer say "I," when he realizes that he can be stopped from throwing himself and what he is into play against the world around him. The hungry fox who destroys the body operates as the threat behind the action of the tale, but the hungry fox who numbs the mind and its language, hence its freedom, provides the real threat that underlies the rhetoric with which the narrator bombards us. The fox, in other words, stands for the agent that destroys not only the freedom of the body, but also, by means of language, destroys the freedom of the mind's reaction. The struggle against both kinds of death, ultimately futile, is man's struggle to preserve his freedom. Success, temporary to be sure, allows him to retain the right to his humanity—or rather, as the tale remorselessly forces us to say, to his roosterhood.

The satire against the "explanation" ranges over a wide area in the tale simply because explanations have various effects upon us. Some explanations are irritating (Pertelote's); some so adequately take care of the matter at hand that immediately upon finishing them we are free to take up whatever pastime we like because they give us joy (Chauntecleer's explanations to Pertelote fall into this category). Some appeal to our pride (the fox's). But if the explainer gets his teeth into us, then he will kill us. It is this sort of death that the fox threatens from the dream onward, and it is because he represents this threat that he is aptly compared to traitors as well as to murderers.

If the satiric attack on the joyful and moving moments before us in the tale is stronger than we care to think of the cheerful poet Chaucer's employing, we are temporarily relieved by the knowledge that the action of the tale concerns, not the fated moment, but one of the moments of play. It deals, not with the day of death, but with the day of freedom. The Nun's Priest— as is apparent in his extensive satirical use of the Boethian theory of conditional necessity, which we examined in the last chapter—is interested primarily in exploring middle grounds. On this ground, which we may call time, the roles of eater and eaten are not assigned with rigidity, and there is considerable difference in the conscious reaction of speakers and hearers to these momentary roles that reverse or are suspended with startling swiftness. On this middle ground, however, the terms remain constant: fate threatens when original language and thought are throttled, and freedom is in evidence so long as a character can speak.

The two scenes of the tale, with their potential Menippean dialogues, explore these themes of death and language. In the *Consolation*, the purpose of the central dialogue set up by Philosophy is to lure Boethius into a point of view which coincides with her will—to establish, in other words, a master-disciple relationship. Each speaker in the tale, in a similar way, may be said with his or her explanation to take on the role of Philosophy for a moment. In the first scene, which centers on the theoretical explanation of dreams, first Pertelote and then Chauntecleer attempts to rule the dialogue, but neither captures a disciple. In the second scene of the tale, which centers on singing and speaking, the fox successfully sets up a dialogue with Chauntecleer, and Chauntecleer at his escape deviously cooperates in this dialogue with the fox. At the end of the tale, with

Chauntecleer in the tree, Chaucer has the fox stay, in spite of the imminent arrival of the farmhands, and attempt to reestablish the courteous but very dangerous relationship of the Menippean dialogue.[3] Chauntecleer wisely refuses his overtures.

In the opening scene, in spite of their poses as master interpreters of dreams, both Chauntecleer and Pertelote are actually up to something else. Pertelote is trying to mold Chauntecleer into her conception of a husband as one who is brave; Chauntecleer is trying to mold Pertelote into his conception of a wife as one who acknowledges his superiority. Both succeed at their endeavor and get their way: afterwards, Chaunteleer struts bravely about the barnyard, and Pertelote peacefully accepts his treading as before. Even better, neither has succeeded in harming the other through the good intentions of happy exertions. Chauntecleer could not, in an English May, assemble one of Pertelote's three poisonous recipes, even if he tried (only one herb, "lauriol," being available at the time), and she has besides given him a few days respite on a diet of worms (presumably in case he is feigning).[4] Chauntecleer's elaborate piling up of *exempla* proving that dreams do forecast the future has, if possible, as little effect on Pertelote as it does on Chauntecleer himself. He is dutifully surveying the "wortes" under the guidance of a butterfly when he discovers the fox. The "dialogue" of the first scene is in reality a two-level monologue where the prime desire of the one speaker raises no conflict with the prime desire of the other. Both capture a hearer and speak the words of the mentor, but neither captures a disciple for the Menippean dialogue.

In the second scene of the tale, however, the confrontation of the fox and Chauntecleer portrays the Menippean dialogue in satiric purity. The fox attempts to mold Chauntecleer into a meal, and for an extended moment is totally successful. Like Philosophy, he converts Chauntecleer to his point of view with little effort, and Chauntecleer becomes a disciple in the absolute clutches of the master. It might be argued that the fox's motives are basely and obviously ulterior, as Philosophy's are not, or at least are no more so than the motives of any teacher who would try to lure her pupil into what she thought important to him. But in this context that concession, unfortunately, is enough to make the parallel telling. The traditional values which Philosophy represents must, in order to continue living, have pupils who acquiesce in their tenets. The triumphant experience they offer is their celebration of the value of man, and that is exactly the basis of the fox's appeal to Chauntecleer (though for "man," substitute "rooster"). The fox, like Philosophy, is without remorse and has every intent of strangling any disagreements out of his disciple. Each would *say* "for your own good," but the acts of each deny freedom; and to be without freedom to think and act in the chosen way is to be dead. The terms in which the Nun's Priest elects to cast this dilemma are intended to be, and are, startling.

The fox is the enemy of fortune ("Lo, how Fortune turneth sodeynly / The hope and pryde eek of hir enemy!" [3403–4]), hence the agent of order. That the fox, like Philosophy, represents these concepts in this scene may be seen in the two images within the description of the barnyard chase. The pursuers scream "as feendes doon in helle" (3388). The fox in the implicit contrastive image becomes, if not the agent of goodness and harmony, at least the satanic orderer of hell. In the second image, the precise function of the fox is more exactly portrayed. Here, the pursuers scream like Jack Straw and his men, killing Flemings:

> Certes, he Jakke Straw and his meynee
> Ne made nevere shoutes half so shrille
> Whan that they wolden any Flemyng kille,
> As thilke day was maad upon the fox.
> (3394–97)

Again, the pursuers become the disrupters of order, a threat to society and to the state. The fox, like the Flemings, is in a foreign country, but he is peacefully attending to his way of life. That his work, like the Flemings', takes food from the mouth of the mob in no way puts him into such a contemptible category as that of his opponents.

These pursuers are parallel to the disordered masses of plunderers which Philosophy almost immediately draws her disciple into her castle to avoid (bk. 1, pr. 3). The fox, in the same way, is attempting to get his disciple into the wood (his castle), where his own rules will operate in their undistracted rigidity. The barnyard is the place where the rooster blindly revels in the goods of fortune, fame, power, and pleasure, from the thought of whose delights Philosophy wishes to rescue Boethius. The wood toward which the fox takes Chauntecleer is the place where man consciously ceases to exist in his spiritual and physical complexity. For Boethius, man attains Being in the castle; for the Nun's Priest, he attains death—states which, to the un-Platonic eye, are uncomfortably alike. To be is also to have been. But the narrator, unlike Philosophy, allows this no-man's-land between world and castle, where death is perceived but not enacted. Here, all voices have equal power, and masters are vulnerable because of the chaotic forces loose around them.

As Chauntecleer takes over the control of the action, the tale's central concern reaches its climax, namely the presentation of how it is that man stays free in the face of death, literal and symbolic. The four speeches which allude to the explanations he uses for this purpose suggest that for whatever devious reason, he can take medicine or he can talk, can philosophize, epicurize, or heroize himself into a state of blind happiness. But this final scene, the crisis, is a representation of what to do at that crucial moment when the deluded finds death too close and the delusion of language too deadly. The fox has left the barnyard with Chauntecleer between his teeth and is nearly across no-man's-land to the wood. An infernal hubbub surrounds them. The whole world is in hot pursuit. What is said here is relatively unimportant, as may be seen by the neutral quality of Chauntecleer's words to the fox.

> "Sire, if that I were as ye,
> Yet sholde I seyn, as wys God helpe me,
> 'Turneth agayn, ye proude cherles alle!
> A verray pestilence upon yow falle!
> Now am I come unto the wodes syde;
> Maugree youre heed, the cok shal heere abyde.
> I wol hym ete, in feith, and that anon!'"
>   (3407–13)

These words to the fox, unlike every other passage in the tale—
almost, we would say, unlike every other line—do not fall into
an easily recognizable stylistic parody of a categorical "explanation." In fact, this speech is merely a flattened version of
what Chauntecleer says in the analogues Chaucer drew the tale
from. It is sometimes said that Chauntecleer flatters the fox
here, the speech then becoming the third stage in the commentary on flattery. As Chauntecleer flatters Pertelote and gets
what he wants, as the fox flatters Chauntecleer and gets what
he wants, so Chauntecleer flatters the fox and gets what he
wants. But the analogy is false. There is no stylistic similarity
between this passage and the elaborate appeals of Chauntecleer
to Pertelote or of the fox to Chauntecleer. Flattery takes time,
and there is little here. The key to Chauntecleer's success in his
speech to the fox lies in his drawing the fox's attention to the
chaotic mob, which recognizes neither the validity nor the existence of the fox's orderly procedures. The indignation which he
should feel at this desecration of a commendable success is
given voice to by his now devious cohort in the alliance,
Chauntecleer. The rooster, recognizing the fox's belief in their
mutual commitment, does not remind the fox of his own reluctance, either by screeching or by any sort of physical struggle.
The fox, in acknowledgment that the disciple has learned the
ways of the master, opens his mouth to trumpet his protest
against the evil destroyers of his order. Chauntecleer, the dedicated representative of all worldly vices, saves himself, illus-
trating, however, Boethius' last comment on Fortune: It lies in
your power to form for yourself what fortune you please.

The moral of all this would seem to be the usual one in the inner dialogue: if we don't watch out, explanations eat us quite as
effectively as foxes eat chickens if they don't watch out. What is
potentially dangerous about the explanation is not any particular thing it says, but that it puts blinders on us and forces us to
limit our understanding of primary experience to some particular area. Its dangerous imposing of restrictions is what makes it
worthy of satire. The defense against the explanation that robs
us of freedom is the same as Chauntecleer's defense against the
fox. We have wings which, if we think to use them in time, al-

low us to soar into the air and concoct explanations of our own (roughly speaking, Chauntecleer's procedure until the moment when he closes his eyes). If we do not think in time, we can take advantage of the chaotic forces the explainers fear, more because they do not account for the explainers than because the explainers cannot account for them. This chaos, ineffectual though it may be in saving us when we are passive victims, provides an overwhelming potential distraction. This incalculable force which operates against any explanation allows the victim opportunity to exert himself and save his life.

The final scene can only be understood as the inevitable playing out of a dialogue which threatens to take place from the beginning of the tale. It arises in the major premise of the tale, and its stakes are freedom or death. The dream, the most realistic view of death in the tale, establishes death as silence, or in Chauntecleer's case in the dream, the absence of dialogue and the total absorption in terror. As death is silence, so life or freedom is language. The dream, of course, also threatens the physical death of Chauntecleer but, as it does not take place in the dream, is secondary, and in spite of the tale's fable of eaters and eaten, does not occur. In the succeeding scenes of the tale the silence that death threatens is countered by allusions to writings which become increasingly complex: we move from medicine to epic. But each of the speakers is intent on silencing his opponent or, to put it more bluntly, in capturing his prey, to kill him with language. The last scene represents dramatically and allegorically how men may maintain or regain their identity in the face of the engulfing, threatening quality of words.

In the outer dialogue, where we as potential victims listen to the language of the Nun's Priest, we are in a more dangerous position than the characters of the tale, for we can neither talk back nor act so as to escape the master machinations of this eater. A certain thoughtful suspiciousness is in order. Donaldson points out one of our chief difficulties: "Aware that in the personality of the satirist will always exist grounds for rebutting the satire, Chaucer carefully gives us nothing to work on in the character of the Nun's Priest: there is no portrait of him in the *General Prologue*, and the introduction to his tale reveals only the most inoffensive of men."⁵ We discover the narrator in primarily two ways. The more obvious is through the words at the end of the tale, where his address to good men and his invitation to take the morality of his tale suddenly announces his presence. The other, less obvious, is through our perception of a certain insinuatingly peculiar bias that emerges every now and again from under the very funny Menippean attacks on verbal formulations which we have been examining in this and the preceding chapter. Since the import of the narrator's concluding remarks is to be grasped only when we have clarified what attitude it is that gives the tale its strange tone, I will begin with what we learn about the narrator before the final lines.

It seems safe to say, even in this tale where all our critical statements are somehow suspect, that the narrator's primary target is human pride. The characters, as we have seen, are generally involved in the attempt to kill pride, which is what the galline being stands for. Pertelote would kill the pride raised by the dream, Chauntecleer would kill the pride raised by the knowledge of medicine, the fox would kill the pride of Chauntecleer's heroic preeminence (which, it is true, the fox has just manufactured for him). The point of this killing is the gratification of a larger individual desire. Each betrays a specific hunger: the hunger for a brave husband, the hunger for a submissive wife, the hunger for an acquiescent pupil. Each is unsatisfied at the end. Chauntecleer is not brave; he is cunning. Pertelote is not submissive; she is either silent, enjoying their mutual love, or screaming in epic proportions. Chauntecleer is, in spite of a temporary acquiescence, not acquiescent a second time. The fox is still as hungry as when he came into the barnyard. If we may judge by the critics' reluctance to be so offensive as to examine the real premises of this tale, the narrator has done better than his characters. But we should resist his explanations and accept to the full the implications of his "merry tragedy."⁶

The narrator's overt but deceptive (we are not offended—we close our eyes and crow in glee) insult to human pride lies in his use of the combined literary forms, the fable and the mock-epic, to present his views. The fable explains how alike men and animals are; the mock-epic explains how alike are the trivial and the grand event, the subjects which supposedly call forth the low and the high style. This anthropomorphizing of animals and this destruction of the hierarchy distinguishing the great and the trivial are traditional and therefore obvious ways of penetrating man's sense of superiority. The erasing of distinctions suggests that, unhappily, man's claims for the greatness of man, especially the hero, in a divinely appointed scheme are only an illusion to cover his rather undistinctive part in the eons of nature's repetitions. The belittling device of fable is simple. It pricks man's pretensions by presenting the animal combatting and solving the physical and spiritual problems men take to be their exclusive prerogatives.

The belittling devices of mock-epic are more elaborate. Epic, which it mocks, represents man's highest effort to contain within a poem the full sweep of human life in relation to time, space, divinity, and death; its scope is bounded only by a grandeur of conception which insists on both the tragedy and the beauty of the human condition. While the technical devices for mockery which the form allows are much more numerous than the devices the fable offers, the fundamental satire of mock-epic resides in creating a vast discrepancy between form and content. It presents a trivial event in high style or a great event in low style: Penelope and Odysseus talk and act like fishwives, or fishwives talk and act like Odysseus and Penelope. The Nun's Priest employs the latter method, much the less bitter of the two, it is true. A cock, a hen, and a fox have the learned and beautiful vocabularies of the great among men.

All of this insulting belittlement is, of course, obvious, a little too obvious. In fact, we are not really insulted at all. On the contrary, we are laughing and delighted. The glorification of animals, highly amusing animals, and the glorification of a minor event, a near-catastrophe in a barnyard, a catastrophe which will befall us all sooner or later in some barnyard or other, creates a sense of brotherhood and communion. In the end we feel—heaven help us, for the narrator will not—that the tale tells us that all creation is involved in the search for meaning and freedom; we need not feel ourselves so alone. We congratulate ourselves on our fine sense of humor, our ability to laugh at ourselves, our commendable and healthy delight in seeing ourselves doubly mocked.

In this silly, self-admiring mood, we are exactly where the narrator wants us. For we have, at this point, failed to heed two of the three warnings in the concluding scene. The first is, Do not listen to flatterers. This we have ignored completely. It is much too cheering to us to think that, for all our foolishness, the rooster in us prevails over the fox and without any direct help from the widow-god. In the midst of the Nun's Priest's beguilement, we ignore the bitter edge of the ironic forms, fable and mock-epic. We ought not to forget the second injunction: Do not close your eyes when you should see. In other words, the form of the tale is one of the chief means by which the Nun's Priest subdues us to his intents, his engulfing negation of "explanation." In order to get loose from the flattery of this fox, we too need to be cunning. We may assume that Chaucer is the narrator's master and, if an admiring master, that he has nevertheless provided us enough information to achieve our freedom from the beguiling one of the "preestes three."

We note that there is something odd about this merged form which the Nun's Priest uses. Though in teaching this tale, we are quite willing to say that it is a fable and a mock-epic, we never at any other point in our discussion of literature think to use it as an illustration for either form (Aesop and the *Rape of the Lock* always precede it). And this is not altogether due to the narrator's employing the two in combination. I suspect that it is rather that we unconsciously possess a knowledge that we must work very hard to acquire consciously, namely that the fable and mock-epic forms do not quite do in this tale what they ought to. Because they do not, we find the tale funny but are uncertain about the causes of our laughter. This combined form is not the vehicle merely for belittling our pride; its intent is also to get us to shut our eyes. The fox beguiles Chauntecleer with straight heroic values; the Nun's Priest beguiles us with straight mock-heroic values.

The discrepancy between what a fable should be and what a

mock-epic should be is, at least for our purposes here, quite obvious. A fable has a moral; a mock-epic has an issue. Neither requirement is fulfilled by this tale. There is not one moral; there is a plethora of morals, morals related to every conceivable angle of the subject. Some critics, thinking this tale no more complex than the story on which it is based, have seen the moral to be one of the announced ones: "Beware of flattery."[7] Some have seen it as a warning against the state of complacency in which both flattery and jangling are dangers.[8] Some, casting their nets wider, have seen it as a satire on the foolishness of men.[9] Some have seen it as a satire against the counsel of women.[10] I see it as a satire on men's habit not only of making but also of idiotically believing in inane categories and outmoded theories. Of course, all of us are right, just as the six blind men were all right about the elephant. But none of these stated or abstracted morals will account for the narrator's tone. And without the validation of tone, believing in one moral or another threatens to tax the mind beyond endurance, that is, as long as we remain as honest as possible and do not merely select a moral for the most convenient theory. In any case, the ubiquity of potential morals destroys the fable's pristine form.

Similarly, the fact that there is no issue to this action destroys the pristine form of the mock-epic. If all the evidence I have presented so far is examined closely, it will be seen to verge onto one plane where everything is static, everything is the same; where, in a word, primary experience is made to exist in all its insignificance. This statement applies to the story as well as to the commentary. The dream provides no action; the action provides no change. The central episode, the meeting, is an interlude merely; when it is ended, everything goes back to what it was before. Adam does not eat his fruit; Christ is not crucified; Troy does not fall; Carthage is not destroyed; Rome is not burned; Roland does not die at Roncesvalles. All the allusions to the grand tragedies of the human race are flattened because they have no mock parallel, and they, too, become a part of the chaff. The absence of result gives a singularly hollow ring to this tale, a deadly, unreverberant nothingness that blocks our laughter.

The sense of empty commitment lurking under the narrator's

use of fable and mock-epic also lurks under his commentary. As we analyze the tale, we keep looking for some sane locus from which the narrator launches his attacks, but we cannot find it. Lucian's *Hermotimus* provides a useful, contrasting analogy. Here, too, we have an insistent attacker of human theories. Lucian's mouthpiece, Lycinus, with merciless logic demolishes the validity of the philosophical systems to which Hermotimus has dedicated a life of study. The "paralyzing agnosticism" in the attack, as Allinson terms it,[11] has as its end, however, only that Hermotimus leave the mad pursuit of theory and be content with living an ordinary life in an everyday world. But this work, Lucian's most damning attack on dialectic, is also his most brilliant use of dialectic. The balanced relation between attack and method provides an illustration of the Menippean theorem: The terms which define a system can also be used to achieve release from the system and hence the pause where we can begin to think constructively again (*vide* Chauntecleer with the fox). Under Lucian's violent attacks, there is kindness and a sense of joy in the brilliant potential of the human mind. The pronoun *we*, not *you*, governs his attacks.

In the Nun's Priest's attitude, however, the terms of this Menippean theorem are askew. He attacks with the language of his noble victims, but he satirizes it with the reductive forms fable and mock-epic and then satirizes even these forms. The thrust of his satire is always toward nothing. He manifestly absents himself from any responsible suggestion whatsoever. He stands outside. *You* is the pronoun we hear. He observes as an alien being who has no human interest in the pause which heralds the chance for a fresh beginning. Instead, he glories in the destructiveness of his attacks. His enthusiastic delight in chaos is revealed by his lies, his inconsistencies, his covert, sly, and gleeful attacks on serious thinkers, which reduce them to the status of inhabitants of a theological Laputa. His pleasure in trivializing is revealed by his reduction of the hopes of human life to the narrow confines of a barnyard, by his representation of the victory over death as a rooster clutching a tree branch. He stirs his spoon in the chaos, and while he laughs at men's rooster-like concerns and belittles their futile attempts at explanation, he rejoices in the uncontrollable state of affairs in which roosters strive for the truth. His attitude shows him loyal to the insignificance of the world where mere mortals struggle to live and think. The voice of the goodly priest, Sir John, is the voice of the devil. Our sense of the comic in the tale may not be diminished by this knowledge, for like other literary devils, the narrator is a very attractive man. But what he is about should cause us to be wary of laughing too much.[12]

In the final six lines, the Nun's Priest, with his address to good men, "opens his mouth" and becomes willfully guilty of the fox's error: he jangles instead of holding his peace. His sudden switch from his story to an address to his audience jerks us out of our complacent involvement with the central dialogue into the different reality of the frame dialogue; and like Chauntecleer, we ought to fly into the most convenient tree, not stay in the fox's mouth the while, for we have been in the process of being beguiled by a master with intents every bit as wicked as the fox's:

> But ye that holden this tale a folye,
> As of a fox, or of a cok and hen,
> Taketh the moralite, goode men.
> (3438-40)

Those who would hold this tale a "folye"—the "mob" at this point chasing the foxy narrator—would be not only those who disapprove of the "lie" of fiction,[13] all those whose French critical propensities make them believe form should not be tampered with, but also all those masters of the human mind—for the tradition of human knowledge, the "gods" of this world: the philosophers, moralists, scientists, poets, grammarians, logicians —who have dedicated themselves seriously to the ordering of chaos. To this mob, that is, to those who can be expected to hold the tale a "folye," the Nun's Priest addresses the injunction: "Taketh the morality, goode men." This injunction is rather like tossing a baby out of the sleigh to the wolves; they stop their pursuit for a while to eat that; they may even be satisfied. When we fall into the category of cheerful searchers, we exhibit a blindness that exceeds that of Chauntecleer, who at least

knew enough to know the fox's teeth were on his neck.
The Nun's Priest continues by quoting Scripture:

> For seint Paul seith that al that writen is,
> To oure doctrine it is ywrite, ywis;
> Taketh the fruyt, and lat the chaf be stille.
> (3441–43)

He suggests, because St. Paul alludes to sacred writings,[14] that
he has put before us a "sacred" text. But the tale, with its mocking subversion of the potential in human struggles to make life
meaningful, is a sacred text only for the devil. The injunction
"Taketh the fruit and let the chaff be stille" is suspiciously
Edenic, a Satanic injunction to eat the fruit that reveals to us
our embarrassing and uncoverable nakedness whose infinite,
depressing ramifications the tale has supposedly touched only
in the slightest comic way. This fruit is the knowledge that destroys all sense of beauty, all joy, all impulse toward freedom.
This fruit is the morality of the arch-destroyer: all creative
human effort is meaningless. This is the only moral that rever-
berates resoundingly through the logic of the action and the
rhetoric and the narrator's attitude without devouring itself. A
"grotesque" (Robertson's apt description of the man-chicken relation)[15] ignorantly avails himself of such constructive freedom
as exists; no one can sort out any other definitive object of the
satire in the rhetoric. As Donaldson says, "The fruit of the
'Nun's Priest's Tale' is its chaff."[16] The narrator's meaningless
heroism, his perpetual lies, his total lack of consistency, his
empty denigration of all that men have thought worthwhile,
would have given him away at once if he were not so successful
in appealing to our stock responses to laughter. If his immediate desire is for a laughing, unoffended audience, his larger intent is to remove any thought, any effort, that masks the reality
of universal despair. In that most negative of depressions, man
becomes food for the devil.

The Nun's Priest gives himself away finally in the last three
lines of his tale—the devil must appear with a cloven hoof. As
Christian priest speaking from the right side of the fence, he
would have had to say "our lord" in these much-commented-
upon lines:[17]

The Eaters and the Eaten in *The Nun's Priest's Tale*

> Now, goode God, if that it be thy wille,
> As *seith my lord*, so make us alle goode men,
> And brynge us to his heighe blisse! Amen.
> (3444–46; my italics)

"My lord" is the devil's address to his master, Satan. The fiend in the *Friar's Tale* uses the phrase also: "My lord is hard to me and daungerous" (1427). The goodly Sir John evidently has a happier relation with his master.

The Nun's Priest is the greatest rascal among the Canterbury pilgrims. By comparison, even the Pardoner is mild, for the rascality he openly and deliberately describes for himself is, after all, on a level which even the relatively dense can understand. The Nun's Priest equivocates, shall we say, in the realms which only a few enter. Those few are invariably innocent (unlike the Nun's Priest) and suspecting no evil from those gifted with a similar ability to reach this stage. We usually escape him the way the Host does:

> "Sire Nonnes Preest," oure Hooste seide anoon,
> "I-blessed be thy breche, and every stoon!
> This was a murie tale of Chauntecleer.
> But by my trouthe, if thou were seculer,
> Thou woldest ben a trede-foul aright.
> For if thou have corage as thou hast myght,
> Thee were nede of hennes, as I wene,
> Ya, moo than seven tymes seventene."
> (3447–54)[18]

In identifying the Nun's Priest with Chauntecleer rather than with the fox, the Host identifies him with the human struggler, the friend of fortune who bumbles along joyfully making what he can out of the potential of the moment. Confused though the Host is about the Nun's Priest's intents, he is nevertheless right about where we mortals wish to stand in relation to this tale. There may be no theoretical way of disproving the Nun's Priest's diabolical moral "All human effort is meaningless," but we simply do not agree. We wish to stay on the high edge of the human comedy, which in its fullness Chauntecleer's activities for the day have provided. We comfortably dismiss the whole thing as a fable, by commonly accepted medieval definition an account of something that cannot have happened.[19] We leave Chauntecleer convinced that he will go back to the barnyard and that night back to his roost. He will doubtless say, "I told you so," to Pertelote. And there he will live with his wives until his brother the fox or his god the widow shall eat him.

8

Sic et Non: Discarded Worlds in *The Knight's Tale*

That the *Knight's Tale*, a philosophical parody with the *Consolation* and the romance as its models, belongs to the serio-comic tradition of Menippean satire is abundantly evident in much of the critical literature that surrounds the poem. While it has never, to my knowledge, had its particular and peculiar elements explained by being related to this genre, the traits characteristic of the satire are commented on frequently. That the tale is a parody of its ostensible genre, the romance, has been recognized and the presence of the inserted text, the *Consolation*, clearly documented; the multiplicity of tones and voices, often illustrated; the presence of unreconciled oppositions and the difficulty of determining the poem's meaning, frequently observed.[1] The subject of order—the organization that Menippean satire sees men trying to impose on chaos with their theories, explanations, and structures—is central to the tale and also to the critical debate that surrounds it.[2]

Yet, in spite of this help, the implications and directions that Chaucer gives to Menippean conventions in the *Knight's Tale* are more complex to interpret than those of either *Troilus* or the *Nun's Priest's Tale*. With *Troilus*, once the subcategory in Menippean satire, Menippean tragedy, is recognized, the poem becomes susceptible of interpretation. The *Nun's Priest's Tale* propounds a difficult "who am I" riddle, but like all riddles, contains a toughness that holds up until the answer is found. In the *Knight's Tale*, however, the pursuit of what seem to be promising interlinking conventions and ideas usually ends in our being turned out into the cold, very gently, but turned out nevertheless. The tale is not a Menippean tragedy like *Troilus* (or any other kind of tragedy, though it flirts continually with tragic issues).³ Nor does it propound a riddle, as does the *Nun's Priest's Tale*. It lacks the free laughter of Menippean comedy such as we find in Lucian, Boethius, and perhaps even the *Nun's Priest's Tale* (though laughing with the devil eventually provides an unendurable strain on our capacity for amusement).

The Menippean dialogue in the *Knight's Tale* is easily visible and so is the textual parody; certainly for identifying the genre of the tale as Menippean satire, both are important. The dialogue, with Theseus (the counterpart of Philosophy) and Palamon and Arcite (the counterparts of Boethius),⁴ takes as its subject the controlling question of the tale, which knight shall have the lady. Palamon and Arcite struggle for ten years to find a method of resolving their conflict over Emily. The *deus* figures —Saturn, Mars, and Venus—preside over the solution directly. Theseus, who gives the knights' emotional desire a constructive outlet, builds lists, arranges a tournament, and finally convenes a parliament to resolve the issue. The textual parody, created by the large injection into the formal story of serious philosophical issues reminiscent of those raised by Boethius, is constantly before us. The juxtaposition of a lightweight problem from romance and profound philosophical questioning sets up the familiar dialogical milieu of Menippean satire. Yet those common parodic devices become almost immediately, in any insistent thinking about the poem, only parts of a larger satiric interest.

When we compare the tale with more complex issues in Menippean satire, we find that Chaucer adds a dimension of ironic observation, which, for the task of interpreting the tale, has the force and effect of the proverbial monkey wrench. For instance, the juxtaposition of characters with unmatched problems, espousing opposing philosophies of life, whose positions we are required to examine, is a commonplace in Menippean satire, a primary method of filling up its foreground and of portraying its basic assumption, namely that the reality of things is "out there" but unknowable, that there is, therefore, no accurate standard, no recognized true answer, which mortals can use to guide their lives and assess their thinking. Hence, in some desperate and paradoxical sense, which it generally elects to treat as comic, it proposes that if it is our nature to spend our time energetically preparing for this search, there is nevertheless nothing to be found by going out there to look. To counteract this nothingness, the satirists direct our attention to intellectual confrontations, to multivoiced conflicts drawn from the various representations in the spheres of human knowledge. The satirist keeps us, verbally at least, in the midst of this chaos by not bringing to the forefront his own resolutions to the incipient clash between his various theoretical and mythical formulations. When the conflict threatens, he offers us pauses and right-angle turns. Both occur because of new events in the story or because of new decisions of characters who have egos powerful enough or are lucky enough to impose their will momentarily on the minds of those with whom they deal. Because of their unexpectedness, these changes of pace and direction allow brief moments of freedom from the conflict, but they disappear as we adjust to the new tempos. They allow us to hope for a while before we discover that the old problem is still there and the new beginning offers no truthful insight into the complexity of things.

Chaucer's innovation in the *Knight's Tale* is that, in addition to juxtaposing sharply opposed, never reconciled views of the world, he batters and undermines us with the implication that neither oppositions nor possible reconciliations are of any great consequence to the Knight. By a variety of means, Chaucer blurs the focus of the oppositions, ignores or siphons off the energy the active reader commonly dedicates to resolving them, and thus keeps us in the constant experience of anticlimax and abandonment. With this extra dimension, the tale is, in fact, a brilliant *tour de force*, a parody of the energetic interest which Menippean satire dedicates to its dialogical conflicts.

A minor example of what happens on scales large and small in the tale is found in the *demande d'amour* passage that ends part 1. Arcite, released by Pirithous, has left Athens; Palamon is still imprisoned. Both have uttered their Boethian complaints, Arcite about happiness (1223–74), Palamon about justice (1303–33). The Knight at this point requests that we pause and consider:

> Yow loveres axe I now this questioun:
> Who hath the worse, Arcite or Palamoun?
> (1347–48)

He goes on to pursue the facets of the dilemma with the opposing questions, Is it better to see what you want everyday, but be bound in such a way as to be incapable of approaching it? or, Is it better to be free to do whatever you like, but excluded from the sight of what you want? The problem is not without interest; various metaphoric applications spring to mind. But the point is that the narrator deserts us and the dilemma at once to move on in response to unexplained demands, which, since we cannot grasp them, leave us feeling orphaned.

> Now demeth as yow liste, ye that kan,
> For I wol telle forth as I began.
> (1353–54)

What is done on a small scale in the *demande d'amour* passage is done on the largest scales in the poem. A major conflict which turns up again and again—treated, it is true, as if it had no deep import, no power to clarify anything about the problems of the universe we exist in—is the conflict between "love's law" and "positive law," Arcite's names for two opposing world views. Arguing with unconscious profundity, he justifies his right to love Emily by saying early in the poem:

> "Love is a gretter lawe, by my pan
> Than may be yeve to any erthely man;
> And therfore positif lawe and swich decree
> Is broken al day for love in ech degree."
> (1165–68)

Positive law is, according to Robinson, "a technical term. 'Lex positiva,' as opposed to natural law, is that which rests solely upon man's decree" (p. 672). (For instance: If I see her first, she's mine.)

The distinction that Arcite makes recalls the passage in the *Romance of the Rose*, where Reason proves to the lover that Love is superior to Justice. Justice, she tells him, ruled at the time of Saturn. But when his son, Jupiter, castrated him and

Venus was born in the sea foam from his severed genitals, she departed. If this Justice of the Saturnalian Age were to return to earth now, it would, unless men loved one another, cause great destruction. But if men loved as before, "everyone in the world would then live peacefully and tranquilly, and they would never have a king or prince; there would be neither bailiff nor provost as long as people lived honestly. Judges would never hear any clamor. So I say that Love by itself is worth more than Justice, even though the latter works against Malice."[5] The justice of the Olympian Age is little more than positive law. The opposition that Arcite names hints at larger categories of opposition: Golden Age and Iron Age, old gods and new gods, matriarchy and patriarchy—oppositions which all, in their way, appear in the *Knight's Tale*.

Positive law accounts for codes of agreement in the poem— for example, for the codes of brothers, knights, and national alliances. Its high values are legal justice and political—if need be, martial—order. Its gods are the Olympians, with Jupiter as king. In contrast to this world is the world of natural law, within whose scope in the poem fall Emily, beauty, love, happiness. It is a world without rules in a legal or categorical sense, a world which men perceive darkly, but nevertheless, a world which inspires even despair with meaning. Its gods are the gods of the old order, Saturn and his last self-engendered child, Venus. Natural law is the law of the culture that Brewer designates "unofficial" (the culture of women), and positive law, the law of "official culture" (the culture of men). The two are distinguished, he points out, in that unofficial culture wants quick benefits, the joys and delights of the moment, while official culture would extend all benefits until death.[6] The Knight and other Menippean satirists think that it is our fate, male and female, to be able to look at conventional codifications of excluding oppositions and enjoy the benefits and burdens of either side, and perhaps, most joyous of all, be wary enough of truth to see the oppositions as inconsequential, even if amusingly attractive.

Although the outlines of these oppositions are blurred in the tale, they are nevertheless relatively easy to see. The laws or worlds providing the terms of the conflict exist on the private and public levels and are reflected in the heavens when the gods' activities catch fire from the desires of the knights and Emily. The components of these two laws and the worlds they govern set up a number of antitheses which the poem can be said to explore dismissively: beauty and brotherhood (the private problem), love and order (the public problem), happiness and justice (the divine problem). The contrast, conflict, and philosophical interactions of the planes on which the laws operate, planes which seem to intersect only because the same mind is capable of considering both (not because the Knight proposes any kind of strong and deliberate contest between them), are to be discovered in whatever phase of the text we care to consider. The presence of the opposition is perhaps most evident in the knights' attempt to find a way between the dictates of the beauty of Emily and the code of their sworn brotherhood. For this particular confrontation, Arcite's terms for the two laws (love's law and positive law) could suffice, but I have also used the term "natural law" as synonymous with "love's law."

The tale's foreground focuses on the knights' struggle with one another; complicating their problem is each one's inner struggle to relate this new perception to the vision of life he had before. In all phases of their relation to the goal represented by Emily, their attitudes differ radically and consistently. In the first part of their private ordeal, which takes place in prison, each becomes identified with one of the two systems: Palamon with love's law and Arcite with positive law. Palamon, mistaking Emily for Venus, chief goddess of the realm of love, says: "Venus, if it be thy wil / Yow in this gardyn thus to transfigure / Bifore me, sorweful, wrecched creature, / Out of this prisoum help that we may scapen" (1104–7). Arcite, identifying Emily as a beautiful woman, allies himself with positive law. He says accurately to Palamon: "Thyn is affeccioun of hoolynesse, / And myn is love, as to a creature" (1158–59). Their preferences are apparent also in their naming of the god who ruins their lives. Palamon, in his complaint at the end of part 1, names the Titan Saturn as one of the gods whose jealousy places him in prison, and he blames Venus, too, for his unhappiness:

> "But I moot been in prisoun thurgh Saturne,
> And eek thurgh Juno, jalous and eek wood,
> That hath destroyed wel ny al the blood
> Of Thebes with his waste walles wyde;
> And Venus sleeth me on that oother syde
> For jalousie and fere of hym Arcite."
> (1328–33)[7]

Arcite, alone in the grove, invokes the Olympian Mars as one of the two gods whose malice keeps him enthralled: "Allas, thou felle Mars! allas, Juno! / Thus hath youre ire oure lynage al fordo" (1559–60).

But when the knights begin to argue with one another, each adduces the other's law as grounds for giving up Emily. Palamon, in arguing priorities, cites the oaths and codes of sworn brotherhood and tries to persuade Arcite that his actions should be guided by the rules of positive law.

> This Palamon gan knytte his browes tweye.
> "It nere," quod he, "to thee no greet honour
> For to be fals, ne for to be traitour
> To me, that am thy cosyn and thy brother
> Ysworn ful depe, and ech of us til oother,
> That nevere, for to dyen in the peyne,
> Til that the deeth departe shal us tweyne,
> Neither of us in love to hyndre oother,
> .   .   .   .
> This was thyn ooth, and myn also, certeyn."
> (1128–39)

Arcite, on the contrary, in the passage quoted earlier (1165ff.), maintains to Palamon that the law of love preempts any imaginable man-made law. He attempts to persuade Palamon that his actions should be guided by the recognition that this new experience voids all previous commitments under positive law. In this first stage of their private ordeal, the language of their arguments is dictated purely by the desire to be rid of an opponent. But that they have effectively confused themselves by the use of language not native to them is apparent in the second stage of their private ordeal, where they continue to follow the values of the law opposite to their innate inclinations.[8]

On the one hand, Arcite, the representative of positive law, allies himself to natural law by returning to Athens after his release, thus breaking his knightly oath to Theseus and risking death (1394ff.). He dedicates himself helplessly and hopelessly to the adoration of Emily in Thebes and later in Athens. In the same palace with her and, we must imagine, frequently in the same room, he regards her as a distant star whom he can see but not approach. Palamon, on the other hand, to whom this sort of adoration would be practically more appropriate, since in prison he is separated from Emily in such a way as to be able to draw no attention to himself, can think only of the war of positive law as a way to win her. (War, if won, under the terms of positive law compels assent.)[9] He immediately assumes that Arcite, upon his release, will collect an army to obtain her (1285ff.). He himself escapes from prison with the intent to do just that (1483ff.). At their confrontation in the grove, their reiteration of their respective attitudes confirms their confused and individually unnatural allegiances. Palamon, acting as if he holds positive law supreme, charges Arcite with treachery to him: "And art my blood, and to my conseil sworn" (1583); and then to Theseus: "And hast byjaped heere duc Theseus, / And falsly chaunged hast thy name thus!" (1585–86). Arcite, acting as if he holds natural law supreme, defies the bond between them and continues: "What, verray fool, thynk wel that love is free" (1606).

The public stage of their experience and their return to their native frames of reference are initiated by the appearance at the grove of Theseus and Emily, the turning point in the action. The knights, in the encounter with this sterling representative of positive law, Theseus and his order, are released from their hopeless fight with one another into channels where they can constructively explore the way to obtaining Emily. With less trouble than Philosophy, Theseus persuades his charges to return to their abandoned methods of thought. For Palamon, Theseus' proposal removes the necessity of a war to attain Emily, and he can think how to propitiate the necessary gods. He turns once more to the world of natural law. His accompanying king is associated with Saturn, god of the Golden Age, timelessness, and hence the matriarchal system and natural law. In the temple, praying to Venus, he asks for Emily (as an Amazon representative of matriarchal values). Arcite turns back to the world of the Olympians (positive law). The king he chooses is associated with Mars, an Olympian, god of the Age of Iron, and god of war, a major occupation of the patriarchal system and positive law.[10] In the temple, he prays to Mars and asks for victory (being winner is a central concern of patriarchal values).

That this contrast between the knights and the force of the opposing values they represent is muted by Chaucer to the point of near invisibility is evident in the energetic debate of a whole subcategory of *Knight's Tale* criticism: the argument about whether the knights have characteristics distinguishing them from each other.[11] One reason for the disconcerting flattening of the issue is that no one in the tale pays any attention to the profound nature of their differences. Emily has no preference. She prays first to Diana that she not be obliged to marry either of them and then disinterestedly for the one who desires her most, as if hoping that at least the gods can make some distinction between them. For Theseus, they are young, Theban, and in love. Another reason is that they themselves switch allegiance from one law to the other for a time, an alteration which blocks and balances the consistent symbolic impression they would otherwise make. Furthermore, the Knight, who bears the intermediate responsibility for flattening the contrast, does so by lumping the knights together rhetorically as if they were always the same, playing semimythic roles of identical quality and minor significance: hero, prisoner, lover, aspirant, loser. Though Palamon wins Emily, the Knight, in what Elizabeth Salter calls the "bland denouement of the final twenty lines,"[12] fails to celebrate his success in a pointed way. He treats them offhandedly, as if their differences had no deep meaning, no power to clarify anything about the desperate struggles of men in the universe he proposes. In their presentation, Chaucer evokes profound mythic conflicts and symbols but also, by the means just suggested, discards them.

Theseus, chief representative in the public sphere of the evoked and discarded "mythic *disputatio*"[13] of the *Knight's*

Tale, is the most respectable of the parodies of Philosophy in Chaucer's poetry.[14] Significant traits he possesses in common with Philosophy are the objective insight which lets him handle, untouched by doubt, the problem he presides over, a willingness to engage himself in courteous dialogue with those whose views escape his understanding, and the impulse to scoff at world views that do not coincide with his own. The latter is especially apparent in the speech where he laughs at Palamon and Arcite for fighting to the death over a woman who knows nothing of their existence, much less of their love:

> "Who may been a fool, but if he love?
> Bihoold, for Goddes sake that sit above,
> Se how they blede! be they noght wel arrayed?
> Thus hath hir lord, the god of love, ypayed
> Hir wages and hir fees for hir servyse!
> And yet they wenen for to been ful wyse
> That serven love, for aught that may bifalle.
> But this is yet the beste game of alle,
> That she for whom they han this jolitee
> Kan hem therfore as muche thank as me.
> She woot namoore of al this hoote fare,
> By God, than woot a cokkow or an hare!"
> (1799–1810)

Needless to say, his cynical good humor implies a level of perception totally different from the knights'.

Theseus, as is common to the Philosophy figure, is associated with positive law and is, in fact, its champion in the tale. His almost superhuman status as the advocate of the laws of man is evident in the two allusions to events from his mythic past: he fought for the rule of light and reason in Athens by killing the monster-man, the minotaur (980ff.), and for human life by rescuing Pirithous from the gods of death in the underworld (1198ff.). In the events of the tale proper, he appears in the role of mediator, a balancer of the scales; at an abstract level, he is the symbol of the kind of power which makes human law inspiring. In the opening lines, we have a much-abbreviated account of his wars with the Amazons and Thebes. The Amazons are traditionally associated with the values of the matriarchal system, which is the social system of natural law; the Thebans, with the patriarchal system, which is the social system of positive law. Neither group, in myth, is absolutely confined to its system: the Amazons are fond of war, which falls in the province of positive law; the Thebans are periodically persuaded that their positive law is not synonymous with natural law (Antigone and Tiresias).

In the *Knight's Tale*, Theseus acts as mediator in both wars: he marries the Amazonian Hippolyte and kills the Theban Creon, thus accurately acceding to the central tenet of each (peacefully consummated love and primitive vengeance). At the end of the tale, he again symbolically resolves the conflict by marrying off the Theban Palamon to the Amazonian Emily, thus showing at least a political preference for the peaceful solutions of natural law. His resolutions are pragmatic rather than profound, but they lead to acceptable ends. For one thing, when positive law allows love to be the cause of marriage, and natural law endures the bondage of marriage's legal contract, there exists one of the few illusions of happiness which simple social man is capable of holding. For another, while Theseus' decisions do not settle the basic and all-pervasive differences between the laws, his preference for marriage as a resolution at least fits into his aims of political order without war.

In the main story, Theseus acts as mediator in the knights' longings for Emily. His tourney is the perfect example of his political mediation. Its ostensible purpose is to help the knights compete for the right to touch the world of love and beauty, but in the words which introduce the tourney, Theseus does not bother to mention the stakes (nor for that matter does the Knight). The goal of the tourney is left as the private affair of the young. The tourney, for Theseus, is a ceremonial and political occasion which, on the one hand, allows him to show the world his wealth and magnificence and, on the other hand, and much more important, allows him to fulfill an underlying political purpose. As long as he keeps the energies of the heirs of the throne of Thebes directed at each other, they do not fight him, the proper target for their warlike instincts. The tourney itself is the perfect fulfillment of Theseus' aims. The tale makes abundantly apparent that his two tactics in establishing political order are war and alliance. The tourney is a mock war; it will result in an alliance with Thebes.

But other evidence makes it clear that for all his acts of creating order anew, for all the indications that he achieves the summits human law is capable of reaching, he has no accurate understanding of or feeling for natural law. Only as long as women's presence and requests intrude upon his activities, is he both just and merciful. With chivalric good humor, he marries the Amazonian queen he had merely set out to punish for her treatment of men, as we know from the *Teseida*. At the sorrowful pleas of the women in black, he defeats the too-masculine Thebes and regains for the women the right to bury their dead. He spares the bloody knights in the grove at the ladies' request. He thinks to say in his final remark to Emily before her betrothal: "Gentil mercy oghte to passen right" (3089). When he is in touch with women, in other words, pity runs soon in his gentle heart. His seeming understanding, however, is only a good-natured tolerance of the world of love's chief symbol: woman.

Without women's presence, Theseus, acting purely on his rights, imprisons the two young knights of Thebes forever. After Palamon's explanation in the grove, he condemns both knights to death to maintain his political order. And in this same episode, after pity has replaced his anger, he is still unable to see that Emily represents anything more significant than his baby sister-in-law. He sets her as the stock reward of a tournament he proposes on the spur of the moment without even the most elementary notion that her humanity requires that he secure her permission. His insensitivity is caused simply by his middle-aged (as some would have it) or male chauvinist's (as woman's liberation would have it) inability to feel or imagine the symbolic appeal of beauty. He takes the knights' violations of his laws seriously, but their love for Emily excites only his heartfelt laughter. In the latter instance, the structure of the tale forces the reader to view the love in both terms, now ludicrous, now the cause of the bittersweet paradox, wretchedness and aspiration. (The Knight, as usual, remains distant from both views of love.) Theseus' inability to understand makes him a prime example in romance literature of conventional knightly virtue.[15] He has mastered the art of chivalric courtesy—or, in his role as the Philosophy of the Menippean structure underlying the tale, of Menippean courtesy, the art of taking other people's views into account—without going to the trouble of considering them.

We might feel that this irony directed against Theseus is so far no more deadly than that directed against Menippus and Philosophy, that Chaucer's treatment of him makes the constant point of Menippean satire that no answer or position, no matter how authoritative it may seem, can ever provide certainty. Conventionally, this figure in the satires never understands the joys which belong to time and the moment. Menippus, in the *Dialogues of the Dead*, stares at the skull of Helen and questions whether *this*, after all, was worth what was paid for it. Hermes says gently to him, reminding us, at any rate, of the values of the world of time and beauty: "Ah, but you never saw the woman alive, Menippus, or you would have said yourself that it was forgivable that they 'for such a lady long should suffer woe.' For if one sees flowers that are dried up and faded, they will, of course, appear ugly; but when they are in bloom and have their colour, they are very beautiful."[16] But in the *Knight's Tale*, Theseus is subjected to something more than the conventional irony. He is diminished, put to one side in a way that Philosophy and Menippus are not. The effect of this treatment is to make him and his powers as vague and distant as the knights' differences.

For one thing, his position as Philosophy figure is blurred because in the analogies that exist between the *Consolation* and the tale, he doubles for Theodoric as well as Philosophy. He is the imprisoner as well as the liberator. Furthermore, his power is political rather than intellectual, as Philosophy's is, and such intellect as we see him exercise (especially in his final speech) is heavily tinged with what we feel to be only practical ulterior motives. In the confrontations of the tale, it is sometimes as if a Theodoric in disguise as Philosophy had come to Boethius to subvert his despair into an appreciation of Ostrogothic aims for empire. The ambivalence in Theseus' presentation at points leaves the impression of excessive mundanity and second-rate ideals, which causes us to move away from him in mild contempt.

For another thing, Theseus, unlike Philosophy, is shown in the context which includes the gods of the universe. They, not he, determine the issue of the tale, which knight shall have the lady, in answers to prayers of young men whom he has only laughed at. His lack of control over the center calls his power into question, and his ignorance of these divine happenings calls into question the quality of his knowledge. Until the gods mingle in human concerns, he reigns unchallenged before us, manipulating the destinies of all who encounter him. In the way appropriate to Menippean satire, and as with women and love, he gives the gods lip service. He mentions them in his speeches, builds temples to them. But just as he has no comprehension of the meaning of the world of beauty and love, so he has no comprehension that the gods form an order of existence completely alien to his own.

When the infernal fury kills his winner and voids his arrangement to satisfy a law independent of his authoritative contrivance, he is shocked by his failure and turns unconsolable to his father, Egeus, for an answer. All he is given is the inappropriate—for the context—tragical answer: Death is the fate of every man.

> "This world nys but a thurghfare ful of wo,
> And we been pilgrymes, passynge to and fro.
> Deeth is an ende of every worldly soore."
> (2847–49)

Thus Theseus, knowing nothing of the prayers or of the scenes in heaven, is left with this explanation far away from the actual state of affairs. Like his belief that his actions would solve the knights' problem, this answer becomes simply another of his glaring misapprehensions. To see Theseus in a universe where the gods take no note of him, where they, at least nominally, are the resolvers of the tale's major issue, quite independent of his initiative power, where the universe he imagines can be thought by no stretch of the imagination to coincide with the universe they preside in ("over" would suggest they have power which they too do not seem to have) is to diminish his significance, to throw him too into a backwash, away from that focus which would enable us to use his words to interpret the tale.

The diminishing of Theseus' stature in the public phase of the *disputatio* blunts the sharpness of the debate, but it is also blunted by Chaucer's giving him no direct opposite, no one to play Palamon to his Arcite. Hyppolyte, the obvious candidate, is silent. The other women at the center of the dialogue, the meeting in the grove, have no distinctive voice. They object to Theseus' killing the knights, not because they shun the all-too-ready, simplistic male solution "off with his head," but because the knights are men of such "high rank," a strictly patriarchal reason for abstaining. ("No rich man ever hanged" belongs to this syndrome of thought.) They are only secondarily concerned that the knights are in love and wounded. There is dramatic verisimilitude in that the out-group usually has to use the language of the in-group to succeed. But the point is that though Chaucer evokes the opposition of matriarchy and patriarchy, he fails to present the values of women and natural law in such a way as to give them objective status. In a general way, women present an opposing world view in the tale, but it is, as it were, without their knowledge, without the language which would objectify the importance of the opposition.

We view the entry of the gods into the *disputatio* with mixed feelings of relief and absurdity. On the one hand, they bring fresh air into the stalemate of the relations the knights have dwelt in with each other and with the world for so long; they turn the mockery of Theseus' tournament into something significant. On the other, in their farcical way, they solve the problems that mortals have been so unfortunate as to create without thought for human complexity. In the scene in heaven, the arbiters of the action present us with nothing so much as a willful child's temper tantrum being handled by the ingenuity of an evil nursemaid. Yet, perforce, their activities embody the divine aspects of the laws that operate in the human world. Saturn's solution represents happiness and immediate gratification of desire, which wins out over justice, a long-range investigation of the appropriate resolution of the knights' requests, which Jupiter shows no capacity for bringing to bear in the argument. The Golden Age triumphs over the Age of Iron, not because it has any divine values attached to it, but ultimately, it would seem, because of Palamon's more careful prayer. The Knight's absence of commentary, as with Palamon's success at the end of the tale, gives this victory no resonance.

The gods have the ordinary characteristics of *deus* figures in Menippean satire. That is to say that they are actual gods with Roman names, have a dramatic objectivity equivalent to the other characters, and are a part of a traditional mythological system to which the Knight pays no attention. Saturn, instead of uttering the words of a Golden Age god, berates the assembly with an account of the evil he presides over. Jupiter, instead of acting as the awesome controller of all things, is the harried, unsuccessful ruler trying to keep peace in the family. In addition, the gods are, according to the convention, concerned to give those with whom they deal what they ask for. Their first intrusion is in Mercury's appearance in Arcite's dream, proof perhaps that the answer to the *demande d'amour* is "Arcite," because his desire to see Emily again is intense enough to call up a god. Mercury's brief message to him, which, though redolent of that ambiguity for which Lucian attacks divine prophecies ("To Athenes shaltou wende, / Ther is thee shapen of thy wo an ende" [1391–92]), is also in accord with what he wants. In the temple the direct prayers of the knights are again heartfelt enough to create the awaited moment of fulfillment. The final appearance of a god, the fury that Pluto sends at Saturn's request, carries out the scheme, a warning perhaps, about the frightening ramifications of intense longing; for if Palamon desires Emily, he cannot have desired Arcite's death, much less the prolonged and painful suffering that precedes it.

Menippean satire's presentation of its *deus* figures functions as a method of breaking the power of mythic oppositions, of calling into question man's methods of telling the stories of the gods, one of his more elaborate methods of explanation. But in the *Knight's Tale*, Chaucer blurs even this impression, by placing the gods too in a context which moves the parodic concerns of the tale into a further dimension. The elation in the heaven where Saturn seems cleverly to find a way of resolving the dilemma posed by the gods' granting of what appear to be opposing requests stands as direct duplication of signs given in the temple. Palamon's sign shows a delay, but he knows that his boon is granted (2268–69). Arcite hears the dim, low word "Victory" (2431–33). In between, Emily, praying for whichever knight desires her most, receives this sign:

> For right anon oon of the fyres queynte,
> And quyked agayn, and after that anon
> That oother fyr was queynt and al agon.
> (2334–36)

These instant answers reflect exactly what happens later. The scene in heaven cannot be read as occurring simultaneously with the prayers because it is the word "victory" that sets off Venus' weeping.

The duplication—which indicates that these gods do not know what they are about—is a parodic representation of the relation between the Boethian concepts of fate and providence (bk. 4, pr. 6). Fate's function is to implement individual events, and the ability to control all these single manifestations in an orderly way is the function of providence. Mars and Venus have the first power; Saturn has the second. But in the *Consolation* the validity of the distinction between fate and providence depends on positing the existence of two states of being—time and eternity. In the *Knight's Tale* these gods live in time like Homer's gods, as is evident in the argument that rages *after* the prayers. Venus' vision is too confined for her to understand the scope of the pattern she is involved in; Saturn's, not quite providential enough to avoid thought. Because of their ignorance of what goes on at the shrines and because they have no freedom, no capacity to do other than follow out the decrees of destinal forces that operate above them in response to the desires of the young people praying, they, in what they do at least, seem to "function as metaphors of man's will."[17]

As the top of the paradigm of the two laws, this presentation of the gods undermines more drastically than any other of the

Knight's "blurrings" the potential significance of the structure. With a more exalted conception of divinity before us, we could read the movement from private, to public, to divine portrayals of the conflict as the way to understanding. We would move from the knights' hopeless confusion, to the pragmatic blindness of Theseus, to the freedom of the celestial vision which understands the mutual reliance of one law on the other. Or if the peace created by Saturn had any of the depths and grandeur of the "Paradiso" or of the final book of the *Consolation*, we could read the poem as the narrator's account of the spiritual pilgrimage from beauty, to love, to happiness, the worlds which transcend force, legality, and categories. But these gods are far from providing confirmation of such a reading. The vision of Venus weeping at Saturn's knee over Mars' promise gives us either the impression that we view a more elementary stage of affairs than the society of earth must abide, or else an uneasy sensation that the universe is stranger than we think.

Instead of the movement upward, such as we get in Dante and Boethius, where the ideas move in ever-widening circles until at last we feel we are intellectually in the final rung of paradise, we encounter a deliberate parody of the thought that man can rise ever higher. The progression from beauty to love to happiness works only within the private phase of the debate and is represented in Emily. Beautiful in the garden, she inspires the knights' love for ten years. As the occasion for the tourney, she is a cause of peace and sublimation among men; the latent hatred between Thebes and Athens is quiet, the tournament being, of course, a much lesser conflict than war. But there is distracting evidence even at the human level. Emily relieves the knights' boredom and despair in prison, gives them hope, but the actions that love inspires are not such as to excite our admiration. In this period of confusion, the creativity the knights' love looses in them borders on madness: each projects, and Arcite actually lives, another version of actuality. Palamon projects a world in which Thebes is conqueror and Athens the defeated; Arcite becomes a servant, changes his class and name. The tourney Emily presides over in name is a further confusion to them and who they are: rulers of Thebes, enemies to Theseus.

It is in their period of confusion that we find their Boethian speeches, in which, sensing something of the horrors of the universe around them, they question the divine levels of the laws. Placed against the *Consolation*, the immediate effect of the speeches is to diminish the speakers. Boethius faces the loss of all material possessions, the desertion of his friends in the Senate, and the threat of physical death, but, worst of all, he wallows in a state of mind which threatens imminent spiritual death. The knights, like Boethius in prison, have also lost everything, but they are not threatened with either physical or spiritual death. They have indeed lost their friendship, friendship being in Philosophy's eyes of so high a spiritual value that it is beyond the control of Fortune (bk. 3, pr. 2), but they are too angry with one another to feel threatened by even this loss. Their deepest despair is in fact caused by a spiritual renewal, which they have found in their love for Emily. What frustrates them is that they cannot reach the experience they want, not the thought that they can never have it again. They are not saying, "The worst unhappiness is to have been happy," but rather, "The worst unhappiness is to contemplate an unattainable object of desire." The bittersweet despair of this experience is profoundly unlike the despair of total loss.

Seen as parts of a Menippean satire like the *Consolation*, the knights' speeches fare better. They deal with the underlying problem that man must solve when he becomes aware of the dualistic universe about him, when his familiar world turns out not to be the only world that exists. The *Consolation*, against which the speeches are implicitly set, is addressed to answer this problem. In his downfall Boethius becomes aware of a universe in which events in human life are haphazard, a universe in which good actions do not necessarily bring just rewards. The knights make a similar discovery of a chaotic universe that stands in opposition to the world of their former training, where everything was related by rules of kinship, oaths, and war. As Boethius' views are contradicted by Philosophy's arguing, so aspects of the *Knight's Tale* contradict the two speeches (Theseus, however, does not have this function). Palamon is a fatalist whose assumptions are proved wrong by events. Arcite, a man searching for God, is contradicted by the absence of any image that fulfills his hope.

Palamon's speech takes justice as its central theme, and this is in accord with his projective investigation of a world view not native to him, a world set up by the conventions of patriarchal society, a world which somehow bars him from Emily. The speech is parallel to book 1, meter 5, in the *Consolation*, Boethius' prayer to understand why man, who must view the evil triumphing and the good oppressed, is excluded from the goodness of the order that governs all else. But Palamon, unlike Boethius, does not put himself in the position of the innocent questioner. He laments with the belief that he already knows the answers which Boethius must go through the process of learning. The only point in which he admits himself ignorant is that state of affairs after death; otherwise, he thinks everything is fated. Men are no better than beasts; they suffer in innocence with the permission of the gods. Beasts have their will and die without dreams, but man must control himself and suffer torment after death in spite of the torment he had in life. Serpents and thieves who have injured men go free, while the gods oppress him and his city. His bitterness springs from a despair, opened to him by love, about the unpleasantness of the alternate world. The most rigid of the projected conclusions about divine governance of men's affairs, Palamon's thoughts are almost as fatalistic as Troilus'.

But in spite of its desperate seriousness, his speech is in many respects a kind of empty exercise reflecting his frustrated but complacent assurance that his views are the correct ones (e.g., his rigid refusal to enter into discussion with Arcite over the new problems posed by Emily). A belief in fate is a great protector of his biased conviction. His statement that animals have a better life than men is not susceptible of proof or contradiction, and is a maxim always comforting when men try to prove their right to despair. But his statement that the guilty go free and the innocent suffer is not borne out well by the tale. In his own view of things, he deserved Emily because he saw her first; in the end he has possession. This connection is sometimes felt as a poorly realized example of poetic justice in the tale; nevertheless, it refutes Palamon's assumption in the complaint, and is a change that Chaucer makes in the *Teseida*, where Arcite sees Emily first. Palamon's speech climaxes in his description of the gods who imprison him and destroy Thebes. But he succeeds in freeing himself, and while Theseus has destroyed the city, it has not been razed, for Palamon and Arcite set off again "To Thebes, with his olde walles wyde" (1880). He laments, then, not from a feeling of alienation and abandonment in a universe without order, as Boethius does, but from anger at the cruel auspices under which man—in particular, Palamon—is compelled to exist. There is no sense of a helpless involvement in a universal dilemma or, subsequently, of the magnificent power of the human mind to transcend what might appear to be the cruelty of the gods. These two conceptions, of course, distinguish the *Consolation* from the momentarily irritated thoughts of a young man.

Arcite's complaint takes happiness as its central theme, a concern also out of accord with his temperament. The measure of his dislocation is revealed by his tendency at this moment to identify with the world of Emily and all she represents, a world in which happiness is as central a concern as love, beauty, and peace. His extreme unhappiness springs from his inability to understand how to penetrate this world. His lament, as that of a questioner who must work out an answer, is more serious than Palamon's. His subject, happiness, is taken, not from book 1 of the *Consolation*, but from book 3, from words spoken by Philosophy rather than by Boethius. But while Philosophy comfortably elaborates on the subject, Arcite can only ask despairing questions. In Philosophy's discussion, happiness is the initial stage in her argument that all men naturally desire God. Arcite, on the contrary, can only lament at the state of affairs. He is torn by the ironic confusion of means and ends, efforts and attainments. The gods give man something good, and he does not realize it until he has lost it; men ask for something and receive it in a way that they had not contemplated. For all his struggle, Arcite cannot rise to the level of transcendence required of the Philosophy figure or see the majestic implications of his own visions. Surrounding Arcite's Boethianism is mundanity which makes his despair seem trivial in comparison with the discussion in the *Consolation*.

As the comparison with the corresponding passages in the *Consolation* implies, Arcite's speech is based on the need to strive for God. But there is nothing in the tale that embodies this "god." Beauty, love, happiness, and peace seem to us all uncontrovertible ideals, and our underlying tendency, therefore, is to sympathize with Arcite. But the tale offers no evidence that anyone possesses this world—certainly not the women, either Hyppolyte or the women at the grove, to whom its possession has been traditionally ascribed and is so ascribed by the male characters in the tale. Emily, the chief inspirer of visions in the knights, knows nothing of it, and possesses neither power nor inclination to take the knights back to Scythia, as it were. Her prayer to Diana, her one positive act in the tale, betrays only the faintest interest in Theseus' world, where marriage has a status equal to war as a controlling device. But there is no rebellion or antagonism at being used as a pawn. Her pale indifference toward the knights reminds us of the attitude of Tennyson's gods, who listen to man's pleas as a "tale of little meaning though the words are strong." And while, on the one hand, her attitude here will serve to remind us of the strange nature of divinity so often depicted in the tale, it will not, on the other, make us think she could have given Arcite what he sought. It may be argued that he knew that, and chose to worship her at a distance, and did not approach her for the physical purposes of marriage when he returned to Athens in disguise. The scene with the gods—which, in its own callous way, embodies the abstract conflict—offers no resting place for the values toward which Arcite moves. The context of the tale makes Arcite's search an unrealizable dream.

Because of the miscalculation in his prayer, he is the object of the plot's most obvious irony, his life being the example of the truth of his own momentary understanding: "We witen nat what thing we preyen heere" (1260). He is the object of its poetic justice. The answer to his question, "Who may give a lover any law?" is answered in the outcome. It is he who initiates the death of friendship, and it is he who is punished. Although the tale as a whole does not allow Arcite the rank of tragic hero, for the Knight's vision contains too many possibilities, he has his attributes. His failure to find his new world is acknowledged in his death speech; he dies affirming the values of the brotherhood he has rejected and crying out in the arms of Emily for mercy. We may interpret his pleas as the desire for the impossible synthesis of the best of both worlds, devoid of error and ultimate destruction. This synthesis is what a different portrayal of the gods might have given us; instead the Knight presents it only as a dying man's hopeless dream.

The echoes of Boethius in the knights' speeches help to hold in ironic counterpoise the events and descriptions in the tale which relate to them. In this light they are parodies of human attempts at understanding the universe. The speeches, like those in the *Consolation*, represent the tableaux of thought, the Chaucerian speeches less well objectified than Boethius'. In the overall scheme of things, the speeches are fragments which attempt to project a pattern of coherence. In themselves, the uttering of such words helps man for a moment to create the illusion that somewhere or other there is wholeness and clarity. In the face of a chaotic universe, the knights' visions embody aids to the belief in the presence of an ideal system. Behind the tableaux lurk the informalizable, the contradictory, the unimaginable. The narrator's failure to reconcile the dichotomies implied by the presence of a "this world and the other" or even to comment on them sets up a sense of constant contradiction, not to say abandonment. The omission of such explanation and the apparent indifference to the blatant and subtle incongruities that ultimately arise from the continual presentation of unresolved views leaves an uninterpretable universe reduced to intelligibility only momentarily by those who try to describe it.

The mythic worlds, evoked, transmuted by the power of the present to alter any myth, then discarded as if irrelevant to the conflicts they survive from, loom and disappear in the *Knight's Tale*. The texture of the universe portrayed remains vague, uncertain. The ancient oppositions are continually thrusting themselves to the fore: Titans and Olympians, Golden Age / Age of Iron, matriarchy / patriarchy, natural law / human law, Boethius' vision / Philosophy's vision. The first members of each set form a syndrome of overlapping agreements, and so do the second. Historically speaking, the last member of each pair is thought to have superseded the first. But of course, Menippean satire would not for good reason propose that the human race ever suppressed any one of its ideas by any means so simple as the passage of time, much less by a war which ended in a victory both sides agreed to. Nor does the *Knight's Tale*. The oppositions which figure in its structure are continually present for our enrichment and also, inevitably, for our confusion. The Titan Saturn and the Olympian Jupiter coexist in the heavens, intent on a conflict which has nothing whatsoever to do with the war that destroyed the Golden Age and instituted the Age of Iron. An Amazon can marry a Theban, neither having manifested any interest in the opposing values they mythically represent. The laws of love and loyalty set up conflicts which are never resolved. The Boethian knights and their struggles stay in our minds quite as clearly as Philosophy-Theseus' superficial, accidental success.

The effect of the Knight's portrayal of the gods, the diminishing of the Philosophy figure Theseus, his indifference toward the ideals of the knights, his parodic treatment of their efforts to attain the vision of the *Consolation*, is to make the conflict of the laws appear man-created, in medieval terms nominalistic rather than idealistic, arbitrary categories which contain neither any certifiable truth nor the capacity to hold up under continuous application to a universe that will not let itself be controlled by any human idea. This is commonplace thought for Menippean satire, but again we encounter that extra level of perception in the tale, the feeling that while there is a definite need to draw on the oppositions of natural and positive law because there seem to be no others for this story, neither the opposition nor one of the views warrants the energy of desperate commitment. The failure seems not to matter very much.

Chaucer's techniques in the tale, which evoke but then ignore these primal conflicts and categories, have not met with universal approval. Baldwin, for instance, writes: "That Chaucer's voice could falter and be unsure of itself is apparent in the *Knight's Tale*, technically, perhaps, one of the poorest of his works. There the severe abridgement of his source, Boccaccio's *Teseida*, especially with the device of *occupatio*; the incompatibility of such motifs as classical Fortune and romantic chance; and the tendency for the narrative to shift focus awkwardly— these seem to indicate a clumsy voice and an early Chaucer as well."[18] Salter also feels that Chaucer has failed to control the material in the tale.[19] I am myself convinced that the tale is the most heavily revised of all Chaucer's works. There is an extraordinary sense of total control, total lack of spontaneity about it, and consequently an overwhelming feeling of *déjà vu*. But I believe that Chaucer stopped revising because he had succeeded in creating the effect he sought and that this effect was the portrayal of a certain kind of narrator, whose observation adds that level of irony which makes this Menippean satire distinctive.

9

The Knight:
Fragments, Silence, and Beauty

In the Menippean world view, men, in their struggle to confront and contain the chaos of the universe, select a few facts and make theories about what is before them. Their theories are unalike and contradictory and cannot by any stretch of the imagination be thought to succeed in providing a complete description of things, their choices being too limited, their interpretations too blind. The Philosophy figures of these satires have great fun in dismissively exploring these fragmentary theories, but their remarks are characterized by a silence in regard to the questions they pose, which in the end implies their creator's withdrawal or attempted withdrawal from the contemplation of the conflicts and the chaos of the universe. "Il faut cultiver nôtre jardin" is the most memorable expression of this attitude. For Voltaire, this escape lay in the doctrine of work; for Boethius, in the free contemplation of brilliant philosophical theories of man's and God's relation to the universe; for Chaucer, the champion of the Menippean struggler and the glories of time, in the perception of beauty. And it is this view that the Knight-narrator holds.

We have in this tale the most elaborate example in Chaucer's work of the struggle to deal objectively with the dialogical nature of Menippean satire. We have the usual experience-authority complex portrayed in the knights and Theseus, we have two developed sets of universal laws, and we have a narrator who dismisses the absolutes of both systems ironically and indifferently. Yet, as I hope to show here, the narrator struggles against the nominalistic and dialogical nature of knowledge and the chaos of things to find some viable method of proceeding. He accords himself little success, but unlike the narrator of

232

Troilus, usually remains unemotional and at a distance.[1] In *Troilus*, with its predominantly tragic dimensions, we have a narrator who fights hopelessly against his sensation of an intentless universe by trying to hide behind his "story" and to persuade us to believe in his empty, literary, Boethian-based Aristotelian notions of fate.

In the *Knight's Tale*, on the contrary, in which tragedy is only one of several possibilities, we have a narrator with objective alternate views of life's unknowability. He uses the Boethian passages as a device for portraying his terrible, but elegantly ironic, conviction that there is no true or even approximate image capable of containing the experience of man. His narrative technique, consequently, is a technique of joining the fragments of things, the incomplete items of different orders, with consummate, ironic skill. The impact of the technique is disconcerting. When we analyze the tale, the clearest parts of it seem to be put together with jigsaw pieces from different puzzles, whose pictures have been cut on identical patterns. Because the cut is the same, the pieces fit together. The surface order creates the illusion of similarity and smoothness. Looked at from an objective position above, the picture is a kaleidoscope, a deliberate, surprisingly adept assembling of pieces from different puzzles. The technique forces us to concentrate on certain selected aspects of the possibilities inherent in the story, particular places, particular moments, particular tableaux.

The Knight-narrator's tale is approximately a quarter of the length of the *Teseida*, his actual source (2,250 lines vs. 9,896). The cutting inevitably has the effect of raising to prominence certain fragments of the Italian poem.[2] While Boccaccio leisurely strews events through a ten-year period, the Knight narrows the action to three selected years. The main events take place in the month of May in the first, seventh, and eighth years. The Knight likewise opens up to us only a few places of the setting in the Italian poem. The chief scenes in the tale are a battlefield and a palace in Thebes and a palace and a grove in Athens, the grove having by far the major share of the action in the last two and a half books. It is the site of the knights' meeting, of the lists, and of Arcite's funeral pyre. Other aspects of the story which the Knight cut and considerably rearranged result in a similar focus on a particular place, episode, or moment. With sharp, deft strokes he limits the description of the entry of the combatants in the tourney to a description of one man on each side, Lygurgus and Emetreus. Boccaccio strings the account through forty stanzas and describes and alludes to great numbers of participants by name. In the tale the description of the lists and the oratories is a concentrated and highly organized presentation made up by selection from the manifold, intermittent suggestions in Boccaccio.

More important is the cutting of the *Teseida* that strips the young characters of psychological motivation. The fragments of information that remain make them symbolic of certain intellectual attitudes. In the Italian poem, the friendship of the knights holds until just before the meeting in the grove. From the prison window, both see Emily as a goddess (Venus); they attempt to console each other for their sorrow; both weep bitterly at Arcite's parting. They become rivals only when the page Panfilo tells Palamon that Arcite is back in Athens in disguise. And even in the grove, where jealousy finally prompts them to fight, their battle is interrupted by a scene in which Arcite weeps over his stunned friend Palamon and decries the foolishness of a love which can have destroyed their friendship. In the tale, the Knight omits these episodes. In the fell and unbelievable moment after the knights see Emily, the brotherhood founded on lineage, kinship, rank, oaths, and the sharing of the blood and death of battle is irreparably severed. They become enemies, and enemies they remain until their reconciliation as Arcite dies. The alterations have the effect of concentrating our attention on only one aspect of their being, their struggle between two worlds. The tableaux with which we associate them are varied, but they are never a part of any consistent dramatic or psychological progression.

The character of Emily is flattened even more sharply by the cutting. In the *Teseida*, we are told why she is brought to Athens: she is to be betrothed to Acate, Theseus' kinsman, who dies shortly after her arrival. She participates in the love affair with Palamon and Arcite at least to the extent that she overhears their first declarations of love for her. She returns to the garden throughout the summer and autumn to experience this love. She recognizes Arcite when he returns to the court at Athens, revels in his love, and does not reveal him. Her sorrow after the death of Arcite and her initial refusal of Palamon are understandable: two men who have loved her at a distance have died, and she fears Diana's vengeance on the man who dares to marry her. Although she remains something of a pawn, she is a pawn who at least knows that the name of the game is chess. In the *Knight's Tale*, all motivation surrounding her is removed. Her pawnlike quality is deliberately made into her dominant feature. She simply leaves Scythia and comes to Athens; we are given no cause. She does not overhear the lovers' declarations in the garden, does not recognize Arcite in Athens. She learns of the young men's love only when they are forced to reveal it to Theseus; it is quite possible, in fact, that she has not even seen them before. She is given only the barest of conventional reactions at the death of Arcite ("Shrighte Emelye" [2817]) and the wedding to Palamon ("Emelye hym loveth so tendrely" [3103]). She speaks but once—the prayer in the temple of Diana—to say with considerably more justification than Boccaccio's character that she has no preference for either knight, that she would rather not marry at all. Because she is not involved in any kind of natural relation with Palamon and Arcite, she is a symbolic figure, without definite or definitive human characteristics.

The Knight's narrow selection from the *Teseida* of times, places, and characteristics of the players in the drama deepens the story's already inherent improbability and throws into relief a series of momentary events which, because they are not related in logical and obvious ways, invariably provide conflicts of perception. In general, the Knight's emphasis on disconnected moments and tableaux instead of on sequence and motivation has the effect of focusing our attention on the curious dichotomies under whose auspices life and action take place.

The struggle with the absurd contradictions between the fragments which Chaucer defines as the Knight's province of thought is perhaps nowhere so apparent as in his depiction of the first meeting of the major characters at the grove. To explain this meeting, the most improbable event in a plot noted for its improbability, the narrator says, in one of the four long Boethian passages in the poem:

> The destinee, ministre general,
> That executeth in the world over al
> The purveiaunce that God hath seyn biforn,
> So strong it is that, though the world had sworn
> The contrarie of a thyng by ye or nay,
> Yet somtyme it shal fallen on a day
> That falleth not eft withinne a thousand yeer.
> For certeinly, oure appetites heer,
> Be it of werre, or pees, or hate, or love,
> Al is this reuled by the sighte above.
>
> (1663–72)

The stated relation between destiny and providence in the first three lines is that proposed by Boethius: destiny is the projection of divine thought in time (bk. 4, pr. 6). The specific philosophical problem that calls forth the Knight's speech is chance; in the *Consolation*, we are given as an example the story of a man who, in plowing his field, suddenly finds a pot of gold (bk. 5, pr. 1). Philosophy defines chance thus: "As men don any thing for grace of any other thing, and an other thing than thilke thing that men entenden to don bytideth by some causes, it is clepid 'hap.' Ryght as a man dalf the erthe bycause of tylyinge of the feld, and founde ther a gobet of gold bydolven" (p. 374). This definition and example can be applied without any difficulty to the meeting in the grove. Arcite goes to the grove to lament, Palamon to hide, Theseus and Emily to hunt. The accidental result is the meetings. The characters have no more intention of discovering one another than the farmer tilled to find the gold, or the man hid the gold to have it found. After his example, Boethius goes on to say that this seeming chance is in fact only a part of the order which proceeds by an inevitable connection of causes from the fount of providence. The Knight too, in explaining the meeting, speaks of fate's bringing everything about. Since "fatum" and "ordo" in the *Consolation* are approximately synonymous terms, the Knight's version is not, on the surface, anti-Boethian. Nevertheless, the speech produces philosophical parody.

What creates this parody specifically is the exaggeration of Boethian doctrine. In the first place, the passage is more emphatically deterministic than Boethius'. If the desires for peace or war or hate or love—apparently the major social and emotional states of men—are ruled by the sight above, the narrator denies not only the possibility of free action, but also—unlike Philosophy—the possibility of free will. As an explanation for divine order, the statement means that the meetings occur because of laws so absolute that the term *probability* has no meaning. The meetings are fated, foreseen, arranged from the beginning of time, hence at the furthest possible remove from improbability. In the second place, we are led up to this passage with a group of characters whose activities have no elementary focus comparable to the gold in Boethius' illustration; that is, none of the participants possesses as a significant piece of knowledge the thought of "meeting." The result is that instead of one chance event (the farmer finds the gold), we have four chance events. Two sets of characters must not only arrive at the same place; they must arrive at the same time. The explanation is thus twice as deterministic as Boethius', and the event it explains is four times as improbable. The mind boggles at the thought.

In larger terms, the parody created by the passage is produced by the Knight's presenting plot and character in such a way as to deliberately contradict the philosophic beliefs of the passage. Had this presentation accurately reflected the explanation, we would encounter a sequence of events that inevitably lead to one another and characters with psychologies suitably adapted to participation in this inevitability. Instead, we find actions and characters from whom the Knight has deliberately stripped away the traits which would suggest the presence of destiny. He ignores explanation, motivations, and the sequences of cause and effect which prepare for the episode in his source, the *Teseida*. In both stories, the assembly of the four main characters at the grove proves a key encounter in the plot because it releases the action from its turgid circling and allows it to move toward a solution. In the *Teseida*, however, these sequential meetings are carefully motivated. It is established that lamenting in this grove is Arcite's habitual way of relieving the terrible tension he lives under as a mere page in the court of Theseus. Panfilo, Palamon's page, overhears this lament one morning and reports it to Palamon in prison. Because of this information, Palamon is immediately involved in complicated plans for escape, which include feigned illness, the calling of a doctor, exchanging clothes with Panfilo, and Panfilo's intoxicating a guard. Palamon stays at an inn overnight and goes fully armed to the grove to do battle with Arcite. Only the arrival of Emily is purely accidental, for she calls Theseus.

In the *Knight's Tale*, not only are the psychological realities of character which precipitate action suspended, but also all natural cause and effect. Arcite's presence in the grove is accidental. He has no habitual place to lament; nor is it even certain that he habitually laments. His utterance on this particular morning is merely a part of the bittersweetness of May and the unattainability of Emily. Palamon has no page. That he escapes on this particular May morning—he has been in prison for seven years without making any other attempt—is accidental. His choice of the same grove as his hiding place is accidental. Next day, the arrival of Theseus and Emily is accidental. At the human level, the Knight has carefully removed any personal knowledge and any psychological relationships which would suggest that the four are fated to come to the grove. This sequence of scenes is purposely constructed in flagrant violation of the laws of probability.

The Knight's parodic presentation of the *Consolation*'s theories treats them exactly as what they are: words which override actual experience, interpreting it in terms of something else, not in terms of itself. In Palamon's and Arcite's Boethian speeches, the Knight raises questions from within the Boethian system. Palamon and Arcite remain unconscious agents of the parody. We, not they, from the total context of the tale, have the privileged information which reveals their limitations. But the Knight's own Boethian comment provides a higher level of awareness. The limitation is still present, since events here also contradict the explanation, but the Knight is responsible for the discrepancy and is therefore consciously parading it before us. There is a kind of mockery in the absurdity of the juxtaposition which suggests an awareness of a sardonic force manipulating events which is of an order quite different from that embodied in man's pedantic forecasts about, and definitions of, chance. The eerie nature of man's predicament is reflected in his earlier lines: "It is ful fair a man to bere hym evene, / For al day meeteth men at unset stevene" (1523–24). In its irrelevance to the situation which it proposes to explain, the comment satirizes human attempts at truthful and useful theorizing. But the Knight's deliberate insistence on an explanation blatantly incomplete and inadequate turns the satire on the satirizer. The presence of the comment is to acknowledge that in the experience of man the two orders of existence have nothing to do with one another, yet continue to exist. It is to acknowledge openly that this inadequate explanation for all he knows may be the best that man can do with this experience and his theorizing. The random meeting no more destroys the idea of fate than the commentary proves its existence. The satiric butt of the contradiction is man trapped in the continual but failing effort to put his fragments together.

The Knight's method of piecing the inequities and diversities together is to use rhetorical devices which deliberately remind us that there was a great deal more than he cares to tell us. We can hardly read more than thirty lines at a stretch without some kind of statement from the Knight that he is being brief, at any rate briefer than his source.[3] The rhetorical abbreviation common in Chaucer's poetry is one of his chief Menippean devices for forcing us to shift our point of view, to think of another author, another version of the story, to forget temporarily what his own story was making us think about. In the *Knight's Tale* particularly, we are constantly deluged with rhetorical devices of abbreviation, the most elaborate of which is *occupatio*. The longest example falls in his account of Arcite's funeral, where for forty-eight lines (2919–66), the Knight tells us what he will not tell us. The first few lines suffice to illustrate the technique:

But how the fyr was maked upon highte,
Ne eek the names that the trees highte,
As ook, firre, birch, aspe, alder, holm, popler,
Wylugh, elm, plane, assh, box, chasteyn, lynde, laurer,
Mapul, thorn, bech, hasel, ew, whippeltree, —
How they weren feld, shal nat be toold for me;
Ne hou the goddes ronnen up and doun,
Disherited of hire habitacioun,
In which they woneden in reste and pees,
Nymphes, fawnes and amadrides.

(2919–28)

This and other apologies about omissions have the psychological effect of distracting our attention from the need for explanation. His continually verbalized silence covers the presence of the incompatible fragments. But when we analyze the tale's conflicting systems, we are disturbed by the refusal to explain and reconcile divergent points of view, by the lack of interest in making the fragments into a whole.

Unlike the narrator of *Troilus*, who in spite of his unhappiness nevertheless follows his old story with disconcerting closeness, the Knight does not regret or cringe at any part of the story he draws on. In the first lines of his tale, he speaks of the "olde stories" (859) that tell of Theseus. In his account of Palamon's escape, he speaks of the "olde bookes" that tell the story more fully (1463–64). He proves later that Emetreus was with Arcite by saying "in stories as men fynde" (2155). The one writer he mentions, Statius, is only one of the writers of "thise bookes olde" (2294) who tells of Emily's rites to Diana. He seems to regard his "source" as the authentic version of the events in question, the authority, in fact; nevertheless he does not hesitate to leave much out (or for that matter to make changes which he does not mention). He wanders away from it continually, but at the same time is constantly holding it before our attention. This withholding of information which is deliberately dangled before us drives us into meditation on the symbolic nature of this "source." And as we take account of this "old story" of his, the Knight becomes one among many utterers of stories, all of which have a common beginning and a common end. In this light, the "old story" becomes a way of referring to the archetypal experience of man.

There is a great deal in this "story" which the Knight does not think worth mentioning. The subjects which he directly refuses to narrate fall into specific categories. For instance, he refuses to deal with ceremonies and social occasions. He thus describes the funeral rites at Thebes:

> But it were al to longe for to devyse
> The grete clamour and the waymentynge
> That the ladyes made at the brennynge
> Of the bodies, and the grete honour
> That Theseus, the noble conquerour,
> Dooth to the ladyes, whan they from hym wente;
> But shortly for to telle is myn entente.
>
> (994–1000)

He refuses to describe the details of the feast given to the visitors of Athens:

> The mynstralcye, the service at the feeste,
> The grete yiftes to the meeste and leeste,
> The riche array of Theseus paleys,
> Ne who sat first ne last upon the deys,
> What ladyes fairest been or best daunsynge,
> Or which of hem kan dauncen best and synge,
> Ne who moost felyngly speketh of love;
> What haukes sitten on the perche above,
> What houndes liggen on the floor adoun,—
> Of al this make I now no mencioun,
> But al th'effect, that thynketh me the beste.
>
> (2197–2207)

He refuses to describe the ceremonies Palamon follows for his sacrifice to Venus ("Al telle I noght as now his observaunces" [2264]), Emily's cleansing ritual ("But how she dide hir ryte I dar nat telle" [2284]), and the funeral rites of Arcite (2919ff.).

The same rhetorical devices appear in episodes dealing with war and strife. The Knight abbreviates the battles with Scythia

(875–92) and Thebes (985–990); refuses to go on with the account of the verbal strife of the knights over Emily ("Greet was the strif and long bitwix hem tweye / If that I hadde leyser for to seye" [1187–88]); leaves the young men in the grove with the remark:

> Up to the ancle foghte they in hir blood.
> And in this wise I lete hem fightyng dwelle,
> And forth I wole of Theseus yow telle.
> (1660–62)

He refuses to give any more details of the tourney and the arrangements for seeing visitors on their way:

> Of this bataille I wol namoore endite,
> But speke of Palamon and of Arcite.
> (2741–42)

We find the same devices of abbreviation in the accounts of extreme unhappiness. This misery of the two knights causes frequent abbreviation. For instance, the Knight says of Arcite: "What sholde I al day of his wo endite?" (1380); of Palamon: "Who koude ryme in Englyssh proprely / His martirdom? for sothe it am nat I" (1459–60). He curtails the misery of Emily at the death of Arcite: "What helpeth it to tarien forth the day / To tellen how she weep bothe eve and morwe?" (2820–21). He tires of Egeus' account of human woe: "And over al this yet seyde he muchel moore" (2850). He is overcome by the tedium of the infinite series of stories of heartbreak, death, and vengeance on the walls of the temple in the lists. In Venus' temple, he says:

> Suffiseth heere ensamples oon or two,
> And though I koude rekene a thousand mo.
> (1953–54)

In Mars' temple,

> Suffiseth oon ensample in stories olde;
> I may nat rekene hem alle though I wolde.
> (2039–40)

Fragments, Silence, and Beauty in *The Knight's Tale*

In Diana's temple,

> There saugh I many another wonder storie,
> The which me list nat drawen to memorie.
> (2073–74)

Heaven and hell are subjected to a similar treatment; the Knight avoids the account of Theseus' trip to rescue Pirithous from Pluto: "His felawe wente and soughte hym doun in helle,— / But of that storie list me nat to write" (1200–1201). He also will not get involved in the problem of what happens to Arcite's soul after death (2809–11).

Sometimes there seems to be an obvious reason for the brevity. The Scythian war is omitted on the grounds that he has a large field to plow and does not wish to deprive any other pilgrim of his chance to tell a tale (886ff.). His cutting off an account of one character to begin that of another hints that events are moving in such a completely predictable pattern that they need not be pursued. Thus, in the following examples, he suggests that there will be nothing new to report of Palamon in his prison or Arcite in his bliss and therefore leaves them:

> Now wol I stynte of Palamon a lite,
> And lete hym in his prisoun stille dwelle,
> And of Arcita forth I wol yow telle.
> (1334–36)

> And in this blisse lete I now Arcite,
> And speke I wole of Palamon a lite.
> (1449–50)

The same device is used to move the story forward a number of years. For instance, after the account of Palamon and Arcite's perpetual imprisonment, we find: "This passeth yeer by yeer and day by day, / Till it fil ones, in a morwe of May" (1033–34). The rhetorical device conveys to us that what went on over the intervening period of time was identical to what has just been described. In this case, the imprisonment and its attendant sorrow bulk so large that the passing years are filled with no other incidents of importance. Similarly, we move from the description of Arcite's success as Philostrate to Palamon who, we may be somewhat surprised to discover, has been sitting in prison for seven years: "In derknesse and horrible and strong prisoun / Thise seven yeer hath seten Palamoun" (1451–52). The effect of this curtailment is to remind us that the same sorrow and the same despair have dominated the life of Palamon; it had been useless to keep reminding us of the fact.

More violent in effect is the formula "There nis no more to telle." The obvious here has the impact of a *fait accompli*, which makes further comment useless. The phrase is used in the description of Theseus on the way to Thebes: "And forth he rit; ther is namoore to telle" (974). Because he has decided, the destruction of Thebes is certain. After the statement that Theseus, having imprisoned the knights forever, lives happily thenceforth in Athens, the Knight says:

> And ther he lyveth in joye and in honour
> Terme of his lyf; what nedeth wordes mo?
> And in a tour, in angwissh and in wo,
> This Palamon and his felawe Arcite
> For everemoore.
>
> (1028–32)

There is nothing in Theseus that will make him relent. Arcite uses the phrase after his declaration of love for Emily: "I nam but deed; ther nis namoore to seye" (1122). The impact of beauty is such that words are futile: only the act which attains her has a purpose. The phrase is used at the conclusion of Emily's prayer in the temple; the indifference of the goddess's reply offers neither knowledge nor freedom: "And hoom she goth anon the nexte weye. / This is th'effect; there is namoore to seye" (2365–66). It appears immediately before the tournament begins: "Ther is namoore to seyn, but west and est / In goon the speres ful sadly in arrest" (2601–2). This act marks the end of ceremonies and the beginning of fatal action.

This stylistic abbreviation points toward a few conclusions about the Knight's dislikes. He leaves out the parts of the story which there is no hope of resolving, the futile circle of repetition which leads nowhere, the dead ends of conventional ceremony or society (the lady who sat highest, the dog who sat lowest), the wars of the do-gooders, the violent efforts of the young expended on insignificant causes (Arcite's dedication to becoming a first-rate servant), long flights of mournful platitudes from those who do not feel, bright-eyed speculations about the unknowable from those who are not touched. He avoids the description of all activity that blinds the mind to receptivity. Added together, these various dislikes suggest a man who is pessimistic, unwilling to speculate about other realms, weary of the struggle of his profession and life in general, but who is barred at the same time from retiring to court and becoming a ladies' darling by his extreme distaste for ceremonies. Such a portrait is an accurate reflection of the mental impasse with which the Knight struggles. There is a dislike of, an indifference to, a hopelessness about rituals, conflict, extreme emotions, anything that does not pertain to a goal this life might have. But if the Knight is silent on a great number of jarring points, he is silent in such a way as to make us feel that the contradictory fragments from sources, from world views, have, in spite of his failure to help us, some insistent force that no one can ignore.

As a result of his attitude, not the least of the contradictions in the poem is the relation between thought and style. The cutting of the *Teseida*, the rhetorical abbreviation, the emphasis on fragmentary philosophical explanations, would lead us to expect a bare, concise style to match. But on the contrary, the style of the *Knight's Tale* is exceedingly rich; the poem is frequently compared to the elaborateness of a tapestry.[4] For if the Knight is fond of getting on with it as quickly as possible, he is also willing to pause and contemplate certain things at length. There are striking descriptions of spectacle and pageantry, so striking that they have often been held to be the *raison d'être* of the tale. Root's words, which present this classic view, can hardly be bettered:

> It is not in the characterization, but in the description, that the greatness of the *Knight's Tale* resides. The poem opens with the brilliant pageant of the victorious homecoming of Theseus,

thrown into sharp contrast by the band of black-clad widowed ladies who meet him on the way. A never-to-be-forgotten picture is that of Emily roaming in her garden, while the kinsmen look down upon her through thick prison-bars. The meeting and silent encounter of the cousins in the wood, the great theater with its story-laden oratories, the vivid portraits of Emetrius and Lygurge, all the varied bustle of preparation, the vigorous description of the tournament itself,—these, with occasional passages of noble reflection, form the flesh and blood of the poem, of which the characters and the action are merely the skeleton framework.[5]

The spectacle certainly provides not only flesh and blood, but also the heart of the tale, the most obvious symbols of beauty which play the major part in the Knight's ultimate source of tentative peace. The three main passages where we see this penchant at work are the descriptions of Theseus before Thebes, the entry of the two young kings, and the lists. These passages do for us what the simple sight of Emily does for Palamon and Arcite. Emily, as Donaldson remarks, is "one of the ideas that make this world tolerable."[6] For the Knight, these spectacles have a similar function.

All three passages are examples of parallel narrative, a technique which enables the writer to avoid accounts of the obvious, the boring, or the hopeless and which, of course, is closely related by intent to the devices of rhetorical abbreviation. The description of Theseus before Thebes avoids an account of his ride to Thebes from the Temple of Clemency, just as the descriptions of Lygurgus and Emetreus avoid an account of their exploits and travels from the end of the earth (as it were) into Athens. The description of the lists, which fills the fifty-week period between the battle in the grove and the beginning of the tournament, avoids an account of the activities of Palamon and Arcite during that year, the account which fills the same space of time in the *Teseida*. The Knight lets these events pass without help; in the meantime, he has told us something else by giving us sharply defined images to consider.

The description of Theseus before he goes into battle at Thebes is the most frequently quoted of the descriptions in the *Knight's Tale*:

Fragments, Silence, and Beauty in *The Knight's Tale*

The rede statue of Mars, with spere and targe,
So shyneth in his white baner large,
That alle the feeldes glyteren up and doun;
And by his baner born is his penoun
Of gold ful riche, in which ther was ybete
The Mynotaur, which that he slough in Crete.
(975–80)

When he arrives at Thebes, he lights "faire in a feeld" (984) to fight. The descriptions of Lygurgus (2128ff.) and Emetreus (2155ff.), often called the most useless in the *Knight's Tale*, also convey a sense of youth, riches, vast dominions, and great physical strength. Though lesser beings than Theseus, they too have the power of beauty. The brilliance of Theseus is such that it causes light in the field he passes; yet their eyes, their hair, their gold, their jewels, also send forth light. Theseus has conquered the fabulous monster the minotaur, whose existence was a scourge to his city, yet they too have conquered and tamed wild beasts who, though real, present difficulties to weaker men.

The Knight's apparent pleasure in these portraits is not, as it might seem, merely a pleasure in martial glory, a delight in the pageantry of war, or a love for conventional rhetorical elaborations by someone whose profession is fighting. Not all that belongs to war excites his admiration sufficiently to make him dwell on it. As we have seen, he dismisses the Scythian and Theban wars with direct rhetorical abbreviation. Passages related to the tournament which might have contained masterly descriptions of war and preparation for war, notably the accounts of the arming (2491ff.) and of the tourney itself (2601ff.), are instead marvelous sketches of scenes of confusion, which lack the sense of magnificence that lies behind the description of Theseus and of the two young kings.

The third of the set descriptions, that of the lists and the temples of the gods, also shares with the portraits a delight in the magnificence and splendor of visual beauty. But while the set descriptions of Theseus, Lygurgus, and Emetreus approach the effectiveness of art works only because the selective vision of the narrator seizes on accidental conjunctions of human activity for the subject matter of his poetry, the temples and lists are art works as such. The initial lines of the description emphasize

their skillful design and execution, their rich adornment, and
above all, their costliness:

> The circuit a myle was aboute,
> Walled of stoon, and dyched al withoute.
> Round was the shap, in manere of compas,
> Ful of degrees, the heighte of sixty pas,
> That whan a man was set on o degree,
> He letted nat his felawe for to see.
> Estward ther stood a gate of marbul whit,
> Westward right swich another in the opposit.
> And shortly to concluden, swich a place
> Was noon in erthe, as in so litel space;
> For in the lond ther was no crafty man
> That geometrie or ars-metrike kan,
> Ne portreyour, ne kervere of ymages,
> That Theseus ne yaf him mete and wages,
> The theatre for to maken and devyse.
>
> (1887–1901)

The lists are worthy of the patron who supervises their erection,
but they are also something more than Theseus and what he
represents. They have the power of art to evoke responses far
beyond the imagination of those who supply money for paint,
gold for overleaf, and meat and wages for the artist.

In the various spectacles of the set descriptions, we find order, discipline, containment. Each of the objects of the Knight's
delight springs forth from its context to distract us from unresolved complexities. He requires that we *see* in each of these
passages; each contains objects which the eye is capable of be-
holding at its leisure. In each case the object is static, a representation which contains all that it is, may have been, or is to
be. But whatever it has, its rich suggestiveness can be examined
in the simple act of seeing, the importance of which is particularly held before us in the description of the lists by the repeated
use of the "saugh I" formula. This emphasis suggests that
merely to be able to see is the gateway to some sort of triumph;
to feel beauty whenever it manifests itself is the experience that
gives men divinity, and for that moment the confusions of the
earth are left behind. These tableaux, which by accident sud-

denly fall under the eye with their spectacle of color, light, energy, and potential, are the Knight's moments in time, the isolated perceptions that give life whatever deep meaning it has. But for all their beauty, they are moments that have no surrounding illusions. There is even a disconcerting quality about them when we view them with care, because the Knight's pleasure is quite independent of any moral judgment about the good and evil of the things that call them forth. His joy depends neither on what precedes or what follows the moment; he is little interested in the direct reconciliation between the pros and cons of the international causes (or for that matter, any other causes).

Theseus' magnificence has doubtless been the cause of death and unhappiness in Scythia and will cause chaos and destruction in Thebes, but the narrator is silent about these facts, just as he is silent about the merits of a leader whose self-righteous sense of justice leads him to rectify, at whatever cost, the wrong that he sees. In the account of the war with Amazons, he does not mention the provocation at all. In his much-abbreviated account of the Theban war, he does not bother to take an objective view. His silence, his failure to judge, puts the idea of the retaliation of a merciful mediator on a par with the idea of the horror in the destruction of a city. We are left with the thought that in terms of human misery the cost of Theseus' compassion is awful, but the results are too commonplace to be of concern. The young kings, in the idealistic framework which might be said to represent their point of view, champion the causes of men who strive to attain beauty. But too much absurdity surrounds the undertaking for them to be taken seriously very long. They are mentioned only once again; their powers are exerted in the melee of a mock tourney, "mock" because of Theseus' rules, "mock" because the battle goes as the gods have decided it in answer to the prayers of men who are subordinate to the kings. But during the moment of these kings' entry, the insignificance of what they have to do is not apparent; the spectacle and pageantry they create is sufficient beauty unto itself.

The description of the lists is the most striking passage in the poem as a whole, the one we return to again and again for direction about the tale's meaning; yet it is nothing so much as an account of the evil and misery that the artists feel the gods preside over. The artists transcend the evil because they have the power of art to subdue and organize the most rampant violence and unpleasantness the mind is capable of conceiving. In the silence of timelessness and suspended narrative, the terrible power of the gods and the hopeless futility of human love and striving are portrayed in their completeness of these walls. The effect is balanced by the artistic structure, by the skill, honesty, the hopeful suggestion of unknowable magnificence which the imagination of man is capable of lavishing upon the constructions made from the earth's dust. Thus, the gods of the lists both attract and repel at the same time.

The Knight's presentation of the lists is the most objective of the moments of balance, and here lies the clearest key to his omissions, descriptions, and indifference to the reconciliation of conflicts. But the sense of an inability to communicate the meaning of the image characteristic of the Knight is found in his reason for recounting the description: "I trowe men wolde deme it necligence / If I foryete to tellen the dispence / Of Theseus" (1881–83). In describing the lists because they cost a lot of money, he acknowledges his acceptance of one of the lower responses of men. He judges, accurately, that few men are interested in the subject of art's power to grapple triumphantly, at least momentarily, with man's awareness of the earth's evil. His reaction to his view of the lists betrays the same sort of indifference to judging what he sees as is apparent in his view of the contrivings of Theseus. If the indifference at the lists is disconcerting always, there is, in this instance, no possibility that he does not grasp the totality of the problem. It is not naivete, an inability to see or care about pain and life's terrible contradictions. In the temples he dwells on the chaos, the strife, the unhappiness which he so often avoids in other places. He does, it is true, turn away in each temple, but not because of the horror and futility in human life which the gods preside over, but because there are too many stories to recount. He dwells on the lists because the artists have found a way of dealing with pain; they encompass strife and make the moment in which horror can be borne.

In a tale so full of contradictions, it is no surprise that the struggle for the moments of beauty leads the Knight on occasion to deal in detail with the subjects which, in the passages of abbreviation, he refuses to deal with at all. I pointed out earlier that a major share of the rhetorical abbreviations avoid events containing accounts of chaos, strife, misery, and unhappiness. Yet certain very important passages in the tale dwell on nothing else. The passage that leaps out of the account of Thebes is that of the bloody bodies of two young knights found in a heap of the dead. What is most memorable about the aftermath of the tournament, indeed much more memorable than the tournament itself, is the description of the terrible suffering of the dying Arcite. The Knight seizes on fragmentary moments to lift to our attention only when they are associated with an event which breaks free of life's monotony or transcends its pain. He describes the wounded cousins memorably—that is to say, the picture stands out as one of the tableaux of the poem—because they are separate from the same old story of conquest, death, and rot that is symbolized by the battle of Thebes. They are about to begin an experience that will give possibility to their lives for ten years.

The description of Arcite's death nearly undoes the Knight; it is here that the most violent tonal shifts in the tale occur. Nevertheless the beauty of Arcite's effort to put the world back in a little order transcends the ugliness of his dying. In the middle of the description—which begins with the account of his swelling, choking, broken body, and ends with death's cold progress through legs, arms and heart, until his eyes dusk over and his breath stops—lies Arcite's attempt to throw what little weight he has left into uniting Emily and Palamon. He says to her:

"With alle circumstances trewely—
That is to seyen, trouthe, honour, knyghthede,
Wysdom, humblesse, estaat, and heigh kynrede,
Fredom, and al that longeth to that art—

251

So Juppiter have of my soule part,
As in this world right now ne knowe I non
So worthy to ben loved as Palamon,
That serveth yow, and wol doon al his lyf.
And if that evere ye shul ben a wyf,
Foryet nat Palamon, the gentil man."
(2788–97)

But here in this section of the poem more clearly than with the set descriptions, there is a bitterness, an irritation, a mockery which negates our comfort in the small good which Arcite's attempt at reconciliation contrives. All man searches for and loses in the repetitious boredoms of human life are found in Arcite's poignant cry:

"What is this world? what asketh men to have?
Now with his love, now in his colde grave
Allone, withouten any compaignye.
Fare wel, my sweete foo, myn Emelye!"
(2777–80)

A moving final speech, yet the account of the moment is twice broken by mocking shifts of tone. At the physical failure of Arcite's crushed body, the narrator says: "And certeinly, ther Nature wol nat wirche / Fare wel phisik! go ber the man to chirche!" (2759–60). Immediately after Arcite's pleas to Emily for mercy, he comments: "His spirit chaunged hous and wente ther, / As I cam nevere, I kan nat tellen wher, / Therefore I stynte, I nam no divinistre" (2809–11). There are touches of the Knight's faintly macabre Menippean humor, which depends on a dislocating shift in point of view, throughout the tale: the young knights, ankle-deep in blood;[7] the absurd catastrophes depicted in Mars' temple; the gods whom he envisages responding to men's desires; the woodland denizens running about frantically after their trees are felled.[8] In a story that idealizes Emily as woman to a degree unparalleled in other medieval romances, there are cracks like: "For wommen, as to speken in comune, / Thei folwen alle the favour of Fortune" (2681–82). But here at the death of Arcite the total shift registers a violent irritation. It is as if he—who in his continual travels has seen the vast empty spaces of the earth and felt in the rhythm of riding and of the sea the monotony of moving for days on end from one place to another, the monotony of the landscape, the monotony of what men who "pray, plow, and perish," think to be earthshaking—has unexpectedly been taken in by the idiocy of hope once more.

Again in this section there would seem to be a kind of frustrated awareness that it is difficult to make such a moment have significance for anyone, either the narrator or the audience. The remarks create the impression that all death, even as the climactic experience of a quester like Arcite, is unpleasantly like any other death (the same old story). And then too, Arcite learned what he did learn too late (also the same old story). The qualified success of the experience is evident, because none of the other characters is enlightened by the event which they witness. After Arcite's death Palamon and Emily can do nothing better than fall into the patterns of conventional lament: the one howls, the other shrieks (the same old story). The powerful Theseus is momentarily at a loss; it is in his favor, of course, that he is disconcerted, but he falls in immediately with the same old conventional gloom in the advice which Egeus offers him. The Knight's cynical banter seems to be his method of protecting himself against his own deeper involvement.

The contradictory attitudes toward pain and misery which we find in various passages in the tale contain different strata of the Knight's conception of man. He does not bother to deal with death, evil, and repetition when they are only part of the all-too-familiar drabness of the earth. When the episodes represent, strive for, or hint at that pure and perfect freedom of man untrammeled, he turns his attention to describing them. As these episodes show, the two highest values of the Knight's universe lie in the experience of the striving Arcite, who tried to reach the final crossroad in this life, and in the work of the artist. The Knight surveys one further moment where peace may be sought, Theseus' final speech.

The speech is the fourth of the long Boethian passages in the poem.[9] It is by no means a resolution to the tale's disconcerting events and philosophical questioning. What it is is Philosophy-

253

Theseus' *consolatio*, an eclectic selection of random philosophical thoughts the primary purpose of which, here as in the *Consolation*, is to free the listeners from their emotional impasse. Its ulterior purpose, as with all Theseus' activities, is political. He calls a parliament a number of years after Arcite's death to settle the question of alliances with other countries and to "have fully of Thebans obeisaunce" (2974). In order to marry off a Theban to his Amazonian sister-in-law and thereby secure the allegiance of both countries, he needs to convince his emotional listeners—in particular, Palamon and Emily—that Arcite's early death makes this the best of all possible worlds. Drama is first in order; so we have the hush, the pause, the staring into the distance, the sad face, the sigh, and finally his argument (2981ff.), which we may summarize as follows.

The First Mover joined all things together. Things have a certain duration which they may not exceed, but may cut short. Therefore this order comes from a stable and perfect Mover, because nature proceeds from the perfect to the corruptible; therefore things endure by successions. Oaks, stones, and people wear away. Jupiter puts everything in its place. Make virtue of necessity and take well what is given. All should be glad Arcite died young rather than when he was old; he was famous and lucky to get out of the prison of this life. Sorrow no more:

> "I rede that we make of sorwes two
> O parfit joye, lastynge everemo."
> (3071–73)

The "sentence" of this exceptionally illogical speech (Troilus' faults in the free will speech are, by comparison, nonexistent) is "God makes you die, so marry." Palamon, Emily, and the onlookers can hardly have been converted from firmly held contrary thoughts by these dubious appeals. But Theseus does what the good administrator often succeeds in doing with his drama and high-flown phrases; he provides the disjunctive lull in which reverse actions can begin, actions which embody what people wanted to do all along anyway.

While the inadequacies of this speech are evident at every turn,[10] the Knight nevertheless lets Theseus speak in semi-Boethian

Fragments, Silence, and Beauty in *The Knight's Tale*

terms for 105 lines. It is abundantly clear that he portrays Theseus as incapable of comprehending the levels of complexity in
the universe which intrude upon the life surrounding him, but
his failure to stop Theseus with much the same offhandedness
as he stops Egeus and even himself is therefore noteworthy.

At the end of part 3, the Knight tentatively suggests that the
concluding section will reveal his positive intention in telling
his story.

> Now wol I stynten of the goddes above,
> Of Mars, and of Venus, goddesse of love,
> And telle yow as pleynly as I kan
> The grete effect, for which that I bygan.
>
> (2479- 82)

What this "great effect" is is not immediately obvious; even the
Knight wearily indicates that it is difficult to make clear. The
events that occur in part 4 are Theseus' tournament, the intervention of the gods, Arcite's death and burial, and the epilogue
of several years later. If we judge all these events from the point
of view of plot, we can only observe that each one is something
of an anticlimax, certainly not an event we have been prepared
for from the beginning of the tale as the "great effect." Theseus'
plans for the tournament are wrecked as the gods, quite impervious to the havoc they cause among men, carry out their promises; Arcite's fatal accident occurs at the moment of his victory,
and his subsequent death does not meaningfully alter anything.
Theseus' speech on order is a reductive commentary on the reality the Knight has represented to us in the tale; the convention-
ality of the final marriage only ties off a few superficial threads
and leaves unaffected the conflicting strata of ideas from which
the tale is pieced together.

But the phrase "the great effect" is echoed in Theseus' speech,
and that passage would seem, therefore, to be the obvious point
of departure:

> "The Firste Moevere of the cause above,
> Whan he first made the faire cheyne of love,
> Greet was th'effect, and heigh was his entente."
>
> (2987–89)

With these words, Theseus projects the divine embodiment of an ideal vision. His conception of God is that of Aristotle and Boethius, the First Mover whom Theseus calls Jupiter. The great effect is created by the great chain of love, which binds the elements in their places, oversees the mutability of things and takes them back to their beginning in God. This projection is Theseus' theological version of his own activities. His concern with the chain of love appears in his marriage to Hippolyte, in his concern for the knights after the intervention of the women at the grove, and in the tourney for love. The great chain's disintegration in time is represented by the spoiling of his plans for the outcome of the tournament and by the death of Arcite. The cycle in which everything returns to its beginning is represented both in the eternity of the memory of Arcite perpetually young and perpetually famous and in the final marriage of Palamon and Emily. So Theseus would have us believe. But not the Knight.

As with the other Boethian speeches, events in the tale call Theseus' words into question. The obvious contrast to his conception of God is the scene in heaven: Jupiter, struggling to stop the strife of Mars and Venus, has little in common with Theseus' Jupiter the King. His Boethian version of nature and the world as the divine projection of eternal Providence also contrasts with the rulers we see in heaven. Like Homer's gods, they dabble with a world given to them. Living in time like men, they are no more able than the gods of Homer to make the future different from what it is to be. They have power, but not absolute foresight, as is obvious in the possibility of the misunderstanding that rages among them immediately after the prayers in the temple. The smooth and purposeful order of Theseus' explanations of how Arcite's death is a part of the goodness of things stands in contrast to the petty panic and machinations of the gods who actually watch over that death.

The "great effect" would seem to be the Knight's ironic term for man's propensity—the propensity so often satirized in Menippean satire—for creating divinity out of his own profane abilities. Theseus, unable (also unwilling, like all "fair-haired" children) to try to penetrate the reality that surrounds him, like a demigod patterns a few fragments and calls them order, imposing a similar inventiveness on the god whom he imagines to create his universe. Yet the underlying truth of this irony is that this speech is given in a universe too terrible to allow us to expect even so much. Whole truths, with their rawness and ugliness, their inhumanity and darkness, drive men into an appreciation of beautiful half-truths which make life a little more bearable. Whatever the incapacities of Theseus,[11] there are moments, as we think of the speech, when we, sensing the predicament of man, accept him. Men and women alone in a universe that does not trouble them with answers have as their optimistic, blind recourse the option of creating a conception of God that is beautiful. Theseus' desire is too mild—since, like all Philosophy figures, he assumes he is right—to create a mirroring scene in heaven. Had it been stronger, perhaps the divinities of the tale would have been more noble. But those with the capacities of the Philosophy figure are by definition incapable of yearning for something they feel unable to have. In terms of this satire (*vide* Troilus), it would only mean that they change positions and become neophytes in the struggle with mortality and its ways to joy. That the Knight allows Theseus to speak is not an indication of acceptance but of a kind of wishful, still weary acquiescence in the little good that man is capable of imagining. Theseus is not very perceptive, but he means well. Within the limits of his conceptions he dedicates himself to making the world a better place. The Knight is silent in the face of Theseus' final explanation, much as Boethius is silent in the face of Philosophy's final explanation. Neither is true, but both have a certain attractive purposefulness, and at least the Theseus and Philosophy figures of the world manage to sound as if they believed them. By their dedication to the creation of order out of the chaos of this world, they have earned the ambiguous right to a final word.

By using the words of the *Consolation* that loom behind the tale, Chaucer juxtaposes a supreme example of man's intellectual success at transcending his blindness in a universe without light and a series of characters who cannot achieve such intellectual release. Westlund's suggestion that the tale "presents the continual subversion of noble efforts to bring order out of disorder"[12] is an accurate description, not so much of the tale's intent, as of the power of the subverting milieu which surrounds the acts of Philosophy-Theseus. Palamon only passively and accidentally wanders into his success as Boethius figure. Arcite, though he rejects the *status quo* and sees the absurdity in the quarrel with Palamon (esp. 1172–80), cannot find a way to objectify his perceptions. He hangs between, a shadow Philosophy, a failed Boethius. The Knight, the proposed creator of this Menippean satire, possesses the dialogical perception of Boethius, but his focus is different. His blurring of raised distinctions, his silence, his quietly pessimistic and ironic observation of the facets of man's struggle create metaphors for weariness in the mind of someone who has seen too much, hoped, and watched all fail. If no theoretical projection offers him the joy of authoritative release, neither does the totality of experience which calls it forth. His only recourse is to assert the power of beauty and make isolated attempts to achieve an ideal perception. Yet his low-key choice is not without power. Chaucer dropped the epic machinery of the *Teseida*, but in this restless narrator searching pessimistically for some momentary peace, he achieves an epic scope which far exceeds that of the much longer and superficially more elaborate Italian poem.

Chaucer's allusions to the *Consolation*, here and elsewhere in his poetry, act as the grain of sand in the oyster, as both irritation and stimulant. When the *Consolation* springs into prominence in the midst of a poem, it shatters various sorts of fictional, philosophic, and local illusions. It provides areas of different perspective, unveils insistent irrelevancies, and augments the number of fragments which have managed before to appear whole. Its optimum effect is achieved when, in the act of its interference, it reveals and shores up some vision of the world not heretofore in evidence. As inserted text, it provides another point on that grid with which Chaucer as Menippean satirist charts out that area where truth lies like a ghostly artifact from a forgotten civilization.

Notes
Index

Notes

CHAPTER 1: MENIPPEAN SATIRE AND MENIPPEAN SATIRISTS

1 See Northrop Frye, *Anatomy of Criticism* (Princeton, 1957), pp.
   308–9. Ernst Curtius, to whom one habitually turns for information on all things classical and medieval, does not mention Menippus or Menippean satire at all in *European Literature in the Latin
   Middle Ages*, trans. W. R. Trask (London, 1953). See M.L.W.
   Laistner's review of this work in *Speculum* 24 (1949): 261. One
   reason for the silence is, perhaps, that the works which established
   the tradition are lost. The few fragments of Menippus' works are
   collected by A. Riese in his edition of Varro, *M. T. Varronis Satu-
   rarum Menippearum reliquiae* (Leipzig, 1895); and those of Varro
   by F. Buecheler in his edition of the *Satyricon, Petronii Saturae*
   (Berlin, 1922). There are, however, a few hints to indicate that the
   tide is turning. For instance, Morton W. Bloomfield, Piers Plowman *as a Fourteenth-Century Apocalypse* (New Brunswick, 1961),
   remarks on the presence of Menippean satire in *Piers Plowman* and
   goes on to say that the genre "is just as common in the Middle Ages
   as the vision genres and like them has its forebears in classical
   times, perhaps most notably in Lucian's romances" (p. 23).
2 Some obvious candidates are Philip Roth, Thomas Pynchon, John
   Barth, and Kurt Vonnegut.
3 See Frye, *Anatomy*, pp. 308–12; M. M. Bakhtin, *The Problems of
   Dostoevsky's Poetics*, trans. R. W. Rotsel (Ann Arbor, 1973), chap. 1.
4 See, for instance, Bakhtin, *Problems*, pp. 4–5; 56–60.
5 Frye, *Anatomy*, pp. 309–12.
6 For instance, Karl Mras, "Varros Menippeische Satiren und die
   Philosophie," *Neue Jahrbücher für das Klassische Altertum* 33
   (1914): 391.
7 Bakhtin, *Problems*, pp. 88–89.
8 Bakhtin's list and the quotations appear on pp. 93–97.
9 Roth says of Kepesh: "For him there is no way out of the monstrous
   situation, not even through literary interpretation. There is only
   the unrelenting education in his own misfortune." Philip Roth,
   Reading Myself and Others (London, 1975), p. 69.
10 Arrowsmith, countering the idea that the *Satyricon* is only "the

story of the misadventures of a trio of picaresque perverts told by a pornographer of genius," remarks that sexuality is a matter of taste; "if the taste happens to be a queer one, you watch it with detached amusement much as you might watch a pair of crocodiles copulating: after all, it *is* odd in a familiar sort of way. And if you happen to be a satirist (and a satyrist into the bargain), what better way of reporting the lovely, natural, human chaos of this vivid world's insanity than through the prejudiced eyes of a first person pederast?" William Arrowsmith, trans., The Satyricon *of Petronius* (New York, 1960), p. xiv. The contrast in tone between a Menippean satire and a derivative work can be seen in *Lucius or the Ass* (wrongly attributed sometimes to Lucian, who never sees himself as an ass). The mating between ass and woman takes place in graphic terms, and the comic twist is achieved through the woman's refusing Lucius, now back in human shape, because of the decrease in his dimensions.

11 Bakhtin, *Problems*, p. 94.

12 See Mras, "Varros Menippeische Satiren," p. 391; H. F. Stewart, *Boethius* (Edinburgh, 1891), pp. 75–76.

13 H. F. Stewart and E. K. Rand, with a new translation by S. J. Tester, *Boethius*, Loeb Classical Library (London, 1973), p. 163.

14 Bakhtin, *Problems*, pp. 93, 236.

15 These are the major philosophic systems to which Boethius alludes. Sometimes a specific work lies behind the text, as the *Timaeus* behind bk. 3, m. 9 or the *Gorgias* behind the early part of bk. 4; more usually, the allusion is to a philosophical technique or point of view. This technique of abstraction and allusion has had the effect of driving many scholars into the search for Boethius' exact sources, a search which, on the whole, has been unrewarding.

16 Bakhtin, *Problems*, p. 153.

17 By contrast, Lucian treats his "giants" the way small boys, knights, and heroes have always treated giants, fighting them at a distance, snipping away at them until they prove vulnerable and fall. Chaucer shares neither Lucian's maniacal glee, nor Boethius' optimism. His poetry is neither funny for very long, nor tragic for very long. We experience short bursts of laughter, short bursts of pity and terror. The states his poetry does excite consistently are two: one, a state of uneasy suspense about the answers to all things human; the other, a state of sadness or, at best, wistful hope. The uses to which Chaucer puts the Menippean dialogue explain in great measure this effect of his poetry.

18 Both Dante in the *Divine Comedy* and Jean de Meun in the *Romance of the Rose* use the Boethian model of the Menippean dialogue, with the author's persona in a position inferior to that of his mentors. Both refer to the *Consolation*; Jean translated it after finishing the *Romance*. Immediately obvious analogies between the *Comedy* and the Menippean tradition are the trilevel construction, frequent references to historical events, combinations of the lyrical and the prosaic, mixed styles, and conflicting views of life, held in check here to some degree by the level of Hell, Purgatory, or Paradise to which Dante assigns them. Jean continually plays off ideologies against one another, conflicts which are not resolved, but simply ignored by the choice of action in the grand obscenity of the conclusion. "I taught the way to take the castle and pluck the rose," Jean says in the prologue to his translation of the *Consolation*. ("Je Jehan de Meun qui jadis ou Rommant de la Rose, puis que Jalousie ot mis en prison Bel Acueil, enscignai la maniere du chastel prendre et de la rose cueillir.") V. L. Dedeck-Héry, ed., "Boethius' *De Consolatione* by Jean de Meun," *Mediaeval Studies* 14(1952): 168. Though Jeun is embarking upon a translation of a work where reason in the person of Philosophy reigns supreme, he reminds the reader with this statement of the choice he made in the *Romance*, a choice which presents Reason as the figure whose words are most at odds with the desires of the lover and which allows the lover, the character in the dialogue who stands for time, to triumph.

19 B. L. Jefferson, *Chaucer and* The Consolation of Philosophy (Princeton, 1917), p. 150.

20 F. N. Robinson, ed., *The Works of Geoffrey Chaucer* (Boston, 1957).

21 Minor works, at least on the fringes of the tradition, are those that belong to the extensive debate literature of the Middle Ages, e.g., the debates between knight and cleric, wine and water, summer and winter, body and soul. See, for instance, Michel-André Bossy's analysis of the complex tones and shifts of emphasis in the body-soul debate generally known as the *Visio Philiberti*: "Medieval Debates of Body and Soul," *Comparative Literature* 28 (1976): 145–51. Other works are the prosimetra and those that belong to the cento literature, which Domenico Comparetti, *Virgil in the Middle Ages*, trans. E.F.M. Benecke (London, 1895), finds so objectionable, and which Octave Delepierre, *Tableau de la Littérature du Centon chez les Anciens et chez les Modernes* (London, 1894), vol. 1, finds such an amusing illustration of the human propensity for playing games.

22 As far as we know, Chaucer could not read Greek. W. W. Skeat, for instance, writes: "As regards the languages in which Chaucer was skilled, we may first of all observe that, like his contemporaries, he was totally ignorant of Greek. There are some nine or ten quotations from Plato, three from Homer, two from Aristotle, and one from Euripides; but they are all taken at second-hand, through the medium of Boethius. The sole quotation from Herodotus in the *Canterbury Tales* is copied from Jerome." *The Complete Works of Geoffrey Chaucer* (1894; rpt. Oxford, 1963) 6: xcviii. Translations of Lucian into languages that Chaucer could read are not recorded until later. For example, R. R. Bolgar in "The Translations of the Greek and Roman Classical Authors before 1600," *The Classical Heritage and Its Beneficiaries* (Cambridge, 1954), pp. 506–41, lists 1497 as the earliest translation of *Icaromenippus* (Italian) and 1520, of *Menippus* (English).

23 Texts and translations of these works may be found in the following books: *Petronius and Seneca*, Apocolocyntosis, trans. Michael Heseltine (rev. E. H. Warmington) and W.H.D. Rouse (London, 1969); for the *Satyricon*, the Arrowsmith translation already cited and J. P. Sullivan, The Satyricon *and the Fragments* (Baltimore, 1969); L. Apuleius, *The Golden Ass*, trans. W. Adlington, rev. S. Gaselee (London, 1935); *The Golden Ass*, trans. Jack Lindsay (Bloomington, 1965). The following section contains brief summaries and descriptions of some of the Menippean features of these works. My purpose is not to make full readings, but only to illustrate certain features of Menippean satire described earlier in this chapter, which are aspects of the tradition that Chaucer inherited.

24 Sullivan, *Satyricon*, p. 11. E. Courtney, "Parody and Literary Allusion in Menippean Satire," *Philologus* 106 (1962): 86–100, deals at length with textual parody in the *Satyricon* and other classical Menippean satires.

25 Sullivan, *Satyricon*, p. 127.

26 Because this work contains so little verse, J. W. Duff, *Roman Satire* (Berkeley, 1936), p. 104, refuses to class it as a Menippean satire. But to refuse it a place shows an excessive reliance on Quintilian, who names only the mixture of prose and verse as a trait of Menippean satire: "There is however another and even older type of satire which derives its variety not merely from verse, but from an admixture of prose as well. Such were the satires composed by Terentius Varro, the most learned of all the Romans." *Institutio Oratoria* 10. 1. 95. Menippean satire is certainly a mixture, but it is a

mixture of styles high and low, of genres serious and comic, of philosophies profound and banal, mixtures for which the term "prose and verse" is hardly adequate.

27 Lindsay, *Golden Ass*, p. 17.

28 *Decameron* 5. 10; 7. 2; see Lindsay, *Golden Ass*, p. 27.

29 B. E. Perry, *The Ancient Romances* (Berkeley, 1967), p. 251.

30 Donald Howard, *The Idea of the* Canterbury Tales (Berkeley, 1976), pp. 159–61, gives an excellent account of what Chaucer does not tell us about the events of a usual Canterbury pilgrimage.

31 Texts and translations may be found in the following books: A. Dick, *Martianus Capella* (Leipzig, 1925 [a new edition is being prepared by J. A. Willis]); W. H. Stahl and R. Johnson with E. L. Burge, *Martianus Capella and the Seven Liberal Arts*, 2 vols. (New York, 1971–77), vol. 1 (commentary), vol. 2 (translation); J. H. Mozley and Robert R. Raymo, *Speculum Stultorum* (Berkeley, 1960); J. H. Mozley, *A Mirror for Fools* (Oxford, 1961); and G. W. Regenos, *The Book of Daun Burnel the Ass* (Austin, 1959).

32 Mozley and Raymo, *Speculum Stultorum*, p. 5.

33 Ibid., p. 6.

34 Stahl, *Martianus*, 1: 27. The Menippean satires of Varro, also an encyclopedist, survive only in fragments. For discussion of the fragments, see Barbara P. McCarthy, "The Form of Varro's Menippean Satires," in *Philological Studies in Honor of Walter Miller*, ed. Rodney P. Robinson, University of Missouri Studies, vol. 11 (Columbia, 1936), pp. 95–107. For recent work on the fragments, see Jean-Pierre Cèbe, *Varron, Satires Ménippées*, 2 vols. (Rome, 1972–74).

35 Stahl, *Martianus*, 1: 21–23.

36 Ibid., p. 42.

37 The *Marriage* raises a quality of ire and exasperation which has seldom been accorded a work of this importance. Fanny LeMoine points out that most have found the work "so tasteless, turgid, and unintelligent" as to be "unworthy of further consideration." *Martianus Capella* (Munich, 1972), p. 3. While Menippean satirists are continually being castigated for the way they use sources, I have never seen any other charge to equal the one LeMoine (p. 2) quotes from J. A. Willis's summary of charges: "Our author is capable of such stupidity in use of his sources it is a credible assumption that Martianus was not a 'sanus homo.'" "Martianus Capella and His Early Commentators" (Ph.D. diss., University of London, 1952). This air of disapproval and irritation also surrounds much of

Stahl's commentary; see Charles Witke's review, *Speculum* 49 (1974): 156.

38 C. S. Lewis, *The Allegory of Love* (Oxford, 1938), p. 78.

39 LeMoine, *Martianus*, p. 7.

40 Ibid., p. 14.

41 English translation from Stahl, *Martianus*, 2: 381.

42 LeMoine, *Martianus*, p. 229.

43 Frye, *Anatomy*, p. 311, mentions Chaucer in his section on Menippean satire, commenting that he was a favorite author of Burton, "the greatest Menippean satirist in English before Swift." Derek Brewer, in his article "Gothic Chaucer," in *Geoffrey Chaucer*, ed. Derek Brewer (London, 1974), pp. 1–32, citing Frye, has recently commented on Chaucer as Menippean satirist (pp. 28–30). Those qualities labeled "Gothic" in Chaucer coincide to a large degree with the traits of Menippean satire. The great advantage of the latter term is that it designates a literary, not an architectural tradition.

44 Norman Eliason, *The Language of Chaucer's Poetry* (Copenhagen, 1972), p. 10.

45 B. H. Bronson, *In Search of Chaucer* (Toronto, 1960), p. 32.

46 Ibid., p. 22. The standard work on Chaucer's varied styles is, of course, Charles Muscatine's *Chaucer and the French Tradition* (Berkeley, 1957).

47 Eliason, *Language*, pp. 138–42.

48 Robert Jordan, *Chaucer and the Shape of Creation* (Cambridge, Mass., 1967), p. 117; Eliason, *Language*, p. 144.

49 Gilbert Highet, *The Classical Tradition* (Oxford, 1949), p. 95. Thomas Lounsbury drew similar conclusions in "The Learning of Chaucer," *Studies in Chaucer*, 3 vols. (1892; rpt. New York, 1962), 2: 160–426, esp. pp. 416ff.

50 Their classification as writers of the second class is not entirely a matter of critics' mistaking the intents of their genres. The truth is that their cited authors are more massive than they. Lucian's dialogues are brilliant little dialogues; the *Consolation* is a brilliant little book. The judgment in favor of length may reflect only our need to avert the thought that all we (and the human race in general) have to say could just as well be contained in one sentence. Nevertheless I think it true that no one, however oblivious to the intents of Menippean satire, would announce without considerable explanation that the *Republic* was a greater work than the *Brothers Karamazov*.

51 Elizabeth Salter, *Chaucer:* The Knight's Tale *and* The Clerk's Tale
    (London, 1962), p. 69.
52 Georgia R. Crampton, *The Condition of Creatures* (New Haven,
    1974), p. 71.
53 Roger S. Loomis, "Was Chaucer a Laodicean?" in *Essays and
    Studies in Honor of Carleton Brown* (New York, 1940), pp. 129–48.
54 For a discussion of the relation between the conflicts of the time
    and the impulse to write Menippean satire, see Bakhtin, *Problems*,
    pp. 22–23. For a description of Lucian's time as a moment of con-
    verging ideas, see Barry Baldwin, *Studies in Lucian* (Toronto,
    1973), p. 117. Boethius was confronted throughout his life with the
    conflict of Ostrogoth and Roman, the conflict between Arian and
    Catholic, and the dissensions in government which grew out of
    those confrontations and culminated in his exile and execution.
    Chaucer lived in times unsettled by the changing economic condi-
    tions brought about by the Black Death, the Peasants' Revolt, Wy-
    cliffe and the Lollards, and the dissensions in government that led
    finally to the murder of Richard II. See Loomis's article cited
    above and M. E. Thomas, *Medieval Skepticism and Chaucer* (New
    York, 1971).
55 For an interesting analysis of the different points of view taken by
    Menippean and non-Menippean writers on death, see Bakhtin's
    hypothetical Dostoevskian reconstruction of Tolstoy's short story
    "Three Deaths" (*Problems*, pp. 56ff.).
56 Russell Peck has recently discussed the relation of nominalism and
    Chaucer. He cautions at once, however: "If nominalism is to be
    understood as that ontological exercise which refutes realist prem-
    ises that universals are things of creation, proving to the contrary
    that only individual things exist and are experienced, and that con-
    cepts beyond the individual are names only (concepts which exist
    exclusively in our heads), then nominalism is probably a matter
    which lies apart from Chaucer's particular interests." "Chaucer
    and the Nominalist Questions," *Speculum* 53 (1978): 745.
57 "Universals," *Encyclopedia of Philosophy* (New York, 1967), vol.
    8, p. 204.
58 Tzvetan Todorov puts the issue thus: "Genre represents, precisely,
    a structure, a configuration of literary properties, an inventory of
    options. But a work's inclusion within a genre still teaches us noth-
    ing as to its meaning. It merely permits us to establish the existence
    of a certain rule by which the work in question—and many others
    as well—are governed." *The Fantastic* (Cleveland, 1973), p. 141.

CHAPTER 2: LUCIAN AS MENIPPEAN SATIRIST

1 For an account of Lucian's life, see Jacques Schwartz, *Biographie de Lucien de Samosate* (Brussels-Berchen, 1965), and Barry Baldwin, *Studies in Lucian* (Toronto, 1973). For the major bibliography, see H. D. Betz, *Lukian von Samosata und das Neue Testament* (Berlin, 1961), pp. 218–51. Lucian's relation to Greek philosophy is discussed by W. H. Tackaberry, *Lucian's Relation to Plato and the Post-Aristotelian Philosophers* (Toronto, 1930). For an excellent short introduction to Lucian and his works, see H. W. Fowler and F. G. Fowler, trans., *The Works of Lucian of Samosata* (Oxford, 1905), 1: vii–xxxviii. Three recent selections from Lucian's works in paperback provide useful material and insights in their introductions: Paul Turner, trans., *Lucian* (Baltimore, 1961), pp. 7–20; Lionel Casson, trans., *Selected Satires of Lucian* (New York, 1962), pp. xi–xviii; Bryan P. Reardon, trans., *Lucian: Selected Works* (Indianapolis, 1965), pp. vii–xxxiv. The monumental classics on Lucian are Rudolf Helm, *Lucian und Menipp* (Leipzig, 1906), and J. Bompaire, *Lucien Ecrivain* (Paris, 1958). For a useful and suggestive critical account of Lucian's satire, see Ronald Paulson, *The Fictions of Satire* (Baltimore, 1967), pp. 31–42.

2 See Tackaberry, *Lucian's Relation to Plato*, pp. 38–41. Tackaberry mentions some twenty works as Menippean satires. The Fowlers, using M. Croiset's categories in *Essai sur la vie et les oeuvres de Lucien* (Paris, 1882), list ten works under the heading (*Works of Lucian*, 1: iii); Reardon, *Lucian*, pp. xix–xxii, lists fifteen. A. Oltramare, *Les origines de la diatribe romaine* (Lausanne, 1926), contains a list of the themes of the Cynic diatribe.

3 A. M. Harmon, K. Kilburn, and M. D. Macleod, eds., *Lucian*, 8 vols., Loeb Classical Library (London, 1913–67), 3: 43. The volume and page number will henceforth be given immediately after citations.

4 See Karl Mras, "Varros Menippeische Satiren und die Philosophie," *Neue Jahrbücher für das Klassische Altertum* 33 (1914): 391–93.

5 Paulson, *Fictions of Satire*, p. 41.

6 Reardon, *Lucian*, p. xxx.

7 See Northrop Frye, *Anatomy of Criticism* (Princeton, 1957), p. 310.

8 The classic statement of this negative view is found in Helm, *Lucian und Menipp*. He was answered by Barbara P. McCarthy, "Lucian and Menippus," *Yale Classical Studies* 4 (1934): 3–58. See

also Reardon, *Lucian*, p. xx, and Tackaberry, *Lucian's Relation to Plato*, pp. 39ff. Baldwin, who is favorably disposed to Lucian, nevertheless makes such statements as "The comparison between Lucian and Voltaire hardly stands up, unless one is disposed to disparaging the latter. Lucian was not a deep thinker, and did not pretend to be one." *Studies in Lucian*, p. 103. Gilbert Highet, *The Anatomy of Satire* (Princeton, 1962), pp. 42–43, is damning. Contrast with this passage, however, his earlier words on Lucian: "There is more gentleness in his voice and kindness in his heart than we feel in his Roman predecessors. His work is unlike nearly everything else that survives from Greco-Roman literature." *The Classical Tradition* (Oxford, 1949), p. 304.

9   Tackaberry, *Lucian's Relation to Plato*, p. 7.
10 Ibid.

CHAPTER 3: THE CONSOLATION OF PHILOSOPHY AS MENIPPEAN SATIRE

1   The *Consolation* is called a Menippean satire by writers as diverse as H. F. Stewart, *Boethius* (Edinburgh, 1891), p. 74; Northrop Frye, *Anatomy of Criticism* (Princeton, 1957), p. 312; M. M. Bakhtin, *The Problems of Dostoevsky's Poetics*, trans. R. W. Rotsel (Ann Arbor, 1973), pp. 93, 110; and Pierre Courcelle, *Late Latin Writers and Their Greek Sources*, trans. H. E. Wedeck (Cambridge, Mass., 1969), p. 296. For general accounts of Boethius' life and works, see Helen M. Barrett, *Boethius* (Cambridge, 1940); Courcelle, *Late Latin Writers*, pp. 273–330; M. Manitius, *Geschichte der Lateinischen Literatur des Mittelalters* (Munich, 1911), 1: 22–36; E. K. Rand, *Founders of the Middle Ages* (Cambridge, Mass., 1929), pp. 135–80; and Stewart, *Boethius*. For the Consolation, see Peter Elbow, *Oppositions in Chaucer* (Middletown, Conn., 1973), pp. 19–48; Monica E. McAlpine, *The Genre of* Troilus and Criseyde (Ithaca, 1978), pp. 47–85; and Winthrop Wetherbee, *Platonism and Poetry in the Twelfth Century* (Princeton, 1972), pp. 74–82. Additional works on Boethius' sources and influence are H. R. Patch, *The Tradition of Boethius* (New York, 1935); Pierre Courcelle, La Consolation de Philosophie *dans la tradition littéraire* (Paris, 1967); E. T. Silk, ed., *Saeculi Noni Auctoris in Boetii* Consolationem Philosophiae *Commentarius* (Rome, 1935), pp. ix–lxi; Jan Sulowski, "The Sources of Boethius' *De Consolatione Philosophiae*," *Sophia* 29 (1961): 67–94; and B. Kottler, "The Vulgate Tradition of the *Consolatio Philosophiae* in the

Fourteenth Century," *Mediaeval Studies* 17 (1955): 209–14. Herman Usener in *Anecdoton Holderi* (Bonn, 1877) established the authenticity of Boethius' *Theological Tracts* and put a stop to the argument (but not to the reports of it) about whether Boethius was a Christian. Courcelle, *Late Latin Writers*, pp. 318ff., gives a thorough and interesting analysis of the issues and the writings of those involved in the controversy. Historical accounts of the events that led to Boethius' downfall are found in Maurice Dumoulin, "The Kingdom of Italy under Odovacer and Theodoric," *The Cambridge Medieval History* (New York, 1936), 1: 432–55; Charles H. Coster, "The Trial of Boethius," *The Iudicium Quinquevirale* (Cambridge, Mass., 1935), pp. 40–63; and Thomas Hodgkin, *Italy and Her Invaders* (Oxford, 1885), 3: 517–72.

2 Usener, *Anecdoton Holderi*, dismissed the *Consolation* as nothing but a compilation: it contains, he thought, an inferior introduction and some bad poetry, which he allowed to be original; a section based on Aristotle's lost *Protreptikos*; and a section based on a Neo-Platonic source. E. K. Rand, in "On the Composition of Boethius' *Consolatio Philosophiae*," *Harvard Studies in Classical Philology* 15 (1904): 1–28, showed that the work is far more complex than Usener supposed, that it is highly original in its selectivity and arrangement of the ideas of preceding writers Boethius draws on. The closest Rand came to mentioning the *Consolation's* Menippean character was to say that though it is called both a "consolation" and a "protreptikos" (an incitement to the study of philosophy), those "who discuss either of these literary species in the large have little to say of the work of Boethius. This is because it is a mixture" (p. 8). Rand went on to call it a "theodicy," not a term that, initially, we would think of applying to Menippean satire in general, but not totally inappropriate.

3 Paul Turner, trans., *Lucian* (Baltimore, 1961), p. 13.

4 See J. E. Sandys, *A History of Classical Scholarship*, 3rd ed. (Cambridge, 1921), pp. 255–56; Courcelle, *Late Latin Writers*, pp. 295ff. There is little unanimity among scholars about Boethius' exact sources. Courcelle remarks on the disagreement: "So many contradictory views demand the utmost caution in an investigation of the sources and indicate that we have to deal with commonplaces easy to find in the most dissimilar writers" (p. 298).

5 Stewart, *Boethius*, p. 106.

6 Edward Gibbon, *The Decline and Fall of the Roman Empire*, Modern Library (New York, 1932?), 2: 471–72.

7 Boethius is "one of the rare cases where an imitator succeeds in sur-
passing his prototype and in purifying the literary course struck out
by his predecessor [Martianus Capella]." Karl Mras, "Varros Menippeische Satiren und die Philosophie," *Neue Jahrbücher für das
Klassische Altertum* 33 (1914): 391. See also Barrett, *Boethius*, p.
76; Stewart, *Boethius*, p. 75; Silk, *Saeculi*, p. 4.
8 On the abrupt close of the *Consolation*, see McAlpine, *Troilus*, pp.
83–85.
9 H. F. Stewart and E. K. Rand, eds., with a new translation by S. J.
Tester, *Boethius*, Loeb Classical Library (London, 1973), p. 135.
Henceforth, book and prose or meter will be given after quotations.
10 A. M. Harmon, K. Kilburn, and M. D. Macleod, eds., *Lucian*, 8
vols., Loeb Classical Library, (London, 1913–67), 4: 99–101. Volume and page number will henceforth be given after citations. In
the *Consolation*, as in this passage, Fortune uses Croesus as an
example.
11 Boethius had direct access to primary texts and also to later Neo-
platonic and Christian synthesizers, the most notable of whom is
Augustine. For the Neoplatonic influence see Courcelle, *Late
Latin Writers*. For the influence of Augustine, see Etienne Gilson,
History of Christian Philosophy (New York, 1955), p. 102; Richard Green, trans., *The Consolation of Philosophy* (New York,
1962), pp. xv–xix; and E. T. Silk, "Boethius' *Consolatio Philosophiae* as a Sequel to Augustine's *Dialogues* and *Soliloquies*," *Harvard Theological Review* 32 (1939): 19–39. For the distinctions
between "open" and "closed" systems, see Whitney J. Oates, "Introduction," *Basic Writings of St. Augustine* (New York, 1948), 1:
x–xii.
12 W. P. Ker, *The Dark Ages* (London, 1904), p. 57.
13 Harmon, *Lucian*, 2: 267.
14 See McAlpine's analysis of this passage, *Troilus*, pp. 50–52.
15 Bakhtin writes: "The phenomenon of reduced laughter has rather
great significance in world literature. Reduced laughter has no direct expression, it does not, so to speak, 'ring out,' but traces of it
remain and can be discerned in the structure of the image and the
word. Paraphrasing Gogol, one can speak of 'laughter which is invisible to the world.'" *Problems*, p. 236.
16 The mostly apocryphal stories of a tenth-century encyclopedist,
Lucian's earliest biographer, voice the outrage of convention: "Lucian of Samosata, otherwise known as Lucian the Blasphemer, or
the Slanderer, or, more accurately, the Atheist, because in his dia-

logues he even makes fun of religion. He was born somewhere about the time of Trajan. He practiced for a while as a barrister at Antioch in Syria, but did so badly at it that he turned over to literature, and wrote no end of stuff. He is said to have been torn to pieces by mad dogs, because he had been so rabid against the truth —for in his *Death of Peregrinus* the filthy brute attacks Christianity and blasphemes Christ Himself. So he was adequately punished in this world, and in the next he will inherit eternal fire with Satan." Quoted by Turner, *Lucian*, p. 7.

17 J. P. Migne, ed., *Patrologiae Cursus Completus: Series Latina*, 2nd ed. (Paris, 1891), 64. 433.

CHAPTER 4: FORTUNE, HAPPINESS, AND LOVE IN
TROILUS AND CRISEYDE

1 The titles of this and the following chapter are taken from the subjects of the major Boethian passages in the poem.

2 Charles Muscatine, *Chaucer and the French Tradition* (Berkeley, 1957), p. 129; see also pp. 142–53. Robert Payne discusses the style of the poem in *The Key of Remembrance* (New Haven, 1963), pp. 188–216, esp. pp. 198–201. Monica McAlpine's *The Genre of* Troilus and Criseyde (Ithaca, 1978) discusses at length the combination of comedy and tragedy in the poem; see especially the chapters entitled "The Boethian Comedy of Troilus" and "The Boethian Tragedy of Criseyde."

3 Muscatine, *French Tradition*, p. 136. The Bethell citation is from *Shakespeare and the Popular Dramatic Tradition* (London, 1944), pp. 26–29, 63–67, and 108–12. Intellectual conflicts in the poem are treated in Donald Rowe's *O Love, O Charite: Contraries Harmonized in Chaucer's* Troilus (Carbondale, Ill., 1976) and in Peter Elbow's *Oppositions in Chaucer* (Middletown, Conn., 1973), pp. 49–72.

4 The attitude and technique both are hard on conservatives. Barry Baldwin, *Studies in Lucian* (Toronto, 1973), p. 117, points out that Photius concluded that Lucian believed in nothing. In Boethius' case, the uneasy sensation that disbelief of some sort lurks in his text led several generations of scholars to occupy themselves with whether he remained a Christian until the end, a pursuit, at least literarily speaking, wide of the mark, but a not inappropriate response to the impression the text gives that Boethius was not taking the finality of his own death with sufficient seriousness. For a

discussion of the Christian controversy that surrounds Boethius, see Courcelle, *Late Latin Writers*, pp. 318ff.

5 B. L. Jefferson, *Chaucer and* The Consolation of Philosophy (Princeton, 1917), p. 150, lists 289 instances of general and verbal influence, almost one-third of the total instances of citations from the *Consolation* in Chaucer's poetry (1,041 in all). For the influence of Boethius on Chaucer, see the books by Elbow and McAlpine cited above and Ida L. Gordon, *The Double Sorrow of Troilus* (Oxford, 1970), pp. 24–60.

6 See R. K. Root, *The Textual Tradition of Chaucer's* Troilus (London, 1916), pp. 155ff., 216ff.

7 Noting that both works have five books, a number of critics have examined possible parallels; see, for instance, John P. McCall, "Five-Book Structure in Chaucer's *Troilus*," *MLQ* 23 (1962): 297–308; and H. R. Patch, "Troilus on Determinism," *Speculum*, 6 (1931): 242. William Provost, however, provides words of caution about the basic facts of such comparison: "If one assumes structural parallelism between the two works, interesting results can be deduced, but the evidence for establishing a *prima-facie* case is simply not there." *The Structure of Chaucer's* Troilus and Criseyde (Copenhagen, 1974), p. 21. Charles A. Owen calls the notion of exact parallel into question by suggesting that Chaucer's original draft contained four books, later extended to five; see "The Significance of Chaucer's Revisions of *Troilus and Criseyde*," *MP* 55 (1957): 1–5. Because we have the account of the aftermath and of Philosophy-Pandarus' failure, *Troilus* may, in fact, be said to go on two books longer than the *Consolation*.

8 T. A. Stroud, "Boethius' Influence on Chaucer's *Troilus*," *MP* 49 (1951–52): 4.

9 This and subsequent quotations of *The Consolation of Philosophy* are from the Middle English translation in *The Works of Geoffrey Chaucer*, ed. F. N. Robinson, 2nd ed. (Boston, 1957). Hereafter, page references to this work will be indicated in parentheses in the text.

10 The most important work on the relation of *Troilus* and the *Filostrato* is Sanford B. Meech's *Design in Chaucer's* Troilus (Syracuse, 1959). See also C. S. Lewis, "What Chaucer Really Did to *Il Filostrato*," *Essays and Studies* 17 (1932): 56–75; and Karl Young, "Chaucer's *Troilus and Criseyde* as Romance," *PMLA* 53 (1938): 38–63. For Chaucer's changes raising the social position of his heroine, see Young, pp. 49–56.

11 For Pandarus' tendency to change positions, see Muscatine, *French Tradition*, p. 145, and Payne, *Key of Remembrance*, pp. 210–11.

12 John P. McCall, "Chaucer's May 3," *MLN* 76 (1961): 201–5.

13 I am indebted for this suggestion to R. Howard Bloch's paper entitled "Love Courts and Law Courts," given at the Kalamazoo Medieval Conference, May 9, 1974.

14 For discussions of this speech, see Peter Elbow, "Two Boethian Speeches in *Troilus and Criseyde*," *English Institute Essays* (New York, 1967), pp. 27, 98ff. (a later version of this essay appears in Elbow's book cited above, *Oppositions in Chaucer*); and Gordon, *Double Sorrow*, pp. 29–30.

15 In his notes, Robinson remarks that the comparison was conventional (*Works*, p. 825); Root, whom he cites, gives various medieval references. The ultimate source, however, was almost certainly Genesis and its commentaries, which saw jealousy as Satan's chief motive for the seduction of Adam and Eve.

16 For analyses of Troilus' Hymn to Love, see John M. Steadman, *Disembodied Laughter* (Berkeley, 1972), pp. 69–70; H. R. Patch, *The Tradition of Boethius* (Oxford, 1935), pp. 69ff.; and Gordon, *Double Sorrow*, pp. 33ff.

17 Elbow, "Two Boethian Speeches," p. 106.

18 The centrality of this unresolved conflict, a necessary condition of Menippean satire, cannot be overemphasized. Winthrop Wetherbee, having written about what he calls the "darker side" of the *Consolation*, remarks in conclusion: "There is a strong Neoplatonic element in Boethius' thought, and a definite quasi-mystical suggestion in the *De consolatione* that the bonds of nature in their very harmony are finally as confining to the human spirit as the bonds of vice and ignorance. But read as a work of imaginative literature, the dialogue seems to me more convincing as a dramatization of the psychological experience of the attempt, than as an exposition of the means of such transcendence." A few lines later he writes that Philosophy's "use of myth to punctuate her argument has the effect of a double exposure of the course she urges. For her the heroic images she presents are models of decisive, liberating action, repudiations of fortune and the ties and fears of earthly life. For the prisoner, and for us, they are also images of the difficulty of such renunciation and transcendence. Boethius' use of dialogue, moreover, and his testing of the efficacy of Philosophy's lessons by their effect on the doubts and confusions of a mortal subject, make it difficult for the reader to acquiesce fully in even the most power-

ful affirmation of the Timaean vision." Winthrop Wetherbee, *Platonism and Poetry in the Twelfth Century* (Princeton, 1972), p. 82.

CHAPTER 5: FREEDOM IN *TROILUS AND CRISEYDE*

1 In the epilogue (so-called) to the poem, certain aspects of which I shall consider at the end of the chapter, both the narrator and Troilus escape in some degree the consequences of their refusal, but their release does not move the poem into the realm of the comic. The poem is, as Chaucer says (5. 1786), a tragedy.

2 Walter C. Curry, "Destiny in *Troilus and Criseyde*," in *Chaucer and the Medieval Sciences*, 2nd ed. (New York, 1960), pp. 241–98; B. L. Jefferson, *Chaucer and* The Consolation of Philosophy (Princeton, 1917), p. 120. H. R. Patch's article, an answer to Curry, redresses the balance somewhat; see "Troilus on Determinism," *Speculum* 6 (1931): 225–43. Monica McAlpine, *The Genre of* Troilus and Criseyde (Ithaca, 1978), esp. pp. 140–42, 148–51, notes the strong presence of freedom in the poem. For the reasons given in n. 1, above, however, I disagree with her that Troilus is a "Boethian comic hero"; I see him instead as a Menippean tragic figure.

3 T. R. Lounsbury calls it "the grossest instance of the failure on the part of Chaucer to comply with the requirements of his art." *Studies in Chaucer* (New York, 1892), 3: 372. G. L. Kittredge defends it to some extent: "Doubtless the passage is inartistic and maladjusted; but it is certainly not, as some have called it, a digression. On the contrary, it is, in substance, as pertinent as any of Hamlet's soliloquies." *Chaucer and his Poetry* (Cambridge, Mass., 1915), p. 115. H. R. Patch defends the passage on the grounds that it reveals to us Chaucer's subtle humor in portraying a very young man's struggle with logic. "Troilus on Predestination," *JEGP* 17 (1918): 399–422. For analyses of the speech, see Sanford B. Meech, *Design in Chaucer's* Troilus (Syracuse, 1959), pp. 90–92.

4 For related discussions of this speech, see in particular Peter Elbow, "Two Boethian Speeches in *Troilus and Criseyde*," *English Institute Essays* (New York, 1967), pp. 85ff.; John Huber, "Troilus' Predestination Soliloquy: Chaucer's Changes from Boethius," *Neuphilologische Mitteilungen* 66 (1965): 120–25; David Sims, "The Logic of *Troilus and Criseyde*," *Cambridge Quarterly* 4 (1968–70): 126–33.

5   Patch, "Troilus on Predestination," p. 405.
6   *The City of God* 5. 9, Modern Library (New York, 1950), pp. 152ff.
7   For an account of Troilus' struggle with logic in the speech, see Patch, "Troilus on Predestination," pp. 414–21.
8   For Chaucer's undermining of Calchas, see S. B. Greenfield, "The Role of Calchas in *Troilus and Criseyde*," *Medium Aevum* 35 (1966): 143–44, 147–48. For the narrator's tendency to overdetermine even insignificant events, see Elbow's analysis of the first meeting of the lovers, in "Two Boethian Speeches," p. 89.
9   Joseph S. Graydon makes this point in "A Defense of Criseyde," *PMLA* 44 (1929): 153.
10 For discussions of the treatment of time in book 5, see Gerry Brenner, "Narrative Structure in Chaucer's *Troilus and Criseyde*," *Annuale Medievale* 6 (1965): p. 8; Meech, *Design*, pp. 230–33; and William Provost, *The Structure of Chaucer's* Troilus and Criseyde (Copenhagen, 1974), pp. 43–52.
11 As McAlpine points out (*Troilus*, p. 172), Troilus can be thought to mistake the identification of the central figure of his earlier dream about being alone among enemies (a perfect description of Criseyde's plight rather than his), and here does not see that the boar can quite easily be himself.
12 Patch, "Troilus on Determinism," pp. 225–26. Stephen A. Barney discusses the complex of limitations Chaucer refers to, including man's natural limitations and his appetites, in "Troilus Bound," *Speculum* 47 (1972): 451–54.
13 Morton W. Bloomfield, "Distance and Predestination in *Troilus and Criseyde*," *PMLA* 72 (1957): 14–15.
14 Graydon, "Criseyde," esp. pp. 158ff.; for Troilus' tendencies to unreasonable jealousy, see pp. 160ff.; the summary of events in book 5, placed in chronological order, is presented on pp. 175–76. This is an important article, one which, for me, brought the final book of the poem into focus.
15 The epilogue has excited nearly as much comment as the free will soliloquy; see, for instance, Curry, *Medieval Sciences*, pp. 294ff.; John Steadman, *Disembodied Laughter* (Berkeley, 1972); E. Talbot Donaldson, *Speaking of Chaucer* (New York, 1970), pp. 84ff.; Meech, *Design*, pp. 452–55, for a summary of views; Peter Dronke, "The Conclusion of *Troilus and Criseyde*," *Medium Aevum* 33 (1964): 47–52; Patricia M. Kean, "Chaucer's Dealings with a Stanza of *Il Filostrato* and the Epilogue of *Troilus and Criseyde*," ibid., pp. 36–46; McAlpine, *Troilus*, pp. 237ff.

16 See, in particular, W. Farnham, *The Medieval Heritage of Eliza-*
    bethan Tragedy (Berkeley, 1936), pp. 137ff.; and McAlpine's
    book, *Troilus*, which deals extensively with *de casibus* tragedy
    and Chaucer's transformations and alterations of this theory of
    tragedy.
17 C. S. Lewis, *The Allegory of Love* (Oxford, 1938), p. 195.
18 D. W. Robertson's essay "Chaucerian Tragedy," *ELH* 19 (1952):
    1–37, views the poem in Fortune's terms, seeing the "fall" as Troi-
    lus' falling in love. Analogically precise, the identification sur-
    prises those with nonexegetical leanings.
19 Various Menippean influences on *Hamlet* can be cited. W. Sher-
    wood Fox points out that the gravedigger scene is based on the ma-
    cabre humor of Lucian's *Dialogues of the Dead*. "Lucian in the
    Grave-scene of *Hamlet*," *PQ* 2 (1923): 132–41. The soliloquy
    "How all occasions do inform against me" is based on the topos of
    the view from the heights which surveys the tiny spaces in which
    the triviality of human endeavors is carried on. (See *Icaromenip-*
    pus.) There are various echoes of the *Consolation*, e.g., "Nothing is
    good or bad but thinking makes it so." Most important of all, how-
    ever, is the absence of what T. S. Eliot called the objective cor-
    relative.
20 M. M. Bakhtin, *The Problems of Dostoevsky's Poetics* (Ann Arbor,
    1973), p. 138.

CHAPTER 6: FOREKNOWLEDGE AND FREE WILL: THREE THEORIES
            IN *THE NUN'S PRIEST'S TALE*

1 Sir William Hamilton, *Discussion on Philosophy and Literature,*
   Education and University Reform, quoted in *The Idea of Free-*
   dom, ed. Mortimer J. Adler (New York, 1961), 2: 474–75.
2 Gordon Leff, *Bradwardine and the Pelagians* (Cambridge, 1957),
   p. 15. For a brief account of Bradwardine's philosophy, see H. R.
   Patch, "Troilus on Determinism," *Speculum* 6 (1931): 225–43.
3 Augustine, *The Free Choice of the Will (De libero arbitrio)*, in *The*
   Fathers of the Church, trans. R. P. Russell (Washington, 1968),
   59: 173.
4 *Sources and Analogues of Chaucer's* Canterbury Tales, ed. W. F.
   Bryan and Germaine Dempster (New York, 1958), p. 658.
5 In the last prose of the *Consolation* (bk. 5, pr. 6; p. 382), Philosophy points out that God's foreknowledge of things in time is to be
   called "providentia," rather than "praevidentia"; that is, the word
   describes a spatial rather than a temporal relation.

6   See, for instance, John Speirs, *Chaucer the Maker* (London, 1951), pp. 189ff.
7   Mortimer Donovan, "The *Moralite* of the Nun's Priest's Sermon," *JEGP* 52 (1953): 498–508.

CHAPTER 7: THE EATERS AND THE EATEN IN *THE NUN'S PRIEST'S TALE*

1   Quoted in W. C. Curry, *Chaucer and the Medieval Sciences* (New York, 1960), p. 199. See *Macrobius' Commentary on the Dream of Scipio*, trans. W. H. Stahl (New York, 1952), pp. 87ff., esp. p. 90.
2   Ibid.
3   J. Burke Severs, in "Chaucer's Originality in the *Nun's Priest's Tale*," *SP* 43 (1946): 38, points out that in the analogues the fox runs away at once.
4   For a discussion of the times and dangers of Pertelote's herbs, see, for instance, Corinne E. Kauffman, "Dame Pertelote's Parlous Parle," *Chaucer Review* 4 (1970): 41–48.
5   E. Talbot Donaldson, *Chaucer's Poetry* (New York, 1958), p. 944.
6   R. T. Lenaghan so terms the "hybrid genre" the Nun's Priest employs in the tale. "The Nun's Priest's Fable," *PMLA* 78 (1963): p. 305. Both terms are appropriate synonyms for "Menippean satire."
7   See John M. Steadman, "Flattery and the *Moralitas* of the Nonne Preestes Tale," *Medium Aevum* 28 (1959): 172–79.
8   Lenaghan, "Fable," pp. 306–7.
9   Curry, *Medieval Sciences*, pp. 227–30.
10 Severs, "Originality," pp. 22–41, esp. pp. 29ff.
11 Francis G. Allinson, *Lucian, Satirist and Artist* (New York, 1927), p. 174.
12 The narrator's speaking as the devil explains various small points, such as his inability to say anything against women immediately after the Garden of Eden allusion: "Thise been the cokkes wordes, and nat myne." ("Cok" equals male human being.) More important, I believe that the sense of evil implicit in the tale because of the narrator's tack also explains the soberness with which the tale has been treated; the critic feels obliged to compensate with his own virtue for the open-ended laughter. I am aware that I have frequently been fully engaged with the narrator's point of view. *Mea culpa.*
13 For a discussion of the attacks on fiction, see Stephen Manning, "The Nun's Priest's Morality and the Medieval Attitude toward Fables," *JEGP* 59 (1960): 403–16, esp. p. 404.

14 Ibid., pp. 414–16.
15 D. W. Robertson, *A Preface to Chaucer* (Princeton, 1963), p. 252.
16 E. Talbot Donaldson, "Patristic Exegesis in the Criticism of Medieval Literature: The Opposition," in *Critical Approaches to Medieval Literature, English Institute Essays*, ed. Dorothy Bethurum (New York, 1960), p. 20.
17 For instance, Nevill Coghill and Christopher Tolkien write: "*As seith my lord* is apparently an insoluble puzzle. In the Ellesmere manuscript the words *scilicet Dominus archiepiscopus Cantuariensis* are written in the margin, but nobody has been able to explain why the Archbishop of Canterbury should be referred to here, and it seems likely to be no more than a guess. As a reference to Christ, *my lord* for *our lord* would be otherwise quite unknown." *The Nun's Priest's Tale* (London, 1959), p. 132. See also M. Hussey, ed., *The Nun's Priest's Prologue and Tale* (Cambridge, 1965), p. 88; Robinson, *Works*, p. 755.
18 It is interesting to speculate, since this is one of the "cancelled" links, that Chaucer may have been contemplating a knowing response by one of the pilgrims, e.g., the Knight, or the Clerk and Pardoner, who deal with devil figures of their own.
19 Lenaghan, "Fable," p. 302.

CHAPTER 8: *SIC ET NON:* DISCARDED WORLDS IN *THE KNIGHT'S TALE*

1 The most extensive analysis of the tale as a parody of romance is by Paul T. Thurston, *Artistic Ambivalence in Chaucer's* Knight's Tale (Gainesville, Fla., 1968). For Chaucer's use of the *Consolation* in the tale, see, in particular, B. L. Jefferson, *Chaucer and* The Consolation of Philosophy (Princeton, 1917), esp. pp. 130–32; R. E. Kaske, "The Knight's Interruption of the *Monk's Tale*," *ELH* 24 (1957): 260–68; and E. T. Donaldson, *Chaucer's Poetry* (New York, 1958), pp. 901–5. The conflicting voices of the tale are treated by Elizabeth Salter, *Chaucer:* The Knight's Tale *and* The Clerk's Tale (London, 1962), pp. 23ff.; and by Georgia R. Crampton, *The Condition of Creatures* (New Haven, 1974), pp. 63ff. Discussions of the oppositions in the tale are found in Peter Elbow, "How Chaucer Transcends Oppositions in *The Knight's Tale*," *Chaucer Review* 7 (1972): 97–112; and in the writings of those interested in the analogy between Gothic art and Chaucer's poetry, especially J. M. Jordan, *Chaucer and the Shape of Creation* (Cambridge, Mass., 1967); and Derek Brewer, "Gothic Chaucer," in *Geoffrey Chaucer* (London, 1974), pp. 1–32. Donald W. Rowe

deals with the *concordia discors* theme in the tale in *O Love, O Charite: Contraries Harmonized in Chaucer's* Troilus (Carbondale, Ill., 1976), pp. 30–34. William Frost comments on the debate about the poem's meaning: "What may be the point of the story is frequently debated, votes having been registered for the Tale as allegory, as a riddle, as a pseudo-epic (marred by omission of too much of Boccaccio's material), and as a piece of realism (marred by an excess of epic machinery)." "An Interpretation of Chaucer's *Knight's Tale*," *RES* 25 (1949): 291. Also see Salter, *Knight's Tale*, p. 12; W. F. Bolton, "The Topic of the *Knight's Tale*," *Chaucer Review*, 1 (1967): 217; and Douglas Brooks and Alastair Fowler, "The Meaning of Chaucer's *Knight's Tale*," *Medium Aevum* 39 (1970): 123–24.

2 Charles Muscatine's much-quoted words form one view: "Order, which characterizes the structure of the poem, is also the heart of its meaning. The society depicted is one in which form is full of significance, in which life is conducted at a dignified, processional pace, and in which life's pattern is itself a reflection, or better, a reproduction, of the order of the universe." *Chaucer and the French Tradition* (Berkeley, 1957), p. 181. Jordan, *Shape of Creation* (esp. p. 153), writes in a similar vein, as does D. Everett, *Essays on Middle English Literature* (Oxford, 1955), pp. 168–69. On the other side, Richard Neuse answers: "The geometric design of the *Knight's Tale* functions more as a comic 'mechanism' than as a means for expressing a concept of order." "The Knight: The First Mover in Chaucer's Human Comedy," *University of Toronto Quarterly* 31 (1962): 306. Salter, *Knight's Tale*, p. 33, and Crampton, *Condition of Creatures*, p. 71, also remain skeptical about the ultimate seriousness of order as the controlling concept.

3 The critics disagree about whether the tale is tragic. For example, Frost, *Knight's Tale*, pp. 292, 299–302; H. R. Patch, *On Rereading Chaucer* (Cambridge, Mass., 1939), p. 201; and Ian Robinson, *Chaucer and the English Tradition* (Cambridge, 1972), pp. 108ff., say yes. Salter, *Knight's Tale*, p. 32, and Neuse, "The Knight," p. 309, say no.

4 The clear-cut relations between the *Consolation* and the *Knight's Tale* are often mentioned; see, in particular, John Halverson's discussion, "Aspects of Order in the *Knight's Tale*," *SP* 57 (1960): 616ff.; also, Dale Underwood, "The First of the *Canterbury Tales*," *ELH* 26 (1959): 463ff.; and R. M. Lumiansky, "Chaucer's Philosophical Knight," *Tulane Studies in English* 3 (1952): 47–68.

5 Guillaume de Lorris and Jeun de Meun, *The Romance of the Rose*, ll. 5555ff., trans. Charles Dahlberg (Princeton, 1971), p. 113. Homer makes Venus the daughter of Zeus and Dione, rather than the daughter of Saturn. The Knight, with a fine lack of discrimination, uses both traditions. Saturn calls Venus "daughter" (2453); in her temple the artists have portrayed her as "naked, fletynge in the large see" (1956). Palamon, however, identifies her as an Olympian (2222). The artists have portrayed her in the temple as presiding over the miseries of love in the Age of Iron.

6 Brewer, "Gothic Chaucer," pp. 17-18.

7 I am unable to get much resonance out of their both citing Juno, since she plays no part in the tale. She was, however, traditionally associated with both marriage and war. Perhaps each preempts one aspect of her power for his own purposes.

8 In this phase of their experience, they do survive intact to the extent that they pray to the right god, Palamon to Saturn, Arcite to Mars. The passages were quoted above.

9 This is a tradition of the patriarchal West; in countries where matriarchal values are stronger, the agreement is void. The Russians defeated Napoleon at Moscow, in effect, by not assenting, by not showing up to surrender. Since that victory is generally laid to the Russian winter, the recent skirmish in Vietnam at least should add a chapter to the history of Western warfare. The war there could not be won because the Vietnamese would not assent to American and Western assumptions about the significance of their victories. The truth is that you can only fight your brother satisfactorily under the agreement of Western traditions.

10 For this astrological identification of the two kings, see W. C. Curry, *Chaucer and the Medieval Sciences* (New York, 1960), pp. 130ff.

11 The first of these articles seems to have been H. N. Fairchild's, "Active Arcite, Contemplative Palamon," *JEGP* 26 (1927): 285-93. Many have followed. Some critics see the knights as undistinguishable. For instance, Muscatine, *French Tradition*, p. 180, argues that Chaucer's "crowning modification" of the *Teseida* "is the equalization of Palamon and Arcite." Others do perceive differences. Halverson, "Aspects of Order," pp. 606ff., sees them involved in a folk combat in which Arcite represents winter and Palamon summer. Nevill Coghill proposes that each represents a medieval secular ideal, Arcite, chivalry, Palamon, courtly love. "Chaucer's Narrative Art," in *Chaucer and Chaucerians*, ed. D. S. Brewer (London,

1966), p. 123. (I will point out that "winter" and chivalry fall in the sphere of positive law, "summer" and love, in the sphere of natural law.) One reason for the debate is that it is not usually realized by those who attack the Fairchild position that the knights exist in a state of confusion from the time of their argument over Emily until the meeting with Theseus at the grove.

12 Salter, *Knight's Tale*, p. 33.
13 The phrase is Frederick Turner's, in "A Structuralist Analysis of *The Knight's Tale*," *Chaucer Review* 8 (1974): 282.
14 Affrican runs Theseus a close second; the Eagle, Pandarus, and the fox, for instance, are in a lesser category of respectability.
15 His competitors for first place are Calidore in the Pastorella episode of the *Faerie Queene* and Feirefiz in *Parzival* (at the grail castle).
16 M. D. Macleod, *Lucian*, Loeb Classical Library (London, 1961), 7: 23.
17 Neuse, "The Knight," p. 307.
18 R. Baldwin, *The Unity of the* Canterbury Tales (Copenhagen, 1955), pp. 68–69.
19 Salter, *The Knight's Tale*, esp. pp. 32–34.

CHAPTER 9: THE KNIGHT: FRAGMENTS, SILENCE, AND BEAUTY

1 The one exception would seem to be his reaction to the death of Arcite.
2 For a description of the relation of the *Knight's Tale* and the *Teseida*, see R. A. Pratt, "Chaucer's Use of the *Teseida*," *PMLA* 62 (1947): 598–621; also see *Sources and Analogues of Chaucer's* Canterbury Tales, ed. W. F. Bryan and Germaine Dempster. (New York, 1958), pp. 82–105.
3 For Chaucer's habit of abbreviating, see W. Nelson Francis, "Chaucer Shortens a Tale," *PMLA* 68 (1953): 1126–41.
4 Elizabeth Salter, *Chaucer:* The Knight's Tale *and* The Clerk's Tale (London, 1962), p. 12.
5 R. K. Root, *The Poetry of Chaucer* (New York, 1906), pp. 171–72.
6 E. Talbot Donaldson, *Speaking of Chaucer* (New York, 1970), p. 49.
7 As Donald Howard points out, this is "a circumstance hard to arrange even in a bathtub." *The Idea of the* Canterbury Tales (Berkeley, 1976), p. 233.
8 Edward E. Foster, "Humor in the *Knight's Tale*," *Chaucer Review*

3 (1968): pp. 88–94, tabulates instances of the humor. Foster and others—for example, Judith S. Herz, "Chaucer's Elegiac Knight," *Criticism* 6 (1964): 212–24; and Paull F. Baum, *Chaucer: A Critical Appreciation* (Durham, N.C., 1958), pp. 84–104—have taken the tonal contradictions in the tale to indicate that Chaucer places the Knight on the wrong side of the humor. But this conclusion, whatever the considerable interest of the information turned up in proceeding to it, fails to recognize the premise of dialogical opposition characteristic of this tragicomic form, Menippean satire.

9 Theseus' speech parallels primarily bk. 4, pr. 6, which explains the relation of fate, providence, order, fortune, and man; but there are allusions to other parts of the *Consolation*. For instance, Theseus' reference to the fair chain of love which binds the elements parallels bk. 3, m. 9, and bk. 4, m. 6. His reference to the perfection of the eternal God from whom the mutable world proceeds parallels material in the third book (bk. 3, m. 9, pr. 10; also bk. 4, m. 6). His insistence on the value of making virtue of necessity comes from the last prose in the fourth book (bk. 4, pr. 7). For a discussion of the relationship, see J.A.W. Bennett, ed., *Chaucer: The Knight's Tale*, 2nd ed. (London, 1958).

10 A. C. Spearing, ed., *The Knight's Tale* (Cambridge, 1966), pp. 75–78, discusses the illogical nature of Theseus' speech.

11 I have suggested some of Theseus' inadequacies in the preceding chapter. The first of the articles that seriously questioned the role of noble Theseus seems to have been H. J. Webb's, "A Reinterpretation of Chaucer's Theseus," *RES* 23 (1947): 289–96. Many have done so since; see, for example, Dale Underwood, "The First of the *Canterbury Tales*," *ELH* 26(1959): 459ff.; and Edmund Reiss, "Chaucer's Courtly Love," in *The Learned and the Lewed*, ed. Larry D. Benson (Cambridge, Mass., 1974), p. 104.

12 Joseph Westlund, "*The Knight's Tale* as an Impetus for Pilgrimage," *PQ* 43 (1964): 526.

Index

Index

Index

Dream visions, 10, 13–14, 19, 27, 31, 32, 33

Eliot, T. S.: objective correlative, 156
Emma, 58
Encyclopedic satire, alternate name for Menippean satire, 5
Encyclopedist: Boethius, 85; Varro, 265n34; Lucian's earliest biographer, 271n16
Epic, 3–5, 35, 141, 143, 197, 199
Euripides, 33, 48, 60
Existentialist, 120
Explanations: danger of, 196; force against, 197; as fragments, 239, 245, 257; non-explanation in *Nun's Priest's Tale*, 196; satiric attack on in *Nun's Priest's Tale*, 159, 170, 175, 178–80, 190–92, 200, 202–3
—as human defense against chaos: *Knight's Tale*, 207, 222, 237; *Nun's Priest's Tale*, 186–89, 195, 197; *Troilus*, 123, 124, 142, 154

Fable: Martianus, 30; *Nun's Priest's Tale* as, 14, 164, 166, 167, 181–82, 189, 199–202, 205–6
Faerie Queene: Calidore and Theseus, 282n15; Prince Arthur and Philosophy, 84
Fatalism, 153
Fatalist, 226
Fiend: fox as, 172; Pandarus as, 134. *See also* Devil; Satan
Formulations: attack on, 166, 175, 198; as creative act, 87, 120, 127, 131; fixation on one, 53, 123, 156; fragments, 209
Freedom: contrasted with forces of restriction, e.g., fate, foreknowledge, death, theories, 45, 77–79, 84, 86, 104, 106, 111, 114, 124, 126–39, 146–52, 159, 160, 161, 162, 163, 164, 166, 169, 178, 184,

186, 187, 191, 192, 194, 196, 197, 200, 204, 223
—intellectual: as attainment, 7, 82, 85, 114, 166, 177, 178, 179, 200, 209, 224, 244, 253; as burden, 10, 12, 114, 122–158; as reward of Menippean satire, 4, 6, 10, 16, 18, 26, 36, 52, 53, 54, 275n2
Frye, Northrop. *See* Menippean satire: critics on

Gargantua and Pantagruel, sixteenth-century Menippean satire, 3
Gibbon, Edward: comment on tone of *Consolation*, 57
Gogol: work as analogue for Roth's *The Breast*, 14; 'laughter invisible to the world,' 271n15
Golden Age: in *Knight's Tale*, 211, 214, 222, 230; in *Nun's Priest's Tale*, 167
"Gothic" Chaucer, 266n43, 279–80n1

Heroes: Chauntecleer: 188; Menippean satire not interested in, 6, 18
Heroism: ants and, 45; fox on, 187; Menippean satire does not value, 18; Nun's Priest's, 204
Historian: *Troilus'* narrator as, 150
Homer, 14, 15, 19, 33, 36, 45, 60, 191, 223, 281n5
Horace: contrasted to Lucian, 39; source for *Consolation*, 56
Humpty Dumpty: example of extreme nominalist, 36

Iron Age: in *Knight's Tale*, 211, 215, 222, 230, 281n5

Jean de Meun: *Romance of the Rose*, thirteenth-century Menippean satire, 20, 55, 210, 263n18, 281n5

Index

Juvenal: contrasted to Lucian, 39; source for *Consolation*, 56

Kafka, Franz: work as analogue for Roth's *The Breast*, 14
Kipling, Rudyard: parody of "If you can keep your head when all about you / Are losing theirs . . . Yours is the earth and everything that's in it," 12

Landor, Walter: *Imaginary Conversations*, 6–7
Laodicean: Chaucer accused of being, 35
Law: human law, 216, 218, 230; love's law, 210–13; natural law, 210–18, 221, 230, 281–82*n11*; positive law, 210–17, 230, 281–82*n11*
Lollius, supposed author of *Troilus'* narrator's old story, 14
Longchamps, Nigel: *Speculum Stultorum*, twelfth-century Menippean satire, 27–28, 265*n31*
Lucian, 3, 9, 11, 14, 19, 21, 33, 35, 36–37, 38–54, 58–62, 66, 68–69, 77, 81–83, 84, 208, 262*n17*, 264*n22*, 266*n50*, 267*n54*, 268–69*n8*, 271*n16*, 272*n4*; *Carousel*, 26; *Council of the Gods*, 50; *Dialogues of the Dead*, 16, 38, 47–49, 68, 219; *Double Indictment*, 38–39; *Downward Journey*, 38, 49; *The Fisherman*, 13, 38; *Hermotimus*, 13, 202; *Icaromenippus*, 8, 26, 38, 41–45, 51, 62, 76, 81, 109, 264*n22*, 277*n19*; *Menippus*, 26, 38, 41–43, 51–52, 62, 81, 264*n22*; *Philosophies for Sale*, 8, 13, 26, 38, 87, 90, 96; *Zeus Catechized*, 13, 15–16, 38, 45–47, 68; *Zeus Rants*, 38, 50
Lucius or the Ass, 25, 262*n10*

Macrobius: on dreams, 183–84, 278*n1*
Martianus Capella: *Marriage of Philology and Mercury*, 26, 27, 28–31, 57, 265*nn30,37*, 271*n7*
Menippean satire: critics on: Bloomfield, 261*n1*
—Bakhtin: list of traits, 7–9; non-Aristotelian catharsis, 156; textual parody, 19–20; mentioned, 3, 4, 5, 17, 18, 83, 261*n3*, 267*nn54,55*, 269*n1*, 271*n15*
—Brewer: Chaucer and, 266*n43*
—Frye: summarized, 6–7, mentioned, 3, 5, 59, 261*n1*, 266*n43*, 268*n7*, 269*n1*
—Martianus: comment on his book, 30
—Muscatine: comment on genre of *Troilus*, 86
—Quintilian, definition, 264*n26*
Menippus, author, 26, 38, 261*n1*
Mentor figure: know-it-all, 9–10, 12, 13–14, 17, 32, 36, 51–52, 108; stock figure in Menippean satire, 91–95; Philosophy figure, 75–77, 89, 216, 219, 232, 257–58; mentioned, 40, 45, 48, 58, 59–60, 96
Mock-epic, 14, 167, 181, 199, 201–2
Myth: of *Consolation*, 57; of Garden of Eden, 172; in *Knight's Tale*, 229; Menippean satire's attack on, 7, 15, 40, 43, 45, 47, 83, 178

Neophyte figure: stock figure in Menippean satire, 36, 68, 257–58; mentioned, 12, 13–14, 48, 50–52, 58–59, 75, 77, 82, 149, 232
Neo-Platonists: source for *Consolation*, 56
Nominalism: incompatible with Menippean satire, 36, 267*n56*

Objective correlative: absent in *Troilus* and *Hamlet*, 156, 277*n19*

Index

DESIGNED BY ED FRANK
COMPOSED BY METRICOMP, GRUNDY CENTER, IOWA
MANUFACTURED BY CUSHING MALLOY, INC., ANN ARBOR, MICHIGAN
TEXT IS SET IN CALEDONIA, DISPLAY LINES IN MELIOR

ⅢⅢ

Library of Congress Cataloging in Publication Data
Payne, F   Anne, 1932–
Chaucer and Menippean satire.
Includes bibliographical references and index.
1. Chaucer, Geoffrey, d. 1400—Humor, satire, etc.
2. Satire—History and criticism.
3. Lucianus Samosatensis—Influence.
4. Boethius, d. 524. De consolatione philosophiae. I. Title.
PR1933.S27P39   821'.1   79-5412
ISBN 0-299-08170-2